Especially for

From

Date

WORRY LESS PRAY MORE

FOR MORNING & EVENING

A DAILY DEVOTIONAL

BARBOUR
PUBLISHING

Devotional thoughts and prayers are from *Worry Less, Pray More: A Woman's Devotional Guide to Anxiety-Free Living, Daily Wisdom for Women: 2017 Devotional Collection, Daily Wisdom for Women: 2018 Devotional Collection, Daily Wisdom for Women: 2019 Devotional Collection, Daily Wisdom for Women: 2020 Devotional Collection,* and *Daily Wisdom for Women: 2021 Devotional Collection* published by Barbour Publishing, Inc. All rights reserved.

Scripture quotations marked KJV are taken from the King James Version of the Bible.

Scripture quotations marked NKJV are taken from the New King James Version®. Copyright © 1982 by Thomas Nelson, Inc. Used by permission. All rights reserved.

Scripture quotations marked NIV are taken from the HOLY BIBLE, NEW INTERNATIONAL VERSION®. NIV®. Copyright © 1973, 1978, 1984, 2011 by Biblica, Inc.™ Used by permission. All rights reserved worldwide.

Scripture quotations marked MSG are from *THE MESSAGE.* Copyright © by Eugene H. Peterson 1993, 1994, 1995, 1996, 2000, 2001, 2002. Used by permission of NavPress Publishing Group.

Scripture quotations marked NLT are taken from the *Holy Bible.* New Living Translation copyright© 1996, 2004, 2015 by Tyndale House Foundation. Used by permission of Tyndale House Publishers, Inc. Carol Stream, Illinois 60188. All rights reserved.

Scripture quotations marked NASB are taken from the New American Standard Bible, © 1960, 1962, 1963, 1968, 1971, 1972, 1973, 1975, 1977, 1995 by The Lockman Foundation. Used by permission.

Scripture quotations marked AMPC are taken from the Amplified® Bible, Classic Edition © 1954, 1958, 1962, 1964, 1965, 1987 by The Lockman Foundation. Used by permission.

Scripture quotations marked ESV are from The Holy Bible, English Standard Version®, copyright © 2001 by Crossway Bibles, a publishing ministry of Good News Publishers. Used by permission. All rights reserved.

Scripture quotations marked PHILLIPS are taken from The New Testament in Modern English by J. B. Phillips copyright © 1960, 1972 J. B. Phillips. Administered by the Archbishops' Council of the Church of England. Used by permission.

Scripture quotations marked GW are taken from GOD'S WORD®, © 1995 God's Word to the Nations. Used by permission of God's Word Mission Society.

Scripture quotations marked HCSB are taken from the Holman Christian Standard Bible ® Copyright © 1999, 2000, 2002, 2003, 2009 by Holman Bible Publishers. Used by permission.

Published by Barbour Publishing, Inc., 1810 Barbour Drive, Uhrichsville, Ohio 44683, www.barbourbooks.com

Our mission is to inspire the world with the life-changing message of the Bible.

MORNING AND EVENING. . .
A WORRY-FREE LIFE IS YOURS!

*Evening, and morning. . .will I pray, and cry
aloud: and he shall hear my voice.*
PSALM 55:17 KJV

This lovely *Worry Less, Pray More for Morning & Evening* devotional will
help you experience an intimate connection to the heavenly Father, the
Anxiety-Reliever Himself, with a brief devotional thought, prayer, and
scripture—twice a day for every day of the calendar year.

Enhance your spiritual journey with the refreshing readings, and come
to know just how deeply and tenderly God loves you.

Read on. . .and discover the worry-free life today!

MORNING
TWENTY-FOUR-HOUR SECURITY

*Where can I find help? My help comes from the LORD, the maker of heaven
and earth. . . . The LORD guards you from every evil. He guards your
life. The LORD guards you as you come and go, now and forever.*
PSALM 121:1–2, 7–8 GW

Imagine having a bodyguard with you twenty-four hours a day. One who is all-powerful, all-knowing. He can see the future, the present, and the past. He never sleeps or takes catnaps.

You *have* such a bodyguard. His name is God. He's all the help and protection you need. With the Creator of the universe guarding you, surrounding you with His magnificent presence and power, nothing can touch you—in heaven or on the earth!

I rest easy, Lord, knowing You are always with me, keeping me from harm. Thank You!

EVENING
CULTIVATING CALM

*I've cultivated a quiet heart. Like a baby content
in its mother's arms, my soul is a baby content.*
PSALM 131:2 MSG

Psalm 131 was written by King David, who trained himself to trust God, to put all things in His hands. David saw God as a stable, ever-present, and powerful force for good and right in his life.

That's why David could say, "My soul waits calmly for God alone" (Psalm 62:1 GW). He looked for no other outside influence to rescue him.

You too can cultivate a quiet heart and calm soul by making God your sole Rock and Stronghold. Pray to Him, and remind yourself that He alone can—and will—handle everything that comes your way.

You alone, Lord, are my Savior. Be calm, my soul. Be content, my heart.

DAY 2

MORNING
GIVING—AND GETTING—PLEASURE

Be energetic in your life of salvation. . . . That energy is God's energy,
an energy deep within you, God himself willing and working
at what will give him the most pleasure.

PHILIPPIANS 2:12–13 MSG

Worrying can sap all your energy, using up all your strength and making you too bleary-eyed to see God's blessings and too weak to do what God's called you to do!

God didn't save you so that you could spend your life half asleep. He wants you to be strong, steady, and stable. So tell God all your concerns, all your imaginary what-ifs. Dig deep within, recognizing God's presence energizing you and giving you the power to let your worries melt away. Then open your eyes, and you'll see all the great tasks and blessings God has put before you.

I'm digging deep, Lord, freeing my frets and experiencing Your awesome energy!

EVENING
PEACE FROM THE INSIDE OUT

"Your threat means nothing to us. If you throw us in the fire, the God we serve
can rescue us. . . . But even if he doesn't, it wouldn't make a bit of difference,
O king. We still wouldn't serve your gods or worship the gold statue you set up."

DANIEL 3:16–18 MSG

Shadrach, Meshach, and Abednego refused to worship King Nebuchadnezzar's idol, so he threatened to throw them into a furnace. But the three men refused to lose their peace. They knew God could rescue them. And if He didn't, so be it.

No matter your circumstances, don't let your fears and anxieties get the best of you. Keep your faith and your peace. You may have to walk through fire, but Christ will be there with you, and you'll come out unharmed (see Daniel 3:25–29)!

Lord, here I am, claiming and holding on to Your eternal peace.

MORNING
BLESSINGS TO GOD'S BELOVED

Except the Lord builds the house, they labor in vain who build it. . . .
It is vain for you to rise up early, to take rest late, to eat the bread of
[anxious] toil—for He gives [blessings] to His beloved in sleep.
PSALM 127:1–2 AMPC

To live and work a worry-free life, ask God how He'd like you to use the gifts with which you've been blessed. Then follow where He leads, taking on the job or ministry He's directing you toward.

Once you're in the space God has provided, invite Him into every moment of your workday. Put your efforts and their outcome in His hands. Then you'll have the peace and rest God is so willing and able to give those He loves.

I'm resting in You, Lord, my Provider, my Love.

EVENING
NOTHING TOO HARD FOR GOD

Alas, Lord God! Behold, You have made the heavens and the
earth by Your great power and by Your outstretched arm!
There is nothing too hard or too wonderful for You.
JEREMIAH 32:17 AMPC

Sometimes the many things going *right* in your life and your world are overshadowed by that one thing that's going wrong. You begin to question whether God has the power or know-how to change things for the better or get you out of whatever mess you're in.

That's when you need to begin focusing on the right things. Trust that along with all the wonderful things God has done, is doing, and will do, He will turn any mishaps, errors, or darkness into something right, correct, and light.

You see, there is nothing too hard for God. Simply pray, and leave everything in His mighty hands.

Thank You, God, for reminding me nothing is too hard for You.

MORNING
NEVER SHAKEN

*Those who trust the LORD are like Mount Zion, which can never
be shaken. It remains firm forever. [As] the mountains surround
Jerusalem, so the LORD surrounds his people now and forever.*

PSALM 125:1–2 GW

Sometimes worry can lead you to literally shake in your boots, but God wants you to know that if you trust in Him, you will *never* be shaken. You can stand firm, leaning on His power.

When you put all your trust, hope, and confidence in the God who actually *created* the mountains, you begin to feel His awesome presence surrounding you. You begin remembering all the things He has done for you and all the others who've gone before you. Knowing this, you need no longer shake in your boots but walk sure and barefooted on the highest mountains (see Psalm 18:33).

I'm trusting in You, Lord. In doing so, I feel Your power and presence surrounding me.

EVENING
A MATTER OF COURSE

*"So don't worry and don't keep saying, 'What shall we eat, what shall
we drink or what shall we wear?'! . . . Your Heavenly Father knows that
you need them all. Set your heart on the kingdom and his goodness,
and all these things will come to you as a matter of course."*

MATTHEW 6:31–33 PHILLIPS

The apostle Paul, the author of Philippians, wasn't the first one to come up with the idea of praying instead of worrying (see Philippians 4:6–7). It was Jesus!

First, Jesus taught His followers how to pray. Then He said, "Stop being perpetually uneasy (anxious and worried) about your life" (Matthew 6:25 AMPC).

Your duty is to seek God more than anything—or anyone—else, knowing and trusting that if you will but ask, you *will* receive!

*Help me, Lord, to find a way to put my concerns
in Your hands, knowing You'll find a way!*

MORNING
A STUDENT OF PRAYER

*Then He was praying in a certain place; and when He stopped, one of
His disciples said to Him, Lord, teach us to pray. . . . And He said to them,
When you pray, say: Our Father Who is in heaven, hallowed be Your name.*
LUKE 11:1–2 AMPC

Through the example of Jesus and His disciples, it's clear that prayer is the antidote
to worry. The stronger you are in prayer, the less your concerns will weigh you down.

Today, come to Jesus as a willing and worthy student. Ask Him to teach you how
to weaken your worries and build up your faith as you learn to pray with power. Pray
this "Disciples' Prayer" (see Luke 11:2–4), knowing Abba God is longing to hear what
you have to say.

Abba God, hear my prayer. "Our Father Who is in heaven. . ."

EVENING
THAT SECRET PLACE

*When you pray, go into your [most] private room, and, closing
the door, pray to your Father, Who is in secret; and your Father,
Who sees in secret, will reward you in the open.*
MATTHEW 6:6 AMPC

No doubt, your life is busy. There are errands to run, emails to send, projects to finish,
meals to plan. . .and more! Yet to do all these things well, you need to unload some of
the clutter crowding your mind.

Jesus tells you to detach from the world without and the thoughts within. Find
that secret chamber He's opened just for you where you can have a spirit-to-Spirit talk
with God, shutting yourself away from the world and shutting yourself in with Him.

Find that place and you'll find your reward—the focus to do and peace to be!

Father, help me find that secret place where it's just You and me.

MORNING
GIVING GOD THE DETAILS

Hezekiah took the letters from the messengers, read them, and went to the Lord's temple. He spread them out in front of the Lord and prayed to the Lord.
2 Kings 19:14–15 GW

Hezekiah was the king of Judah. He received letters filled with threats of attack from Sennacherib of Assyria. After reading them, Hezekiah didn't panic but went to the temple of the Lord, where he spread out the threatening messages before the Lord and prayed, acknowledging God as the supreme Ruler and Creator of heaven and earth. He asked God to listen to him, to open His ears and hear Sennacherib's message, and to come to the rescue of His people. And God did.

When you have a massive problem, don't panic. Go to God and lay all the details before Him. Ask Him to save you—and He will.

Lord of all, here's what's happening. . . . In You alone will I find help.

EVENING
WORTHY THOUGHTS

Keep your thoughts on whatever is right or deserves praise: things that are true, honorable, fair, pure, acceptable, or commendable.
Philippians 4:8 GW

It's easy to get caught up in the bad news that surrounds us: rumors of wars, school shootings, drug addiction, crime, and terrorism, to name just a few. It's enough to keep you in bed, under the covers. Either that or you find yourself forever fretting about people and situations over which you have no or little control.

Take those news items to God. Ask Him to be in the situation, to help the victims, to bring justice. Then leave it all in His hands, knowing He can handle anything—and everything. Then look for some *good* news stories. And fix your focus on *those* things that are good, honorable, and commendable, praising God in the process.

Lord, help me fix my thoughts on those things that deserve my praise and focus! Amen.

MORNING
REASSURANCE TIMES THREE

*You know when I leave and when I get back; I'm never out of your sight. . . .
I look behind me and you're there, then up ahead and you're there, too—your
reassuring presence, coming and going. This is too much, too wonderful.*
PSALM 139:2, 5–6 MSG

People come and go, but there is a three-in-one person who remains: God, Jesus, and the Holy Spirit.

Wherever you go, God sees you. Whatever you're experiencing, Jesus is familiar with it. Whatever comfort you need, the Spirit is there, giving it to you. When you believe these things, when you have faith in God's presence always with you—before and behind you—all worries fade away.

*My worries fade, Lord, and vanish into nothing when I acknowledge
Your presence, Jesus' love, and the Spirit's power. Be with me now.*

EVENING
THE ONE WHO COMFORTS

*"I, yes I, am the one who comforts you. So why are you afraid of
mere humans, who wither like the grass and disappear?"*
ISAIAH 51:12 NLT

God understands you. He knows your worries, fears, hopes, dreams, and passions. He sees what's going on in your life. That's why Father God wants to fill you with assurance that He alone is the One who can and does comfort you.

So when you are worried or fearful about what some person might say or do next, draw close to the "one who comforts you" like no other. Lean into God, His power, promises, and protection. Remind yourself of who He is and the solace He and His presence provide. Allow His love and light to pour over you as you pray.

*Abba God, pour Your love, light, and protection over me.
In You I find the comfort that melts all fears and worries.*

MORNING
TRUSTING THE MASTER PLANNER

*Blessed is the person who places his confidence in the LORD and
does not rely on arrogant people or those who follow lies. You have
done many miraculous things, O LORD my God. You have made
many wonderful plans for us. No one compares to you!*

PSALM 40:4–5 GW

You've made a few plans, but it feels like it's taking forever for things to fall into place. If you're not sure you're on the right path, share your concerns with the Master Planner. Place all your trust in Him, relying on His wisdom, for He's already done some marvelous things in your life. If your plans are aligned with His will and Word, you can rest easy. He'll give you the patience and peace you need to see things through—in His time and way.

*You have many wonderful plans for me, Lord.
I'm trusting You'll help me see them through.*

EVENING
INSIDE THE CIRCLE OF PROTECTION

*GOD met me more than halfway, he freed me from my anxious fears. . . .
When I was desperate, I called out, and GOD got me out of a tight spot.
GOD's angel sets up a circle of protection around us while we pray.*

PSALM 34:4, 6–7 MSG

When you're weighed down by anxiety, God is ready to meet you "more than halfway." All you need to do is cry out to Him; tell Him everything that's on your mind, all your fears, worries, and troubles.

Once you do, God will rescue you and fill you with His peace; His angel will set up a protective circle around you until you are able to rise again in strength. Don't neglect the privilege and benefit of prayer. It's a lifesaver.

Here's what's happening, Lord. . . . Save me!

MORNING
THE FATHER WHO LISTENS

I love the LORD because he hears my voice and my prayer for mercy.
Because he bends down to listen, I will pray as long as I have breath!
PSALM 116:1–2 NLT

Listening has almost become a lost art among humans. But there's one person who will *always* pay attention to what you have to say: God.

Fix firmly in your mind that image of God bending down to you. See yourself as the woman-child that so desperately needs her Father to hear all her woes and worries. "The LORD protects those of childlike faith" (Psalm 116:6 NLT).

When you put all your trust in Father God, when you tell Him that you believe in Him and are deeply troubled (see Psalm 116:10), you'll come away free from fretting, and your soul will "be at rest again" (Psalm 116:7 NLT).

Lord, I want the soul rest only You can supply.

EVENING
THE BIG ASK

"Ask and it will be given to you. Search and you will find.
Knock and the door will be opened for you."
MATTHEW 7:7 PHILLIPS

In these days of information overload, your mind is likely overly cluttered with various what-if scenarios swirling around in your head. It's likely that you're not even conscious of all these unchecked worries.

Fortunately, you have a Father God who can give you peace of mind, heart, spirit, and soul. As His daughter, you have the privilege to come before Him in prayer.

Jesus says that when you give God your worries and **A**sk for His peace, you'll get it. If you **S**eek the Father's presence, you'll find Him. If you **K**nock on the door of His home and love, He'll open it to you.

Ask, Seek, and Knock (ASK)—and be blessed with clarity, peace, and hope.

Here I am, Lord, giving, asking, seeking, and knocking. Hear my prayer.

MORNING
OUT OF SELF AND INTO JESUS

Jesus. . .said to them, If anyone intends to come after Me, let him deny himself [forget, ignore, disown, and lose sight of himself and his own interests] and take up his cross, and. . .follow with Me [continually, cleaving steadfastly to Me].

MARK 8:34 AMPC

You worry you won't be promoted, you won't get the house you bid on, you'll never get ahead monetarily, and so on. In this land of worry, it's all about you. But Jesus wants you to realize it's really all about Him. If you want to be His follower, you're to lose sight of yourself and your own interests.

That's a tall order, but it is possible and so much more freeing than fretting. When you empty yourself of your concerns, you have more room to hold what God wants to give you.

Get out of yourself and into Jesus. You won't regret it.

Jesus, help me focus on You alone.

EVENING
PROOF OF THE PROMISE

And how bold and free we then become in his presence, freely asking according to his will, sure that he's listening. And if we're confident that he's listening, we know that what we've asked for is as good as ours.

1 JOHN 5:14–15 MSG

In Mark 11:24, Jesus said that you'll get what you ask for if you really believe. This promise was proven by a woman who'd been bleeding for twelve years. She'd been to lots of doctors and not one had been able to help her. Hearing Jesus was coming, she sneaked up to Him, saying to herself, "If I only touch his garment, I will be made well" (Matthew 9:21 ESV). Jesus saw her and said, "Take heart, daughter; your faith has made you well" (Matthew 9:22 ESV). And in that instant, she was!

Take your concerns to God. Then leave everything in His hands.

Jesus, You prove the promises, so I'm bringing You all my concerns.

MORNING
EXPECT THE UNEXPECTED

*Seeing Peter and John about to go into the temple, he asked to receive alms.
And Peter directed his gaze at him, as did John, and said, "Look at us." And
he fixed his attention on them, expecting to receive something from them.*

ACTS 3:3–5 ESV

When you bring your worries to God, chances are you also let Him know how you'd like things worked out before you leave them all in His hands. In other words, you let God know what you expect to happen. But sometimes what you expect is not the best thing for you.

Rest assured that when you hand your troubles over to God, He'll go deeper, to the very core of your desire, and discover what you really want. Expect God to give you the unexpected, the better thing.

Lord, when I give You my concerns, help me expect the unexpected!

EVENING
BECOMING A BLESSING

*The LORD said to Abram, "Leave your land, your relatives, and your father's
home. Go to the land that I will show you. I will make you a great nation,
I will bless you. I will make your name great, and you will be a blessing."*

GENESIS 12:1–2 GW

Most of your worries are about you and your own life, and that's normal. But after you've come to God in prayer and dropped off your worries with Him, He wants you to leave the land of You-ville behind.

Freed from your own concerns, you'll have room and time to bring the concerns of others to God. When you use the kingdom power of prayer on behalf of others, you become a blessing to others and God.

God's ready. Are you?

I have friends I'd like to bring to You tonight, Abba. They need Your blessing.

MORNING
POWER AND PEACE ARE YOURS

The Lord will give power to his people.
The Lord will bless his people with peace.
PSALM 29:11 GW

God is ruler over all. And you're His daughter. So on days when you're weakened by worry, you can go to God for all the strength you need. He'll give you the power to persevere and prevail, and He'll bless you with peace today and all your days to come.

There's only one catch. You need to *believe*, to fix these facts firmly in your mind so you'll not feel helpless and veer from the path He's laid out for you.

Drop your worries by the doorstep as you enter God's presence. Take in all the strength and peace that He's *always* waiting to give you. And go on your way in His name and power.

Lord, my God and King, fill me with Your power and peace so I may do Your will.

EVENING
IN HARMONY WITH GOD

"Be in harmony and at peace with God. In this way you will have prosperity.
Accept instruction from his mouth, and keep his words in your heart."
JOB 22:21–22 GW

When you're caught in a cycle of worry and anxiety, you're not in harmony with God. Your fretting actually forms a barrier between you and Him. This keeps you from receiving His full power, strength, and peace.

Tonight, get back in harmony with God. Put your trust in the words and promises of the love letter (the Bible) He's written just for you. Ingest His wisdom and follow it, allowing it to have full sway over your thoughts. Don't just *write* His words on your heart—*keep* them there so when worry flares up, you can quench it with God's wisdom. You'll find yourself prospering more than you ever dreamed or imagined.

I want Your song in my heart, Lord.

MORNING
A FAITH-LIFT

Anxiety in a man's heart weighs him down,
but a good word makes him glad.
PROVERBS 12:25 ESV

Worry is a weight that presses upon your heart. That's why the psalmist wrote that you should "Pile your troubles on GOD's shoulders—he'll carry your load, he'll help you out" (Psalm 55:22 MSG). That's why Jesus told you not to be anxious about anything but to come to Him if you're heavy laden—that He'll give you the rest you need (see Matthew 6:25; 11:28–29). That's why Peter reminds you to "give all your worries and cares to God, for he cares about you" (1 Peter 5:7 NLT).

Find a verse, psalm, or story that speaks to your heart. When you do, you'll find yourself lifted up to the heavenly God who waits to greet you.

Lord, I'm digging into Your Word. Reveal the words I need to lift me up to You!

EVENING
CONFIDENCE IN GOD

I know and rest in confidence upon it that the Lord will maintain the
cause of the afflicted, and will secure justice for the poor and needy.
PSALM 140:12 AMPC

Hearing all the bad news that's out there, you may find yourself worrying not only about your own safety but about the safety of others, as well as justice for the afflicted. It's almost too much to take in!

Your only recourse is to just hand those who are suffering over to God and to rest in the confidence that *He* will take care of all those harmed by evil and violence. It may not happen tomorrow, in your lifetime, or on this side of heaven, but it will happen. In God's time and way.

Meanwhile, begin lifting to God all those who are troubled, and leave the outcome in His hands.

Lord, I'm handing over the afflicted to You. Heal their hearts and bring them justice.

MORNING
GOD IS NEAR

The Lord is close to the brokenhearted;
he rescues those whose spirits are crushed.
PSALM 34:18 NLT

Human beings are fragile creatures. As one such being, your heart can break, your spirit become crushed. Whatever the cause, upon the heels of a broken heart and a crushed spirit, anxiety is sure to follow. You wonder, *Why did it happen? How do I go on from here?*

Know that in the midst of trial, God is right there with you. He's holding you in His arms. He'll heal your heart, restore your spirit, and alleviate your anxiety. You need say nothing more than "Lord. . .help me."

Thank You, Lord, for always being there when I need You. You're the one sure thing
I can count on. You will heal my heart, revive my spirit, and calm my soul.

EVENING
BELIEVE AND LOOK

[What, what would have become of me] had I not believed that I would see the
Lord's goodness in the land of the living! Wait and hope for and expect the Lord;
be brave and of good courage. . . . Yes, wait for and hope for and expect the Lord.
PSALM 27:13–14 AMPC

What would become of you if you didn't believe you'd see God's goodness in the world? What if you let your worries and anxieties have complete sway over you, annihilating any hope that God *will do something* and *you will see* the results?

God's Word says this: "I believe that I shall look upon the goodness of the LORD in the land of the living!" (Psalm 27:13 ESV). Make this verse part of your arsenal. Look to God with complete dependence and trust. Then you'll find the strength and courage to get through anything.

I expect to see Your goodness, Lord. You give me hope!

MORNING
YOUR HIDING PLACE

For you are my hiding place; you protect me from trouble.
You surround me with songs of victory.

PSALM 32:7 NLT

Physically, it's difficult to find a place where you can truly hide from everyone. Yet spiritually, there is one place you can always go to get away from all people and all worry. It's in God's presence where you find yourself surrounded with not just love and encouragement but with songs of victory.

God is your biggest cheerleader and best coach. He says, "I will guide you along the best pathway for your life. I will advise you and watch over you" (Psalm 32:8 NLT). His only caveat is for you not to be stubborn when He tells you which way to go, what to do. But that's a small price to pay to live in victory.

Lord, I come to hide in You. Save me, guide me. Make me putty in Your hands.

EVENING
GOD'S COMMAND FOR YOU

"This is my command—be strong and courageous! Do not be afraid or
discouraged. For the LORD your God is with you wherever you go."

JOSHUA 1:9 NLT

Moses has died, and Joshua is left to lead God's people into the Promised Land. Can you imagine all the thoughts that must have been going through Joshua's head? Perhaps that's why God tells him three times to be strong and courageous and two times that He would be with him (see Joshua 1:5–9).

Chances are your challenges are not as great as Joshua's. But even if they are, these are the words God wants you to take to heart. Know with certainty that God *IS* with you. He will *NEVER* leave you. No matter where you go, God is there. He's got you.

Thank You, Lord, for these encouraging words. Help me get them through my head
so that I can be the strong and courageous woman You've designed me to be!

MORNING
KEEP GOING

*I do not consider myself to have "arrived", spiritually, nor do I
consider myself already perfect. But I keep going on, grasping
ever more firmly that purpose for which Christ grasped me.*
PHILIPPIANS 3:13 PHILLIPS

Do you sometimes worry about the things you've said and done? It's time to leave the past in the past. God knows you aren't perfect. That's why He sent Jesus and then left you His Spirit, so that you'd have supernatural help on your journey through life.

So don't look behind, worrying about the ramifications of your words and actions. Hand them over to God. Then "leave the past behind and with hands outstretched to whatever lies ahead. . .go straight for the goal," heading for the "reward. . .of being called by God in Christ" (Philippians 3:14 PHILLIPS).

Jesus, please help me leave the past in the past. Help me move forward with You.

EVENING
THORNS OF WORRY AND RICHES

*"The seed planted among thornbushes [is another person who]
hears the word. But the worries of life and the deceitful pleasures
of riches choke the word so that it can't produce anything."*
MATTHEW 13:22 GW

Jesus tells a parable about a farmer who sows seed. The seed that fell on the path is grabbed up by birds (the evil one). The seed sown on the rocky ground quickly withers when the sun scorches it. These are people of little faith who lost their way when troubles came. The seeds that fell amid thorns got choked out. These are people who allowed the cares of the world and money to choke God's Word out of their life, making them unfruitful.

Your goal is to grow on God's Word, allowing it to build you up. Then you'll be the fruitful seed, yielding more crops than you ever thought possible.

Help me bear fruit for You, Lord, as I let go of my worries and take up Your Word.

MORNING
POWER TOOLS

For God did not give us a spirit of timidity (of cowardice, of craven and cringing and fawning fear), but [He has given us a spirit] of power and of love and of calm and well-balanced mind and discipline and self-control.

2 TIMOTHY 1:7 AMPC

God has gifted you with tools to help you live out a heavenly life while you're here on earth. He's given you a spirit of power, the same power He used to raise Jesus from the dead (see Philippians 3:10). He's filled you with the spirit of love, which prompts you to please God and put the welfare of others above your own. And He's given you a calm, well-balanced mind.

Use the power tools God has given you. Put worries behind as you pour yourself into God and construct a heaven on earth through prayer.

Lord, thank You for the tools of love and a calm mind.
Help me use them to build up Your kingdom.

EVENING
GOD'S PATHWAY FOR YOU

Your road led through the sea, your pathway through the mighty waters—a pathway no one knew was there! You led your people along that road like a flock of sheep.

PSALM 77:19–20 NLT

Worries sometimes come upon you like mighty waters. Once you were standing in the shallows, then you wandered deeper into the depths, and before you knew it, you were caught in the undertow. How would you ever regain your footing?

Before you let your worries pull you under, go to God. Ask Him to show you the pathway you cannot see with your limited vision. He will clearly reveal the road He's carved out just for you, the path He's provided by dividing waters, obliterating the worry and despair that block your way. Then He'll calm you and carefully and masterfully guide you as any good and loving shepherd would.

I don't want worries to take me under, Lord. Calm my soul. Take my hand. Lead me.

MORNING
EQUIPPED BY GOD

*Then David took his shepherd's staff, selected five smooth stones
from the brook, and put them in the pocket of his shepherd's pack,
and with his sling in his hand approached Goliath.*

1 Samuel 17:40 MSG

David wasn't worried. He was just a young shepherd boy when he convinced King Saul that God would help him defeat Goliath. And when Saul tried to outfit David in kingly armor, David said, "I can't even move with all this stuff on me. I'm not used to this" (1 Samuel 17:39 MSG). He took it off and donned his usual gear: trust in God, a staff, stones, and a sling. With these, David took down the giant.

Just as God equipped David to defeat Goliath, God's given you exactly what you need to face your own challenges!

Thank You, Lord, for giving me all I need to face the challenges before me.

EVENING
AT HOME IN GOD

*You've taken my hand. You wisely and tenderly lead me,
and then you bless me. . . . I'm in the very presence of God—
oh, how refreshing it is! I've made Lord God my home.*

Psalm 73:23–24, 28 MSG

When you worry, look at where you're standing. Have you moved away from God?

Remember the Lord is your Rock, Fortress, and Shelter. When you get close to Him in prayer, He'll take your hand and lead you exactly where you need to go, and then He'll bless you as soon as your feet touch down on the path He's opened for you.

Tonight, get yourself into the presence of God. Allow Him to take your hand. As you do, you'll not only find the refreshment you've been thirsting for but the home your spirit and soul have been longing for—in Him alone.

Lord, when doubts and worries assail me, help me get back to You, my only true home.

MORNING
GOD CALLS YOU AS HE SEES YOU

The angel of the LORD appeared to him and said,
"Mighty hero, the LORD is with you!"
JUDGES 6:12 NLT

The Midianites kept taking all the crops God's people had sown. So Gideon was thresh-ing wheat in a winepress, hiding his grain from the Midianite raiders. That's when God came and called him a "mighty hero." Yet Gideon denied God's estimation of him, telling God he was the least in his family and his clan the weakest of its tribe.

When you worry you aren't good enough to do what God has called you to do, go to Him in prayer. He'll remind you who you are: a mighty hero, a daughter of God. Your job is to believe Him, to trust Him to empower you. Then you'll become the woman God sees you already are.

Help me see myself through Your eyes, Lord, a mighty daughter of a mighty God.

EVENING
GOD HAS A FIRM GRIP ON YOU

"Don't panic. I'm with you. There's no need to fear for I'm your God. I'll give you
strength. I'll help you. I'll hold you steady, keep a firm grip on you. Count on
it: Everyone who had it in for you will end up out in the cold—real losers."
ISAIAH 41:10–11 MSG

God tells you not to panic because He is with you. He'll give you all the strength you need to face whatever lies before you. He has your hand, and He'll never let you go. He'll keep you steady on your feet, give you firm footing to walk where He'd have you go. And those who threaten you today will be gone tomorrow.

Believe, and you will have the strength and peace your heart, spirit, and soul crave.

Lord, in You I find my courage. I'm counting on You alone!

MORNING
PONDERING GOD

I meditate on all Your doings; I ponder the work of Your hands. . . . Cause me to hear Your loving-kindness in the morning, for on You do I lean and in You do I trust. Cause me to know the way wherein I should walk, for I lift up my inner self to You.
PSALM 143:5, 8 AMPC

Today, open God's Word or focus on tried-and-true verses that lift your thoughts and shield your mind. Remember all the great things God has done in the past, and thank Him for what He's doing in the present. Then lean in close. Tell God you trust Him. Ask Him to show you the way you're to go. Listen to what He says as you lift up your inner woman to Him, spirit to Spirit, love to Love.

I'm coming to You before all other things, Lord. Love me, lead me, lift me to You.

EVENING
GOD TO THE RESCUE

Though I am surrounded by troubles, you will protect me from the anger of my enemies. You reach out your hand, and the power of your right hand saves me. The LORD will work out his plans for my life—for your faithful love, O LORD, endures forever.
PSALM 138:7–8 NLT

When you're in the thick of a situation you never saw coming and you're more than worried. . .stop. Take a deep breath no matter where you are or what you're doing. Remind yourself that God will—*is*—protecting you. His power is saving you in that very moment. He's going to work everything out for you. Why? Because He not only loves you but has a good plan for your life. All you need to do is trust Him and live it!

Protect me, Lord, when danger steals in. I know You'll save me. You have a plan!

MORNING
PERFECT, TRUSTING PEACE

You will keep in perfect peace all who trust in you, all whose thoughts are fixed on you!
ISAIAH 26:3 NLT

It *is* possible to have perfect peace. It's a simple formula to remember: The first part is to trust in God. That means committing yourself to Him and His ways, leaning on Him, hoping and expecting Him to move in your life. The second part is keeping your mind on Him. That means planting His Word deep within yourself, spending time with Him, and learning about who He is.

Ask God to change you from a worrier to a woman of peace. He'll then do the unimaginable—for your good and His glory!

Lord, I want the calm only You can provide. Change me,
Lord. Make me a woman of perfect, trusting peace.

EVENING
CONFESS AND REFRESH

So repent (change your mind and purpose); turn around and return
[to God], that your sins may be erased (blotted out, wiped clean), that
times of refreshing (of recovering from the effects of heat, of reviving
with fresh air) may come from the presence of the Lord.
ACTS 3:19 AMPC

If handing your worries over to God in prayer isn't bringing you peace, maybe you haven't told Him all that's been going on in your life. You haven't confessed those things you don't even want to admit to yourself. And so they remain hidden, festering like an unclean wound.

Nothing is hidden from God. He sees all you do, hears all you say (see Job 34:21). But if you want to be refreshed, to have less worry and more peace, ask God to examine you (Psalm 139:23–24) to reveal the hidden missteps you have yet to confess. Know that God *will* forgive you. And you'll come away more refreshed than ever!

Lord, look within me. Help me tell You all.

MORNING
EXPERIENCING GOD'S MANY ASPECTS

*Blessed be the Lord, my Rock and my keen and firm Strength. . .my
Steadfast Love and my Fortress, my High Tower and my Deliverer,
my Shield and He in Whom I trust and take refuge.*
PSALM 144:1–2 AMPC

When you've prayed and you've prayed and still you come away with some dregs of anxiety you can't seem to clear out, perhaps it's time to go slow. To go deep. To experience who God truly is.

See God as your solid Rock that will not be moved. Allow Him to be your Strength. Recognize He is your Steadfast Love, forever and constant. He is your great Protector, your Fortress. In times of trouble, you can run to Him, your High Tower, and be safe. He, your Deliverer and ever-present Shield, will rescue and protect you.

*Today, I'm going deep in You, Lord—my Rock, Strength, Steadfast
Love, Fortress, High Tower, Deliverer, and Shield.*

EVENING
HABITUAL PRAYER

*Be earnest and unwearied and steadfast in your prayer [life], being
[both] alert and intent in [your praying] with thanksgiving.*
COLOSSIANS 4:2 AMPC

If your prayer life is sporadic, so will your peace be. And if you don't pepper your petitions with thanksgiving, your prayers will become a mere litany of selfish desires you'd like fulfilled before you go on your way and in your own power.

So don't go to God just once a day but throughout your day. When you see someone suffering, pray. When worry begins to creep into your mind, pray. While you're with God in all ways all day, thank Him for all He has done, is doing, and will do. In so doing not only will all your worries fade but you'll find yourself walking God's way and in His power.

*Help me, Lord, to be steadfast in my prayer life,
continually giving thanks to You in all ways all day.*

MORNING
GOD—THE CYCLE BREAKER

When I am afraid, I will put my trust in you. I praise God for what he has promised. . . . For you have rescued me from death; you have kept my feet from slipping. So now I can walk in your presence, O God, in your life-giving light.
PSALM 56:3–4, 13 NLT

To steer clear of fear and to keep worry from taking over your life—the life God wants you to live in Him—you need to trust the One who rules and sustains the universe.

When you're afraid, trust God. Remember all the promises He's made to you, including the fact that He goes before you and behind you. That He'll never ever leave nor forsake you.

God has already sent Jesus to rescue you from death and given you the Holy Spirit to guide your feet. So trust Him. As you do, you'll be walking in His life-giving light!

When I'm afraid, I'll trust in You, Lord!

EVENING
A STACK OF BLESSINGS WAITING FOR YOU

Desperate, I throw myself on you: you are my God! Hour by hour I place my days in your hand. . . . What a stack of blessing you have piled up for those who worship you, ready and waiting for all who run to you to escape an unkind world.
PSALM 31:14–15, 19 MSG

Second by second, minute by minute, hour by hour, put yourself into the hands of One who loves and protects you. The One who longs to talk to you, walk with you, and carry you when necessary.

No matter what your troubles or worries, God will find a unique way of making good come out of anything and everything that comes your way. So escape into God, knowing He has a stack of blessings waiting just for you.

My worries evaporate when I put myself in Your hands, Lord.

MORNING
GOD'S RAINBOW IN THE CLOUDS

*"Whenever I form clouds over the earth, a rainbow will appear in the clouds.
Then I will remember my promise to you and every living animal."*
GENESIS 9:14–15 GW

God told Noah the rainbow would be a sign of His promise to never again allow water to destroy all life. And God promises that He'll never give up on you no matter what you've done. He will be there for you no matter how great your flood of worries and troubles. Let God's beautiful rainbow amid the clouds be a reminder that He *will* make something good come out of the storms in your life (see Romans 8:28). Just look up to Him and His spectral arc. He's set something good for you amid your clouds.

*Father God, thank You for making all things work for good.
Help me focus on Your rainbow amid my clouds.*

EVENING
GOD'S GATEWAY OF HOPE

*"I will lead her into the desert and speak tenderly to her there. I will return her
vineyards to her and transform the Valley of Trouble into a gateway of hope."*
HOSEA 2:14–15 NLT

God is so tenderhearted toward you. He desires to spend time with you, to speak to you. So go to Him with your worries. Pour out all the anxious thoughts in your mind. Unburden your heart of all that's concerning you. Tell Him everything that's troubling your spirit and keeping you from focusing on Him.

As you do so, God will come close and listen. Then He will talk to you with a soft voice, pour out His wisdom, and cover you with His love. You'll soon find Him transforming your dark valley of despair into a shining gateway of hope.

*Lord, I come to You, pouring out my heart.
Lead me to the gateway of the hope I have in You!*

MORNING
IN RHYTHM WITH JESUS

"Come to me. . . . I'll show you how to take a real rest. . . .
Watch how I do it. Learn the unforced rhythms of grace. . . .
Keep company with me and you'll learn to live freely and lightly."
MATTHEW 11:28–30 MSG

Worrying is only human, yet it can become an energy zapper if you don't take your concerns to Jesus on a regular basis.

Remember that Jesus doesn't want the evil one to steal or destroy your life with worry. Jesus wants you to come to Him, to let Him carry your load. He came so His followers "can have real and eternal life, more and better life than they ever dreamed of" (John 10:10 MSG). So, for a real rest, get away with Jesus. Get into His rhythm. You'll find yourself living not only right but also light!

I want to be in rhythm with You, Lord.

EVENING
YOUR WORRY LIST

Keep your life free from love of money, and be content with what you
have, for he has said, "I will never leave you nor forsake you." So we
can confidently say, "The Lord is my helper; I will not fear."
HEBREWS 13:5–6 ESV

Do your concerns revolve around money or things you don't really need? Is your discontent rising up because you don't have the latest cell phone, the most fashionable clothes, the best-looking lawn, or the nicest car?

Tonight, consider writing down your worries. See how many things you can cross off, knowing you can be content with what you have. Then hand over to God whatever worries are left, trusting Him, your Helper, to provide whatever you truly need.

Lord, help me be content with what I have and trust
You to provide all things I truly do need. Amen.

MORNING
REAL LOVE

God showed how much he loved us by sending his one and only
Son into the world so that we might have eternal life through him.
This is real love—not that we loved God, but that he loved us.

1 JOHN 4:9–10 NLT

Everyone has times when they're feeling unloved, unnoticed, or uncared for—even by the people closest to them! They begin to worry, wondering if they matter at all!

If you're going through such a time, take heart. God loves you more than you can imagine. You're the apple of His eye. He gave up His one and only Son to save you from death and darkness. He loved you even before you loved Him!

God will never *not* love you. He has His eye on you, cares deeply for you. He provides what you need—before you need it!

Rest easy, beloved daughter. Father God's love has you covered!

Thank You for loving me, Lord, even when I don't love myself!

EVENING
OPEN DOORS

"Behold, I have set before you an open door, which no one is
able to shut. I know that you have but little power, and yet you
have kept my word and have not denied my name."

REVELATION 3:8 ESV

Ever worry that you might be on the wrong path? Have you had a door opened or shut in your face lately? No need to worry.

God has a definite plan for your life. He wants you to be successful, to prosper, to bloom where He's planted you. So instead of worrying if you're on the right or wrong road, go to God. Ask Him to come up behind you and tell you which way to turn, if turn you must. Rest easy, knowing He's guiding you and won't let you go down any rabbit holes.

Lord, I'm trusting You to lead me the right way. Amen.

MORNING
GOD THE REWARDER

No one can please God without faith. Whoever goes to God must believe that God exists and that he rewards those who seek him.
HEBREWS 11:6 GW

Worry comes when you have a problem or situation that seems unsolvable or hopeless. Or when you're uncertain about how long you can hang on before God will help you or provide an answer.

As soon as you enter God's presence and focus on Him, your initial reward is the unsurpassing peace that falls upon you. As you unload your burdens, you realize how small they seem compared to the feats He continually accomplishes and the promises He consistently fulfills. And you now take comfort from the knowledge that God will reward you with an answer to your prayer, a solution to your problem, and strength until they arrive.

I'm seeking Your face before all else, Lord.

EVENING
IT'S GOD WHO SAVES

The LORD said to Gideon, "You have too many warriors with you. If I let all of you fight the Midianites, the Israelites will boast to me that they saved themselves by their own strength."
JUDGES 7:2 NLT

God told Gideon to gather an army to defeat the Midianites, who'd been raiding Israel. But Gideon had too many warriors with him, so many that the Israelites might imagine their own strength had saved them instead of God.

So, through a series of commands to Gideon, God pared down his army from thirty-two thousand to three hundred men, who went on to defeat their enemy.

It's plain to see that when God is in your camp, you need not worry you don't have enough resources to win the day. God will equip you with all the strength, power, and provisions you need—for the victory lies solely in *His* hands!

All I need to win the day is to have You on my side, Lord!

MORNING
A WAY-OUT GOD

No test or temptation that comes your way is beyond the course of what others have had to face. All you need to remember is that God will never let you down; he'll never let you be pushed past your limit; he'll always be there to help you come through it.
1 CORINTHIANS 10:13 MSG

No matter what troubles you encounter as you travel through this life, your experiences are really nothing new. Some other woman has walked that road before. So don't worry, fear, or panic. Others have found a way through, and so will you.

Instead of getting caught up in worry, take all your concerns to God. Remember that He'll never let you down. He'll never let things go too far, beyond what you can handle. And He'll stick with you, strengthening and helping you each moment.

Lord, I know others have walked this road before, and You'll help me find my way out of this trial and into You.

EVENING
LIKE A CHILD

But Jesus said, "Let the children come to me. Don't stop them! For the Kingdom of Heaven belongs to those who are like these children."
MATTHEW 19:14 NLT

Little children don't worry. That's because they trust in their parents for everything— food, clothing, water, protection, and love. They're vulnerable and cannot get far without their mother's or father's help and guidance. So they're happy to take their parent's hand, knowing they'll be safely led across the street, through the store, or up the stairs to bed.

That's how God wants you to be—like a trusting child. He wants you not to worry about anything but to rely on Him for everything. He wants you to be humble, realizing your complete dependence upon Him, knowing you won't get far without your hand in His.

Be like a child, and you'll find yourself growing up securely in God.

Lord, help me be like a little child, trusting You'll safely lead me where You'd have me go.

MORNING
EYES ON GOD

We have no might to stand against this great company that is coming against us. We do not know what to do, but our eyes are upon You.
2 CHRONICLES 20:12 AMPC

Three armies were coming to attack Jehoshaphat, king of Judah. Jehoshaphat recalled God's strength and power. Then he asked for God's help, admitting that he and his people didn't have the strength to fight that which was coming against them. They didn't know what to do, but their eyes would be on God.

When you don't know what to do, you may worry at first. But prayer will get you realigned with God. Seek Him and recall His strength. Admit your weakness and confusion. Then keep your eyes on God, and you'll gain the victory He provides.

Lord, You're strong and mighty, and I'm weak. I don't know what to do, but I'm keeping my eyes on You, knowing that's where victory lies.

EVENING
STAND STILL AND SEE

Be not afraid or dismayed at this great multitude; for the battle is not yours, but God's. . . . You shall not need to fight in this battle; take your positions, stand still, and see the deliverance of the Lord [Who is] with you.
2 CHRONICLES 20:15, 17 AMPC

After King Jehoshaphat prayed, God told the king and his people not to worry or be dismayed because the battle before them was God's. All they were to do was to go where God told them to go, stand there, and watch Him save them.

When you come up against a conflict or challenge, keep these powerful verses in mind. Then put yourself and your battle in God's hands. Knowing He's with you, calmly take your stand and watch God work His wonders.

I don't know what You're going to do, Lord, but I know my role. I'll go where You tell me, calmly stand there, and watch You work.

MORNING
YOUR GREATEST WEAPONS

Jehoshaphat stopped and said, ". . .Believe in the LORD your God, and you will be able to stand firm. Believe in his prophets, and you will succeed."

2 CHRONICLES 20:20 NLT

After God had given King Jehoshaphat his marching orders, he told his people to believe in God, stand firm, and they'd see success in the mighty battle against them. Then he appointed singers to march out *in front of his army* and sing songs of praise to God (2 Chronicles 20:22). By the time the army of Judah got to the battleground, there was nothing left for them to do but gather up the spoils.

Your greatest weapons against fear and worry are prayer and praise. Pray for guidance, and then praise the God you love and believe in. You'll be able not only to stand strong but to find treasures galore.

Lord, thank You for fighting for me. Your faithful love endures forever!

EVENING
LOOK UP

Pursue the things over which Christ presides. Don't shuffle along, eyes to the ground, absorbed with the things right in front of you. Look up, and be alert to what is going on around Christ—that's where the action is. See things from his perspective.

COLOSSIANS 3:2 MSG

Have you ever seen people walking along, looking down at their cell phones? They're so worried they're going to miss the latest text, email, or news bite, so absorbed in what's happening on their mobile device that they aren't watching where they're going. And before they know it, they've either walked into something or fallen into a hole and hurt themselves.

God wants your focus off the ground and onto heavenly things. He wants you checking out what Jesus is doing, seeing things from His point of view. Looking up at Him will keep you from stumbling when God wants you soaring.

Jesus, help me keep my eyes looking up to You, alert to what You're doing.

MORNING
COME AS YOU ARE

Let everyone come who is thirsty [who is painfully conscious of his need of those things by which the soul is refreshed, supported, and strengthened]; and whoever [earnestly] desires to do it, let him come. . .and drink the water of Life without cost.

REVELATION 22:17 AMPC

Have you worried you aren't good enough to come to God and unload your cares and concerns? That you aren't worthy enough to ask for and receive God's mercy, Jesus' love, and the Holy Spirit's help?

God knows you aren't perfect. That's why He sent Jesus to save you and left the Holy Spirit to help you. So don't tarry. Go to God and set your burdens down. Take up His light, and you'll find refreshment for your soul, strength for your spirit, and love for your heart.

I'm coming to You just as I am, Lord. Take my worries and give me Your peace.

EVENING
SPIRITUAL SOWING

He who sows to his own flesh (lower nature, sensuality) will from the flesh reap decay and ruin and destruction, but he who sows to the Spirit will from the Spirit reap eternal life.

GALATIANS 6:8 AMPC

When you're in a state of worry, you're sowing to your flesh, planting worry seeds that will reap only more worry, or worse, grow into outright fear and panic.

So, when worry crops up, do yourself and the world a favor. Take some deep breaths. Dig into the Word. Find a verse that calms your spirit and builds up your faith. Write that verse upon your heart. Then seek God's face and peace. Soon, you'll be sowing in the Spirit and reaping the light of eternal life.

I'm tired of sowing worry, Lord. It only grows up into bigger worries, or worse. Help me grow in You, sowing to the Spirit, reaping Your light.

MORNING
BEING A BLESSING

*We can't allow ourselves to get tired of living the right way. Certainly,
each of us will receive [everlasting life] at the proper time, if we don't give up.
Whenever we have the opportunity, we have to do what is good for everyone.*

GALATIANS 6:9–10 GW

If you allow yourself to be bogged down by worry, you won't have the energy to focus on anything but those things that concern and affect you. With your eyes on only yourself, you can no longer take advantage of—or even *see*—opportunities to help someone else. You stop being a blessing to others.

Today, get out of yourself and into God and others by doing something good for your neighbor, friend, relative, or a stranger. As soon as you start focusing on others, your worries will fade in the light of love.

Lord, show me who I can help and love in Your name.

EVENING
GOD'S PATIENCE

*The Lord isn't slow to do what he promised. . . . Rather, he is patient for
your sake. He doesn't want to destroy anyone but wants all people to have
an opportunity to turn to him and change the way they think and act.*

2 PETER 3:9 GW

Many women come to church alone because their mates don't yet believe in Jesus. Some people call these women "church widows." Perhaps you're one of them. You worry and wonder, *Will my loved one ever believe?*

It's good to be concerned about the salvation of others, but it shouldn't be all consuming. Instead of spending your time worrying about your loved ones, fix your eyes on God. He has tons of patience, *and* He has a plan, wanting to give everyone the opportunity to follow His Son. In the meantime, be the best God-follower you can be.

Lord, thank You for always being with me.

MORNING
GOD MAKES YOUR PATHS PLAIN

Trust in the LORD with all your heart, and do not lean on your own understanding.
In all your ways acknowledge him, and he will make straight your paths.

PROVERBS 3:5–6 ESV

At some point in your life, chances are you asked God to tell you what He would have you do to serve Him. And He answered your prayer, directing you into an area that you already had a passion for. But then, as the years passed, your passion ebbed a bit, and now you're wondering if there is some new road He wants you to take.

Perhaps it's time to ask God again to show you which way to go. Then trust Him to do so—but don't make a move until He's made everything plain. Patience will be your reward.

I'm leaning into and on You, Lord. Show me
the road You want me on. I'm trusting in You.

EVENING
STAND STILL AND CONSIDER

Hear this. . .stand still and consider the wondrous works of God.

JOB 37:14 AMPC

This evening, consider taking a break from the hectic pace of your life and going for a relaxing prayer walk. Head out into nature, whether that is your backyard, a nearby park, a beach, a creek, or a tree planted in the city sidewalk. Once there, stand still and think about all the wonderful things God has created for your provision and enjoyment.

As you prayerfully reconnect with God's creation and consider its vastness, your worries will seem trivial, and your lips and mind will be filled with nothing but praise.

Lord, help me stop worrying and start admiring all
You've done for those You love in heaven and on earth.

MORNING
SUPERHUMAN POWER

When you received the message of God. . .you welcomed it not as the word of [mere] men, but as it truly is, the Word of God, which is effectually at work in you who believe [exercising its superhuman power in those who adhere to and trust in and rely on it].

1 Thessalonians 2:13 ampc

God's Word is everything you need! It saves, guides, warns, rewards, and counsels you. It trains you up into the woman God has created you to be. It revives your spirit, restores your strength, comforts your heart, nourishes your soul, and renews your mind. It strengthens you, gives you joy, and prospers you.

Forget about the worries. Focus on the Word. And God will change you from the inside out!

Lord, take my worries into Your hands and pour out Your Word upon me!

EVENING
SERVING GOD AT SUCH A TIME

"And who knows whether you have not come to the kingdom for such a time as this?"

Esther 4:14 esv

Esther, a beautiful Jewish girl, was an orphan who became a queen. When her cousin Mordecai discovered the Jews were being persecuted, he sent word to Esther, telling her that this may be her time to talk to the king and ask for his help to save her people.

After receiving his message, a resolved Esther told Mordecai to ask her people to fast and pray for three days, saying, "Then I will go to the king, though it is against the law, and if I perish, I perish" (Esther 4:16 esv).

Perhaps you feel God is calling you, willing you to be brave in His name. If so, ask God to replace your worries with His peace, your fears with His courage. Don't miss this opportunity to serve God for such a time as this.

Lord, reveal to me any opportunities You have for me. I will serve You.

MORNING
MEDITATE ON WONDERS

Every day [with its new reasons] will I bless You [affectionately and gratefully praise You]; yes, I will praise Your name forever and ever. . . . On the glorious splendor of Your majesty and on Your wondrous works I will meditate.

PSALM 145:2, 5 AMPC

David loved to talk to God. Many of his psalms speak of his fears, woes, and worries. But David also looked for the good in his life. He actively kept his eyes open for the new and amazing things the Lord was doing every day and praised God for them.

Why not follow David's example? After unloading your worries, actively seek something new to praise God for. Keep your eyes open to His wonders and works around you. Think about them throughout your day. You'll find yourself so busy looking for the good, you won't have time to worry.

Today, I'm looking for new reasons to praise and adore You, Lord!

EVENING
LISTENING TO WISDOM

Whoso hearkens to me [Wisdom] shall dwell securely and in confident trust and shall be quiet, without fear or dread of evil.

PROVERBS 1:33 AMPC

No matter what Bible version you have, the verse above speaks volumes. If you want to live without worry, you need to not just pour out your troubles to God but *listen* to Him when He responds. To follow where His words and voice lead. When you do, you will be free not only from fretting but actually from the fear of evil and disaster. You will no longer find yourself mentally envisioning the worst-case scenario and rehearsing your reaction to it but living securely, quietly, and peacefully, confident that God will give you the *best*-case scenario.

I want to live in quiet confidence. My ears are open to Your wisdom, Lord.

MORNING
THAT SPECIAL GLOW

*"If you are generous with the hungry and start giving yourselves
to the down-and-out, your lives will begin to glow in the darkness,
your shadowed lives will be bathed in sunlight."*
ISAIAH 58:10 MSG

When your worries become a shadow in your life, get out of yourself and into others. Weed a widow's garden, offer to drive a carless person to church, or help support a child who lives in poverty.

As you expend your energy to help others, you will begin to glow in this dark world. Your shadowed life will be bathed in the light of God's Son. And you'll find people saying, "I want what she has." There's no better witness than that.

Lord, I want to get out from underneath this shadow of worry. Open my eyes to the needs around me. What can I do today to help someone, become a powerful force in Your kingdom, and brighten up my own life—all at the same time?

EVENING
FAITH OVER FRET

*"I'm convinced: You can do anything and everything.
Nothing and no one can upset your plans."*
JOB 42:2 MSG

God has made you certain promises. You can find them in His Word. But you must be convinced that God can and will do anything and everything, that no one can mess up His plans for you and the rest of His creation. When you have such certainty, your faith will win over your fretting every time!

To shore up such faith that God's Word trumps your worries, remember what He said in Isaiah 55:11 (MSG): "The words that come out of my mouth [will] not come back empty-handed. They'll do the work I sent them to do, they'll complete the assignment I gave them."

Help me shore up my faith, Lord. Show me how to grow in certainty that You will do what You've promised to do in my life.

MORNING
NEW HOPE EVERY MORNING

There's one other thing I remember, and remembering, I keep a grip on hope: God's loyal love couldn't have run out, his merciful love couldn't have dried up. They're created new every morning. How great your faithfulness!
LAMENTATIONS 3:21–22 MSG

Take heart. Keep your grip on hope by remembering that God's love and mercy never run out or dry up. Every morning, your Creator has a new supply that you can access through spending time in His Word, praying, and meditating. Just give God room and time to speak through the Spirit. Open yourself to some new thoughts. God, in His faithfulness, will meet you just where you need Him the most.

Lord, in times of doubt, trial, and worry, remind me that You are always there for me with a new supply of love and mercy every morning.

EVENING
ROCK ON IN GOD'S TRUTH

For in the day of trouble He will hide me in His shelter; in the secret place of His tent will He hide me; He will set me high upon a rock.
PSALM 27:5 AMPC

When you are filled with worries, torn up by troubles, there's only one place to go: to God in prayer. Let your worries slip off of you and onto Him.

See yourself as hiding in the shelter of God's love. God pulls you up and sets you upon the rock, high above your earthly cares and all the problems, dangers, and trials that want to drag you down.

As you stand upon the rock, God whispers His encouragement, reminding you that you're a strong Christian woman, a sister of Jesus, a beloved daughter of a king, and a conduit of God's Spirit. Rock on in His truth!

I'm running to You, Lord. Remind me who I am in You!

DAY 38

MORNING
GOD RAINS BLESSINGS

*Blessed be the Lord, the God of Israel, Who has fulfilled
with His hands what He promised with His mouth.*
2 CHRONICLES 6:4 AMPC

The land was experiencing a great famine when the Lord said to the prophet Elijah, "Go, show yourself to Ahab, and I will send rain upon the earth" (1 Kings 18:1 AMPC). Elijah followed God's command.

Six times Elijah told his servant to go and look toward the sea. And each time the servant came back, saying he'd seen nothing. But the seventh time, he saw a cloud that was followed by torrential rains.

Don't let worry and frustration cloud your wonder at what God has said He'll do. Just keep looking. God will do "with His hands what He promised with His mouth."

I'm believing in Your promise to me, Lord. I know You'll rain down Your blessing!

EVENING
SWEET-SMELLING INCENSE

Is anyone crying for help? GOD is listening, ready to rescue you.
PSALM 34:17 MSG

Do you sometimes wonder if God is listening to you? Do you worry your prayers are falling on deaf ears?

Don't. It's the father of lies' aim to drive a wedge between you and the Lord. Yet the truth is that every word you utter in prayer rises up to God like sweet-smelling incense (see Revelation 8:4).

As you go to God in prayer tonight, imagine Him eagerly waiting to hear what you have to say. See Him hanging on every word. Then take the time to listen to His response. His words will rescue you, bringing you ever closer to Him.

*"GOD, come close. Come quickly! Open your ears—it's my voice
you're hearing! Treat my prayer as sweet incense rising; my raised
hands are my evening prayers" (Psalm 141:1–2 MSG).*

MORNING
WORDLESS PRAYERS

Likewise the Spirit helps us in our weakness. For we do not know what to pray for as we ought, but the Spirit himself intercedes for us with groanings too deep for words.
ROMANS 8:26 ESV

Sometimes your worries and troubles may be so burdensome that you find yourself not knowing how to put your pleas to God into words. That's where the Holy Spirit comes in. He knows just what your heart, soul, mind, and spirit are trying to express and delivers your yearnings to God.

Never avoid prayer because you don't know how to put your petitions into words. Just go to God as you are. Sit before Him, allowing Him to enter in. Raise your spirit to His, and all things will be made clear—for you and for God.

I'm coming to You, Lord, for a spirit-to-Spirit talk, resting in Your presence, knowing You will understand all that lies within me. Amen.

EVENING
THE REALITY OF FAITH

Now faith is the assurance (the confirmation, the title deed) of the things [we] hope for, being the proof of things [we] do not see and the conviction of their reality [faith perceiving as real fact what is not revealed to the senses].
HEBREWS 11:1 AMPC

Faith is not wishful thinking but *knowing* God has made certain promises to you and that He will keep those promises. So you can accept them as your present reality even if you do not yet perceive them.

As you read the Bible, you begin to see and understand that all God has said and promised came to pass for those who believed. And this same fact holds true for you! So let go of fears and worries and hang on to faith and hope. God is already working on your behalf, transforming His promises into your reality even as you read these words.

I believe, Lord. I believe.

MORNING
BOLDLY BELIEVING

*If you don't know what you're doing, pray to the Father. He loves
to help. You'll get his help, and won't be condescended to when you
ask for it. Ask boldly, believingly, without a second thought.*

JAMES 1:5 MSG

God loves people who come to Him believing, who have no doubt in their mind that He will give them the wisdom and help they need just when they need it.

In this chapter, James (Jesus' brother) goes on to talk about those who doubt, writing, "People who 'worry their prayers' are like wind-whipped waves. Don't think you're going to get anything from the Master that way, adrift at sea, keeping all your options open" (James 1:6–8 MSG). In other words, God delights in people who boldly come to Him in faith, holding no doubt in their minds.

Ask and believe, and you will receive all the guidance and help you need from the Master.

*Lord, I'm trusting You—and only You—for the
help and wisdom I need. Show me the way.*

EVENING
WORDS OF LIFE

*Remember what you said to me, your servant—I hang on to these words for dear life!
These words hold me up in bad times; yes, your promises rejuvenate me.*

PSALM 119:49–50 MSG

There is only one place where you can *always* find comfort: God's Word.

If you're so troubled and worried that you can't even think, then the best Bible book to go to is the Psalms. It's like reading someone's personal journal. The psalmists write of their troubles, fears, doubts, worries, and hardships. Yet they find reasons to praise God for all the wonderful things He is doing and has done in the past and that they are certain He will do in the future.

Hang on to God's words. They will speak to your heart, lift your spirit, and soothe your soul.

Dear God, show me in Your Word what You would have me read, know, and study.

MORNING
LOOKING TO JESUS

Let us strip off and throw aside every encumbrance (unnecessary weight) and that sin which so readily (deftly and cleverly) clings to and entangles us, and let us run with patient endurance and steady and active persistence the appointed course of the race that is set before us, looking away [from all that will distract] to Jesus.

HEBREWS 12:1–2 AMPC

Many faith-walkers that have gone before you have proven the truth of God. Their example should be enough to prompt you to strip off worry and anything else that hinders your own walk in Christ. View worry as just a distraction, something that keeps you from living in God's light and truth. And see Jesus as your focal point—in life and in prayer.

Jesus, thank You for not just saving me from death but from the fears and worries that dog womankind.

EVENING
FELLOW WORRIERS

Peace I leave with you; My [own] peace I now give and bequeath to you. Not as the world gives do I give to you. Do not let your hearts be troubled, neither let them be afraid. [Stop allowing yourselves to be agitated and disturbed. . .and unsettled.]

JOHN 14:27 AMPC

When someone comes along venting worries and it threatens to drag you down, what's a woman to do?

Be a good listener, but don't let someone else's fears trigger your own. Simply pray for your fellow worrier with the realization that the worries are what that person sees as truth. But you know better. For *your* truth lies in the Word of life. You have Jesus to give you the peace you need and the wisdom to know that, in God, all is truly well.

With You, Jesus, I'm a fellow warrior, not a worrier!

MORNING
A GREAT CALM

And He arose and rebuked the wind and said to the sea, Hush now! Be still (muzzled)! And the wind ceased (sank to rest as if exhausted by its beating) and there was [immediately] a great calm (a perfect peacefulness).
MARK 4:39–40 AMPC

Jesus suggested He and the disciples take the boats to the other side of the lake. On the way, Jesus fell asleep in the stern even after a huge storm rose up and water started filling the boats!

So the disciples woke Jesus, saying, "Don't you care if we're about to die?" That's when Jesus got up, calmed the storm, and then asked the disciples, "Where is your faith?"

When worries start to flood into your life, allow faith to anchor you. Remind yourself of Jesus' love and power.

Lord, calm the storm deep within me.

EVENING
GOOD SPIRITUALITY

Be happy [in your faith] and rejoice and be glad-hearted continually (always); be unceasing in prayer [praying perseveringly]; thank [God] in everything [no matter what the circumstances may be, be thankful and give thanks], for this is the will of God for you.
1 THESSALONIANS 5:16–18 AMPC

Instead of worrying, God wants you to rejoice continually, to pray without ceasing, and to thank Him for everything—"no matter what the circumstances may be." That may sound like a really tall order, but if that's what God wants and wills you to do, He'll give you the power and strength to do it! Besides, if you begin to spend all your time rejoicing, praying, and thanking God, you won't have time to worry!

Help me, Lord, to seek constant joy in You. To pray continually, giving You my worries as soon as they creep into my mind, then leaving them in Your hands.

MORNING
REGAINING A FOOTHOLD OF FAITH

When I said, "My feet are slipping," your mercy, O Lord, continued to hold me up. When I worried about many things, your assuring words soothed my soul.
PSALM 94:18–19 GW

When you start to slip into worrying, when your feet of faith start to lose their purchase, tell God all about it. Acknowledge to yourself that His kindness and compassion *will help* you regain a foothold. Allow His words to soothe your soul and nurture your spirit.

No matter when worry, trouble, or danger strikes, God is right there with you in the midst of things. He promises He'll never leave your side.

Lord, thank You for always being there when I need You, loving me, holding me up, helping me out, and soothing my soul.

EVENING
KNOWING GOD

"Give your entire attention to what God is doing right now, and don't get worked up about what may or may not happen tomorrow. God will help you deal with whatever hard things come up when the time comes."
MATTHEW 6:34 MSG

The human imagination has a way of leading you astray by coming up with a myriad of different scenarios that may or may not become your reality. But Jesus says a believer's attention should be focused on God and where He's working right now, in this moment, not on tomorrow and its uncertainties, knowing God will help with whatever happens when it happens.

But how do you get there from here? Move closer to God. Learn all you can about Him. Know Him. And your worries about tomorrow will flee.

Help me, Lord, to keep my focus on You and what You're doing right now. I'm trusting my unknown future to You, the God I know and love.

MORNING
REFUGE, SHIELD, HOPE, AND PEACE

You are my refuge and my shield; your word is my source of hope. . . .
Those who love your instructions have great peace and do not stumble.

PSALM 119:114, 165 NLT

When you're worried, lost, and confused, when you don't know where to go or who to turn to, go to God and open His Word. There you will find the refuge you so desperately seek, the safety you need, the hope you thirst for, and the compass you crave.

You can run to God no matter where you are. He is as near to you as your breath. Within His presence and power, you will be shielded. He will make sure you do not stumble as you follow His instructions and take the next steps.

Thank You, Lord, for being my constant refuge, shield, and hope.
In Your Word alone do I find wisdom and peace.

EVENING
THE OPENER OF EYES, HEARTS, AND THE WORD

"Did not our hearts burn within us while he talked to us on
the road, while he opened to us the Scriptures?"

LUKE 24:32 ESV

After Jesus' death, two of His disciples, confused and sorrowful, headed to Emmaus and talked about what had happened. As they were walking, Jesus joined them, yet they did not recognize Him. Hearing their story about Him, Jesus "interpreted to them in all the Scriptures the things concerning himself" (Luke 24:27 ESV). Later, when He broke bread with them, "their eyes were opened" (Luke 24:31 ESV), and Jesus vanished.

Like those disciples, at times you may feel confused, alone, and worried about what has happened or will happen. But you can take heart, because Jesus will give you hope—for He still walks and talks with you!

Jesus, help me to recognize Your presence walking with me.
Open my eyes and heart as I seek Your Word.

MORNING
GOD'S ARM

*Be the arm [of Your servants—their strength and defense]
every morning, our salvation in the time of trouble.*
ISAIAH 33:2 AMPC

It's obvious that starting your day with prayer, seeking to make God your primary guide and focus instead of your own self, sets you on the right course. Before you're out the door, you'll be armed with God's strength, protection, and saving power. The volume of His voice in your heart, mind, and soul will then rise above all other sounds and whistles, keeping your feet on the right path and worries and other distracters at bay (see Isaiah 33:3).

Lord, be my strength and defense every morning.

EVENING
WISDOM OVER WORRY

*Listen well to my words; tune your ears to my voice. Keep my message in
plain view at all times. Concentrate! Learn it by heart! Those who discover
these words live, really live; body and soul, they're bursting with health.*
PROVERBS 4:20–22 MSG

If you want to have the best life, dig into God's wisdom. You'll find it throughout the Bible but especially in Proverbs. There King Solomon provides insight into how to deal with everyday issues, including how to work, act, talk, think, curb your anger, and so much more.

In the verses above, Solomon strongly suggests you learn some verses by heart. Perhaps you could start by reading Proverbs every day. When you come to a verse that really speaks to you, that gives you guidance or peace about a situation, memorize it. Before you know it, God's wisdom will stand in place of your worry.

I want to live a good life, Lord. Help me replace my worry with Your Word!

MORNING
WARDING OFF WORRIES

O Lord God, my savior, I cry out to you during the day and at night.
Let my prayer come into your presence. Turn your ear to hear my cries.
PSALM 88:1–2 GW

Chances are you brush your teeth in the morning and again in the evening. You were taught to do this as a child and now do it automatically, without even thinking. And that's a good thing, for brushing teeth helps ward off cavities.

So why not start the practice of praying in the morning and then again in the evening? As you do this day after day, it too will become something you do automatically. And it'll be a good thing because doing so will help ward off worries, giving you a focused mind by day and a restful one at night!

Lord, let my prayer come into Your loving presence day and night.

EVENING
GOD ONLY KNOWS

For the Lord sees not as man sees; for man looks on the
outward appearance, but the Lord looks on the heart.
1 SAMUEL 16:7 AMPC

Although people can give you clues—through expression, voice, body language, attitude, or demeanor—as to how they think or feel about you—only God can truly see within peoples' hearts and minds to know what they're really thinking (see 1 Kings 8:39; John 2:24–25; Matthew 9:4).

God doesn't want you to worry about the opinions or thoughts of others or to let them hold you back from what He's calling you to do or say. Your job is to please Him alone (see 1 Thessalonians 2:4). He'll take care of the rest.

Help me, Lord, to not worry about what others may
think about me but to live and serve You alone!

MORNING
THE PEACE OF GOD'S KINGDOM

*Now may the Lord of peace Himself grant you His peace
(the peace of His kingdom) at all times and in all ways
[under all circumstances and conditions, whatever comes].*
2 THESSALONIANS 3:16 AMPC

The philosopher Michel de Montaigne, who lived in the 1500s, said: "My life has been filled with terrible misfortune; most of which never happened."

And there are modern-day statistics to back up Montaigne's statement. A recent study says 40 percent of the things you worry about will never happen; 30 percent are in the past, which you can't change; 12 percent are needless worries about your health; and 10 percent are trivial worries that fall into the miscellaneous category. That leaves you with 8 percent of worries that have actual substance in your life. So tell your worries to hit the road, and walk in God's path of peace.

Lord of peace, fill me with Your presence and the peace of Your kingdom.

EVENING
ALWAYS THERE

*Even if my father and mother abandon me,
the LORD will hold me close.*
PSALM 27:10 NLT

Relationships with others can be difficult at times. Through some misunderstanding or deliberate affront, some family members can become estranged. Others may find themselves divorced. Even friends can fade away. And then, of course, some loved ones are lost through death.

Yet there's no need to worry about being alone. Even if your mother and father abandon you, God will always be there to hold you close. For He, your eternal and loving Father, promises to take you in and care for you. And His Son, your Friend Jesus, will stick closer to you than a brother (see Proverbs 18:24).

*Thank You, Lord, for being the Love and Light
that's forever with me—from beginning to end.*

MORNING
MOMENT BY MOMENT

Whatever you do, put your whole heart and soul into it, as into work done for God, and not merely for men—knowing that your real reward, a heavenly one, will come from God, since you are actually employed by Christ.
COLOSSIANS 3:23–24 PHILLIPS

Are you living in the future or in the present moment?

When worry begins to creep into your day, check to see where you're living. If it's in the future, take a step back. Then ask God to draw you into the present moment. He'll get you back on course.

Lord, help me stay living in the present moment, where You and my peace reside.

EVENING
GIVE GOD A CALL

For you, O Lord, are good and forgiving, abounding in steadfast love to all who call upon you. Give ear, O LORD, to my prayer; listen to my plea for grace. In the day of my trouble I call upon you, for you answer me.
PSALM 86:5–7 ESV

No one is perfect—except God, of course. But you're a mere human. You're bound to make a few mistakes. There will probably be times when you wrong yourself, God, or a fellow human being. Before you realize it, you're caught in a whirl of worry—about the effects of your misstep, what God and others may be thinking about you (and your words and actions), how or what you'll say when you ask for forgiveness, and so on.

To break free of this whirl of worry, call on God. Ask Him to hear your prayer and to bestow His forgiveness, and then expect His answer.

Lord, I'm calling on You, counting on Your love and forgiveness.

MORNING
WELL-EMPLOYED

*"Study this Book of Instruction continually. Meditate on it day
and night so you will be sure to obey everything written in it.
Only then will you prosper and succeed in all you do."*
JOSHUA 1:8 NLT

Unlike worry, meditation will help you not just to prosper but to succeed! Yet you may find it hard to pull yourself out of the world and into God. Fortunately, those who've gone before are here to help. About meditation, St. Francis de Sales advises:

"If the heart wanders or is distracted, bring it back to the point quite gently and replace it tenderly in its Master's presence. And even if you did nothing during the whole of your hour but bring your heart back and place it again in our Lord's presence, though it went away every time you brought it back, your hour would be very well employed."

*"May the words of my mouth and the meditation of my heart
be pleasing to you, O LORD" (Psalm 19:14 NLT).*

EVENING
UNFAMILIAR PATHS

*I will lead the blind on unfamiliar roads. I will lead them on unfamiliar paths.
I will turn darkness into light in front of them. I will make rough places smooth.
These are the things I will do for them, and I will never abandon them.*
ISAIAH 42:16 GW

Worrying about what may happen in the future, what to do in the present, or how to get over the past can make you feel as if you're blind, walking in the dark, lost and confused. Yet you need not worry about stumbling in the dark, unable to see the road ahead of you, because God promises to lead you down unfamiliar paths. In fact, He'll transform the darkness into light right in front of your eyes! He'll make rocky places smooth. And He will never abandon you.

I'm with You, Lord, all the way! Lead me down Your path into Your light!

MORNING
GOD ONE STEP AHEAD

*"I will answer them before they even call to me. While they are still
talking about their needs, I will go ahead and answer their prayers!"*
ISAIAH 65:24 NLT

How wonderful to have a God that answers you before you even cry out for Him! That
while you're busy pouring out your worries, presenting God your what-if scenarios, and
trying to put words to all you feel and are concerned about, He is already answering
your petitions!

That's just who God is! That's just how much He cares about you! If you memorize
today's verse and truly believe it, you can break up whatever worries come your way.

*Lord, I'm taking up my shield of faith in You, knowing that You are already going
before me, answering my prayer, solving my problem, and healing my heart.*

EVENING
LIVING CAREFREE

*So be content with who you are, and don't put on airs.
God's strong hand is on you; he'll promote you at the right
time. Live carefree before God; he is most careful with you.*
1 PETER 5:6–7 MSG

God doesn't want you worrying about the who, what, when, where, how, and why in
your life. He doesn't want you to be unhappy where you are right now, in this moment.
He wants you to totally trust Him, to know and believe He has a plan for your life—and
it's so much better than anything you ever dreamed or imagined.

The same strong hand God used to part the waters and lead the Israelites out of
Egypt and into the Promised Land is the same hand that is now upon you.

*Take my worries, Lord. Then hold me until I can
feel Your peace, love, and strong hand upon me.*

MORNING
MAKE UP YOUR MIND

I have cheerfully made up my mind to be proud of my weaknesses,
because they mean a deeper experience of the power of Christ. I can
even enjoy weaknesses, suffering, privations, persecutions and difficulties
for Christ's sake. For my very weakness makes me strong in him.
2 Corinthians 12:10 Phillips

God gives many gifts to His faithful followers, one of which is that no matter how weak you are, no matter how much you suffer or how often you worry, your very weaknesses give Christ the chance to shine through you. For this formula to work, though, you must have faith and then make up your mind to live it.

God moves when you're truly helpless. He provides when you have no more resources left. He will give you the power to overcome all things—even worry!

I've made up my mind, Lord! I'm going to be content no matter what!

EVENING
GOD MEETS YOUR NEEDS

The Lord is my Shepherd [to feed, guide, and shield me], I shall not lack. He makes me
lie down in [fresh, tender] green pastures; He leads me beside the still and restful waters.
Psalm 23:1–2 AMPC

In 1943, Abraham Maslow proposed a theory in psychology called Maslow's hierarchy of needs. He explained that there are five levels of human needs. The first level, which is physiological—food, water, warmth, and rest—must be satisfied before individuals can take care of needs higher up.

Amazingly enough, those are the *same* needs David covers in the first two verses of Psalm 23! David says he doesn't want for anything because God is his Shepherd who feeds, guides, and shields him. He makes David lie down and rest. He leads David to water.

God will take care of everything! Why? Because He's the *Great* Shepherd!

Lord, thank You for being my Great Shepherd!

MORNING
DESIRES MET

Whatever we ask we receive from him, because we keep his commandments and do what pleases him. And this is his commandment, that we believe in the name of his Son Jesus Christ and love one another, just as he has commanded us.

1 JOHN 3:22–23 ESV

Worried you won't get what you've been praying for? No need to be. You *will* get what you desire if you follow God's commands and do what pleases Him.

That means you must believe in Jesus: that He walked upon this earth, was God's Son, performed miracles, was full of wisdom, and is the example you're to follow. The second command is to love others—including God and yourself.

Examine your life. Talk to God. Live His way. And your desires will be more than met!

Help me examine my life, Lord. I want to live—and pray—Your way.

EVENING
ALL IS WELL

She said, "All is well."

2 KINGS 4:23 ESV

A childless woman went out of her way to provide a room where Elisha, a man of God, could rest when he came into town. To repay her, Elisha told her she'd have a baby. And she did. A boy. But then he died. So she laid her son on Elisha's bed and went to find Elisha. When her husband asked why she was going out, she simply said, "All is well." She repeated the phrase to Elisha's servant, who, seeing her coming, asked if anything was wrong (see 2 Kings 4:26 ESV). And in the end, all *was* well, for Elisha brought the boy back to life.

Go the way of this woman. No matter what's happening, know God has a plan. Somehow, He'll make everything turn out right.

Lord, I know You make all things work out to Your good.

MORNING
PRAYING HANDS

You, O Lord, are a shield for me, my glory, and the lifter of my head. . . . I lay down and slept; I wakened again, for the Lord sustains me. I will not be afraid.
PSALM 3:3, 5–6 AMPC

The world can be a pretty scary place. It's enough to make you wring your hands, leading you to worry about what may be coming around the next corner. But fortunately for you, God is on your side.

Instead of wringing your hands, fold them together and pray. Rest and sleep easy, knowing God sustains you. With Him in your corner, you need not be afraid. His blessing and love are upon you!

You're my shield, Lord. You fill me with joy and keep my head in the right place. Knowing that You're sustaining me, I rest and sleep easy. As I pray, my fears fade.

EVENING
WATCH AND WAIT

In the morning You hear my voice, O Lord; in the morning I prepare [a prayer, a sacrifice] for You and watch and wait [for You to speak to my heart].
PSALM 5:3 AMPC

One of the best places to have a Bible is right by your bed, for then you can connect with God before your feet even hit the floor. To help you springboard into this idea of making reading the Word a morning habit, begin by reading the psalms, specifically Psalm 5:3.

It acknowledges that God hears your voice in the morning as you prepare a prayer for Him. It reminds you not to just read some words and then jump out of bed, but to pray "and watch and wait" for God to speak to your heart.

In the morning You hear my voice, O Lord; in this moment I prepare a prayer for You. And now I watch and wait for You to speak into my heart.

MORING
GOD WALKS WITH YOU

*Yes, though I walk through the [deep, sunless] valley of the shadow
of death, I will fear or dread no evil, for You are with me; Your rod
[to protect] and Your staff [to guide], they comfort me.*

PSALM 23:4 AMPC

God not only satisfies your basic human needs for food, water, warmth, and rest but also walks with you, equipped with two tools to make sure you're safe and heading the right way. He uses the first tool, His shepherd's rod, to stave off any force, power, or evil that threatens your life. He uses the second, His staff, to guide you through the shadows and onto the right path.

So the next time you're worried about your safety or where to take your next step, pray to God—the all-powerful Father and Shepherd who loves and adores you.

*Lord, I feel Your presence by my side. With You walking alongside
me, I know I'll be safe and heading down the right path.*

EVENING
ASLEEP AND AWAKE IN GOD

*When you go, they [the words of your parents' God] shall lead you; when you
sleep, they shall keep you; and when you waken, they shall talk with you.*

PROVERBS 6:22 AMPC

Knowing God's Word and following it can keep you, Father God's child, from letting your worries careen out of control.

Wherever you go, allow God's Word to lead you down the right path. While you sleep, allow it to comfort and protect you. And when you wake, seek God's Word through reading and His voice through prayer, allowing both to talk to you, giving you all the wisdom you need to keep from stumbling, to make the choices God would have you make throughout your day.

*Heavenly Father, help me to lean heavily on Your Word.
Talk to me, guide me, comfort and protect me.*

MORNING
THE RIGHT WOMAN FOR THE JOB

Moses said to God, "Who am I that I should go. . . ?"
God answered, "I will be with you."
EXODUS 3:11–12 GW

From a burning bush, God appeared to Moses, telling him to free His people. But Moses was full of worry and self-doubt, so he asked God, "Who am I that I should go?" Then he came up with a bunch of excuses why he wasn't the right man for the job.

Perhaps Moses didn't know that whomever God calls, He's already prepared.

Is God calling you to do something you're not sure you can do? Are you worried you won't be able to handle it? Don't be. Whoever God calls, He's prepared. And just as God was with Moses, He's with you.

Lord, I know You've prepared me for where You call me. Help me trust in You.

EVENING
WHAT'S IN YOUR HAND?

Moses answered, But behold, they will not believe me or listen to and obey my voice; for they will say, The Lord has not appeared to you. And the Lord said to him, What is that in your hand? And he said, A rod.
EXODUS 4:1–2 AMPC

Maybe God has called you and, like Moses, you still have worries, self-doubts. That's when God calls your attention to the tools you already have, the ones you're very familiar with, the ones in your hand or your company. Your tool might be your pen, voice, talent, vehicle, knitting needle.

Instead of worrying about how you'll do something, look to see what you have in your hand or who you have at your side. Pray for God to reveal your tools, and then use them.

What, Lord, would You have me use to serve You? Reveal my tools for Your glory!

MORNING
NO WORRY LINES

*Let all those who take refuge and put their trust in You rejoice; let them ever sing
and shout for joy, because You make a covering over them and defend them;
let those also who love Your name be joyful in You and be in high spirits.*

PSALM 5:11 AMPC

It's difficult to be joyful in God and in high spirits when worry is clouding not only
your day but your judgment. The fact of the matter is that worry not only mars you
within but without. You've heard of worry lines, haven't you? Who needs them? Why
not replace them with laugh lines?

Today, do just that by running to God. Put your trust in Him alone. You'll soon
find yourself breaking out in song and shouting for joy.

I'm running to You, God, knowing You're my path to joy!

EVENING
GOD'S SHIELD OF LOVE

*For You, Lord, will bless the [uncompromisingly] righteous [him
who is upright and in right standing with You]; as with a shield
You will surround him with goodwill (pleasure and favor).*

PSALM 5:12 AMPC

When you begin seeking God early, expecting Him to speak to your heart, taking refuge
in and trusting Him (see Psalm 5:3, 11), not only will your worries take a backseat to
God's presence in your life, but He will bless you in so many other ways! He will show
you the way to walk and talk. He will surround you with His shield of love and bless
you with His favor!

As your worries fall like scales from your eyes, you will be able to see all the blessings He is putting in your path. Your life will be full of pleasure behind God's shield
of abundant love.

*Lord, surround me with Your shield of love so
that my eyes may see Your blessings in my life.*

BLESSED IS THE WOMAN WHO SEEKS WISDOM

Those who look for me find me. . . . Blessed the woman, who listens to me, awake and ready for me each morning, alert and responsive. . . . When you find me, you find life, real life, to say nothing of GOD's good pleasure.
PROVERBS 8:18, 34–35 MSG

Lady Wisdom was with God before He even formed the earth. She was brought forth before the seas, mountains, and heavens. And she's filled with all the knowledge and understanding you need to keep worries at bay.

But there's a hitch. You need to *look* for her. To listen to her. To seek her each morning. To be alert to her presence and respond to her advice. When you do, Wisdom will bless you with more than material wealth, which is fleeting at best. She will bless you with spiritual wealth. You'll be living a life worth living, a true life, as the recipient of God's favor.

Reveal Your truths to me. Give me Your wisdom to replace my worry.

PREVAIL IN PROMISES

"Don't worry about a thing. Go ahead and do what you've said. But first make a small biscuit for me and bring it back here. Then go ahead and make a meal from what's left for you and your son."
1 KINGS 17:13 MSG

The prophet Elijah approached a poor widow gathering firewood. He asked her to bring him water and something to eat. She told him all she had left was "a handful of flour in a jar and a little oil in a bottle," just enough to "make a last meal" for herself and her son (1 Kings 17:12 MSG).

But Elijah told her not to worry, that God promised her oil and flour would not run out before God sent rain to end the drought. Hearing those words, the widow put aside her worries and obeyed Elijah. For the next two years, God provided as promised. Have faith, woman of God!

Lord, I never want my faith to run dry. I believe in You and Your promises!

MORNING
ARROW PRAYERS

The king said to me, "What are you requesting?" So I prayed to the God of heaven. And I said to the king, "If it pleases the king, and if your servant has found favor in your sight, that you send me to Judah. . .that I may rebuild it."
NEHEMIAH 2:4–5 ESV

When Nehemiah, the king of Persia's wine taster, received word Jerusalem's wall was broken and her gates burned down, he wept then fasted and prayed to God for days. When he later entered the king's presence, he was still sad. So the king, seeing his cupbearer's face, asked him what the matter was. This frightened Nehemiah, for servants were to be cheerful before their sovereign.

Nehemiah sent up an arrow prayer—quick and to the point—to God, knowing he'd get courage and guidance just when he needed it.

Take your challenges to God as soon as they come, knowing your all-powerful Father is waiting and ready to help.

Lead me to pray to You not just daily but the instant I need You, Lord.

EVENING
BEDTIME PRAYER

In peace I will both lie down and sleep, for You, Lord, alone make me dwell in safety and confident trust.
PSALM 4:8 AMPC

You have lots of challenges. Yet you have a God-Father-King-Shepherd you can run to. One who has rescued, encouraged, provided for, and fought for you time after time. He's answered your prayers, has loved you like no other, has gifted you with eternal life, and has made you, His daughter, a princess. You can count on Him to keep you safe, to watch over you.

So when your head hits the pillow, override your worries with God's Word. Bring tonight's verse to mind. Repeat it slowly, absorbing its power, and you will find the peace you need for a good night's sleep.

In You, loving Lord, I find the peace to sleep.

MORNING

MORNING
WEAVING GOD'S WORD WITHIN

Keep my words; lay up within you my commandments [for use when needed] and treasure them. Keep my commandments and live, and keep my law and teaching as the apple (the pupil) of your eye. Bind them on your fingers; write them on the tablet of your heart.
PROVERBS 7:1–3 AMPC

The more ways you work God's Word into your very being, the less you'll find to worry about. God makes it clear you're to follow His words. To store up His wisdom so you can use it when you need it. To keep your eyes fixed on the teachings of His Son and Spirit. To write God's words on the back of your hand and within your heart.

Today, spend time in God's Word. Ask God to reveal the verses He wants you to write upon your heart. Meditate upon them and implant them within you.

God, engrave Your Word upon my heart.

EVENING
PRAYING FOR ALL

I admonish and urge that petitions, prayers, intercessions, and thanksgivings be offered on behalf of all men.
1 TIMOTHY 2:1 AMPC

There may be some people in positions of power or authority with whom you disagree or feel uncomfortable. There may be some you think will lead your town, city, state, or country down the wrong road. You worry that they don't have the best interests of you and other people at heart.

Rather than worry about what leaders may or may not do next, the apostle Paul urges you to go to God. To pray for "kings and all who are in positions of authority or high responsibility" (1 Timothy 2:2 AMPC). For that's the only way you'll be able to live in peace—within and without.

I want to pray for all people in all positions, Lord.

MORNING
A HEART-TO-HEART ATTITUDE

*When Solomon finished making these prayers and petitions to
the LORD, he stood up in front of the altar of the LORD, where he
had been kneeling with his hands raised toward heaven.*

1 KINGS 8:54 NLT

Prayer is a form of worship, and everyone has their own prayer posture. Some pray with eyes closed, hands folded, or head bowed. King Solomon kneeled and raised his hands toward heaven.

Jesus told the woman at the well, "It's who you are and the way you live that count before God. Your worship must engage your spirit in the pursuit of truth. That's the kind of people the Father is out looking for: those who are simply and honestly themselves before him in their worship" (John 4:23 MSG).

Today, go before God for a heart-to-heart talk, conscious of your own heart attitude. Look for places where you might need to be more of who you truly are as you come before God.

Here I am, Lord, coming before You, just as I am.

EVENING
QUALIFIED BY GOD

*By ourselves we are not qualified in any way to claim that we
can do anything. Rather, God makes us qualified.*

2 CORINTHIANS 3:5 GW

The world would have you believe that to be successful, you must have a high degree of self-sufficiency, counting on yourself alone to provide your needs. Yet such an attitude would lead you away from God, your true and loving Provider.

An attitude of self-sufficiency also leads you to worrying about how you'll meet all your needs and keeps you from praying to the One who provides them.

So, the next time worry comes creeping along, look within to see if you're harboring an attitude of self-sufficiency. Ask God to root it out so you can become the woman He created you to be—one dependent upon Him alone.

Keep me leaning on and relying on You, Lord. I can do nothing without You.

MORNING
YOUR BURDEN BEARER, DAY BY DAY

*Blessed be the Lord, Who bears our burdens and carries us day by day, even
the God Who is our salvation! Selah [pause, and calmly think of that]!*
PSALM 68:19 AMPC

How blessed you are to have a God who loves you so much He will not only bear your
burdens but also carry you! Knowing and truly believing this gives you the peace of
mind, heart, body, and spirit you need to live a fabulous life, free of worry! Yet the
benefits don't stop there. Along with God bearing your load, He's decided you will
be strong!

Today, give God your worries. Believe that He's carrying them—and you. Then
enter your day in the strength He gives you.

*Lord, my worries have been weighing me down. Thank You so
much for carrying them—and me—today and every day.*

EVENING
HAPPY AND BLESSED

*"Blessed are you among women. . . . Oh, how happy is the woman who
believes in God, for he does make his promises to her come true."*
LUKE 1:42, 45 PHILLIPS

Gabriel told Mary that God favored her and she would be giving birth to His Son.
When she wondered how that would happen, the angel explained the details. Then he
told her that her once-barren cousin, Elizabeth, had conceived in her old age. "For no
promise of God can fail to be fulfilled" (Luke 1:37 PHILLIPS)!

Mary went to visit Elizabeth, who called her blessed, saying, "Happy is the woman
who believes in God, for he does make his promises to her come true."

You too can be happy and blessed when you give up your worries and submit
yourself to God, who never fails to come through on His promises!

*I lift my whole self up to You, Lord, knowing You
and Your promises come true to those who believe!*

MORNING
BE STILL

God is in the midst of her; she shall not be moved;
God will help her when morning dawns.
PSALM 46:5 ESV

No matter what troubles you're facing or what worries are upon your mind, you have a mighty fortress in God. He's your "refuge and strength, an ever-present help in times of trouble" (Psalm 46:1 GW). He brings His full power, all His angels, all His resources, visible and invisible, material and temporal, to aid you. He shields, empowers, and frees you.

God brings His peace to you, telling you gently, *"I've got this. You need not worry."* He tells you your role in all this. It's to simply "let be and be still, and know (recognize and understand) that I am God" (Psalm 46:10 AMPC).

Today, make it your aim to let be and be still. Know your God is taking care of everything. He's got this.

Oh Lord, help me know You better.

EVENING
COME AWAY WITH GOD

His left hand is under my head, and his right hand embraces me! . . . My beloved
speaks and says to me: "Arise, my love, my beautiful one, and come away."
SONG OF SOLOMON 2:6, 10 ESV

God longs to have an intimate relationship with you. He doesn't want your worries about what may or may not happen to become a barrier between you, to distract you from what He can do and is doing in your life.

To tear down the wall of worry, find a quiet place. Tell God all that's on your mind. Relax as you imagine God right next to you. Spend as much time as you'd like with Him, enjoying His presence, listening for His voice, hearing what He has to say. Then arise, beautiful one, and go with Him wherever He leads.

Father, let me rest in this peace, surrounded by Your presence and love.

MORNING
CONTINUAL CARE FROM ABBA

*I will be a Father to you, and you shall be My
sons and daughters, says the Lord Almighty.*
2 Corinthians 6:18 ampc

When you were little, chances are you ran to your parents when you fell and skinned your knee. They wiped away the blood, cleaned the wound, and bandaged it up.

Now you're a woman, perhaps with children of your own. You may even be taking care of your parents as they once took care of you. And sometimes you find yourself worrying, wondering, *Who'll take care of me when I need help?* The answer is *God.*

You're God's precious daughter. He tells you, "Even when you're old, I'll take care of you. Even when your hair turns gray, I'll support you. I made you and will continue to care for you. I'll support you and save you" (Isaiah 46:4 gw).

Thank You, Daddy God, for always being there for me, ready to help me when I fall.

EVENING
THE MASTER PLANNER

*We are God's [own] handiwork. . .recreated in Christ Jesus. . .that we may do those
good works which God predestined (planned beforehand) for us [taking paths which
He prepared ahead of time], that we should walk in them [. . .for us to live].*
Ephesians 2:10 ampc

God, the Master Planner, had you in mind before time began, designed you, and then re-created you in Christ so you could be a part of His grand plan. He has paths He's prepared for you to take, all so you could live the good life He made ready for you.

You're in God's plan, but your worries are not. So, stop wringing your hands. Give God all you can't handle, and settle down in His peace. Live "the good life which He prearranged and made ready"(Ephesians 2:10 ampc) for you to live.

Lord, I'm amazed at the plans You've made for me.

MORNING
LAUGHING WITHOUT FEAR

*She is clothed with strength and dignity, and she laughs without
fear of the future. . . . Charm is deceptive, and beauty does not last;
but a woman who fears the LORD will be greatly praised.*

PROVERBS 31:25, 30 NLT

Proverbs 31:10–31 describes the glowing attributes of God's ideal woman, giving female followers something to aim for. She's trustworthy, works hard and willingly, takes care of her household and family. . .and more! But the most striking is that "she laughs without fear of the future"! Perhaps you're wondering, *How can I get to where she is?*

It's simple. Fear God. Know Him. Worship Him by obeying and loving Him with all your heart, mind, body, spirit, and soul. Once you truly know and obey God, you will realize that you really have nothing at all to worry about.

I want to know You more, Lord, so I too may laugh without fear of the future!

EVENING
NIGHT WATCHES

*When I remember You upon my bed and meditate on You in the night watches. For
You have been my help, and in the shadow of Your wings will I rejoice. My whole
being follows hard after You and clings closely to You; Your right hand upholds me.*

PSALM 63:6–8 AMPC

In the quiet darkness, it's easy to let your mind wander into the even darker territory of worry. But why not switch up your thought pattern and go from worry to wonder by meditating on God.

Remember how much God has done for you. How He protected and cared for you, helped you, and provided all you needed to make it to this point in your day and in your life. Then see yourself clinging to Him as He holds you up, carries you, and pours out upon you His strength and peace.

Hold me, Lord, as I cling to You, absorbing Your presence and peace.

MORNING
LET PEACE REIGN

I have told you these things, so that in Me you may have [perfect] peace and confidence. In the world you have tribulation and trials and distress and frustration; but be of good cheer [take courage; be confident, certain, undaunted]! For I have overcome the world.
JOHN 16:33 AMPC

Jesus knows you'll have times of trouble. Yet as you live in Him, you'll find that perfect peace and confidence you need to face them. So, no matter what has happened, is happening, or may happen, don't worry.

Instead, take courage. Live the life God has planned for you. Have confidence in Jesus, and have peace within because He has overcome your world. He says, "I have deprived it of power to harm you and have conquered it for you" (John 16:33 AMPC).

Come live in me, Jesus. Help me overcome my worry, and let Your peace reign within.

EVENING
IN STEP WITH GOD

It is the Lord Who goes before you; He will [march] with you; He will not fail you or let you go or forsake you; [let there be no cowardice or flinching, but] fear not, neither become broken [in spirit—depressed, dismayed, and unnerved with alarm].
DEUTERONOMY 31:8 AMPC

Moses was saying farewell to God's people, who would be led into the Promised Land by Joshua. He told them God *Himself* would go before them and give them victory.

As God went before His Israelites, He goes before you. He *marches* with you as you enter His land of promises. Your role is not to worry or fear but to believe God will neither fail nor forsake you. When you trust God with all, keeping in step with Him, you will prevail.

I'm trusting in You, Lord, as we walk in step together.

MORNING
CROSSING SAFELY

I, the Lord your God, hold your right hand; it is I
who say to you, "Fear not, I am the one who helps you."
ISAIAH 41:13 ESV

A mom becomes extra vigilant when it comes to helping her child cross the street. It is she and not the child who can see all the cars coming, understands the rules of the road, and knows the dangers of stepping away from the safety of the sidewalk. Yet the child is neither fearful nor worried. She's totally secure with her hand in her mom's.

Now that you're older, you may not need help crossing the street. But you *do* need help finding your way through life. Fortunately, you have Father God beside you. Allow Him to take your right hand. Hear Him say, *"Fear not, I am the one who helps you."* And you'll find the safety and security you seek.

Lord, take my hand. Walking with You, I have no fear.

EVENING
GOD HAS A PLAN

"I know what I'm doing. I have it all planned out—plans to take care
of you, not abandon you, plans to give you the future you hope for.
When you call on me, when you come and pray to me, I'll listen."
JEREMIAH 29:11–12 MSG

Have you ever tried a new recipe and gotten flustered because you didn't know what you were doing?

Some new challenges in life can be like that. No matter how much you plan or how much effort you put into some new task, job, or project, you worry things will somehow go wrong and you may not be able to fix them!

Fortunately, God knows what *He's* doing—and He's infallible, so you need not worry about anything. God has everything planned out for you. He's going to take care of you. So no worries. Just go to God in prayer.

I'm thankful that You know what You're doing, Lord. I'm counting on You!

MORNING
GOING AFTER GOD

You will seek Me, inquire for, and require Me [as a vital necessity] and find Me when you search for Me with all your heart. I will be found by you, says the Lord, and I will release you from captivity.

JEREMIAH 29:13–14 AMPC

When you *really* go looking for God, seeking His face, pining for His presence, needing Him as you need no one and nothing else, searching for Him with all your heart, you will find Him. And when you find Him, God will free you from everything that binds you, including worry.

Can you imagine living a worry-free life? Living every day for God with courage, hope, joy, and laughter?

Go after God with all that you are and have. Live a life of freedom. You'll never look back!

I'm making You number one in my life, Lord, going after You with all I am and have!

EVENING
THE ART OF LIFE

The steps of a [good] man are directed and established by the Lord when He delights in his way [and He busies Himself with his every step]. Though he falls, he shall not be utterly cast down, for the Lord grasps his hand in support and upholds him.

PSALM 37:23–24 AMPC

Can you imagine exchanging worry for wonder? It's possible!

Instead of focusing on what may or may not happen or how to fix the past, why not wonder what God may be saying to you in the present? Come out of yourself and into God, looking for His message through His Word, for the connection among you, Him, and your life events. See where God's directing you, where He's taking you.

Delight with wonder in every step along the way, knowing that with your hand in Father God's, although you may stumble, He'll never let you fall.

Lord, help me discover Your message as I delight in every step along the way.

MORNING
NO WORD WITHOUT POWER

For with God nothing is ever impossible and no word from
God shall be without power or impossible of fulfillment.

LUKE 1:37 AMPC

When you're between a rock and a hard place and see no way out, look to God. Rest in His presence. Bask in His peace. Remind yourself that there's no feat He cannot perform, no task He cannot undertake, no problem He cannot solve, no challenge He cannot meet. Nothing is impossible for God. He makes all His words and promises come true. And He's your number one fan.

I don't know what to do, Lord. That's where You come in. Help! I'm trusting
in You to make things right. Ease me with the power of Your Word!

EVENING
PERFECT LOVE

And as we live in God, our love grows more perfect.
So we will not be afraid. . . . Such love has no fear.

1 JOHN 4:17–18 NLT

Communing with God, there's no room for anything else—no worries, no fears, no anger, no doubts. God loves you so much that He'll never let anything come between you and Him. Nor will He let anything or anyone snatch you out of His hand.

Tonight, pray that God will help you open your heart to the power and peace of His love, that your spirit and His will meld into one. Then spend some time in God's presence, allowing His love to pour into you, feed and nourish you, and fill you until it spills out of you and onto those around you.

Lord, I want that perfect love I get only when I am living in Your
love and You're living in me. Fill me, Lord, with such love.

MORNING
ONE THING WORTH YOUR ATTENTION

*The Lord said to her, "My dear Martha, you are worried and upset over
all these details! There is only one thing worth being concerned about.
Mary has discovered it, and it will not be taken away from her."*
LUKE 10:41–42 NLT

While Martha was rushing around preparing food for Jesus and the other guests, her sister, Mary, "sat at the Lord's feet, listening to what he taught" (Luke 10:39 NLT). So Martha went to Jesus, saying, "Lord, doesn't it seem unfair to you that my sister just sits here while I do all the work?" (Luke 10:40 NLT). That's when Jesus made it clear that Martha shouldn't be worried or upset. There was only one thing to focus on—Jesus and His words.

Today, turn your worries over to Jesus. Let Him know you're interested in one thing only—listening to what He has to say.

Here I am, Lord, sitting at Your feet. Please speak to me. I'm listening.

EVENING
BECOMING UNSINKABLE

*Jesus immediately reached out his hand and took hold of him,
saying to him, "O you of little faith, why did you doubt?"*
MATTHEW 14:31 ESV

After telling His followers to take the boat to the other side of the lake, Jesus went up on a mountain to pray. When darkness set in, the boat was still far from the shore, caught in a storm.

So Jesus came to them, walking on the water. Jesus told them, "Take heart; it is I. Do not be afraid" (Matthew 14:27 ESV). That's when Peter got brave, saying, "If it's You, Jesus, tell me to come to You." Jesus did, prompting Peter to get out of the boat and begin walking on the water. But then he saw the wind, got scared, and began sinking, crying out to Jesus, "Save me!" And Jesus did!

If you keep your eyes on Jesus, focusing on Him rather than your circumstances, Jesus will enable you to do things you never dreamed possible!

With You, Jesus, I'm unsinkable! Tell me to come to You!

MORNING
SPEAK EASY

"Don't worry in advance about what to say. Just say what God tells you at that time, for it is not you who will be speaking, but the Holy Spirit."
MARK 13:11 NLT

How many times have you had a difficult life scene to play out? So you rehearsed in your mind exactly what you'd say, sometimes even imagining what the other person's response would be.

There are a couple problems with that method. The first is that the conversation that actually ends up taking place is rarely the same as what you imagined. The second is that worrying in advance about what you're going to say and then trying to stick to that script leaves no room for the Holy Spirit to get a word in edgewise!

The best way to handle what may be a difficult conversation is to go to God. Let Him know what's going on, what you're concerned about. Then relax.

Spirit, when I don't know what to say, speak through me, I pray.

EVENING
CHOOSE JOY

"He shall eat curds and honey when he knows how to refuse the evil and choose the good."
ISAIAH 7:15 ESV

Every day you have the freedom to make choices. To choose good over evil, right over wrong, God's Way over your way, and joy over worry. That's a lot of choices, each one having its own set of repercussions. The choosing good over evil, right over wrong, and God's Way over your own seem self-explanatory.

But how do you choose joy over worry? It's simple: you open your eyes to the blessings around you.

Tonight write a list of things that are going right in your life. Then thank God for all He has done for you, and your joy will blossom.

Help me, Lord, to choose joy, to recognize all the good in my life, other people, and this world.

MORNING
BREATHING IN PEACE

*"Peace be with you! As the Father has sent me, so I am sending you." After he
had said this, he breathed on the disciples and said, "Receive the Holy Spirit."*
JOHN 20:21–22 GW

The disciples gathered together behind locked doors, worried what the Jews might do.
It was there the resurrected Jesus appeared, saying, "Peace be with you!" He showed
them His wounds and then repeated His greeting of peace, adding that He was sending
them out. Then He breathed on them, saying, "Receive the Holy Spirit."

As a believer, you've been gifted with the Holy Spirit. Yet to do what you have been
called to do, to be fully focused on the work and not the worry, you're to open yourself
up to the peace and breath of Christ through prayer.

Lord Jesus, bring me Your peace.

EVENING
RADIANT WITH HOPE

*May the God of hope fill you with joy and peace in your faith, that by the power
of the Holy Spirit, your whole life and outlook may be radiant with hope.*
ROMANS 15:13 PHILLIPS

Tired of letting your worries fill your mind, guiding your decisions and keeping you
from living the life God wants you to live? Why not fill your mind with God before
worry has a chance to rear its ugly head?

This morning, before your mind has a chance to run away with itself, fill it full of
God. Begin with a short, "Good morning, Glory!" prayer. Then read a portion of the
Bible, looking for a message from the Author of your faith. Finally, pray as the Spirit
leads, allowing Him to give you His outlook, radiant with hope!

Good morning, Glory! Fill my mind and give me hope!

MORNING
THE TRUE YOU

"That's why my cup is running over. This is the assigned moment for him to move into the center, while I slip off to the sidelines."

JOHN 3:30 MSG

The Bible tells you to offer yourself up to God, to let Him take you over, to allow Jesus to become more while you become less. Yet you may wonder where that will leave you, your personality, your uniqueness.

There's no need to worry. When you let Jesus take over, you can become the true you everyone (including God!) is waiting to meet.

Jesus, help me get out of the way so that You and I can truly shine!

EVENING
EVERY MOMENT BECOMES A PRAYER

Seek God while he's here to be found, pray to him while he's close at hand.

ISAIAH 55:6 MSG

God wants you to seek Him, to pray to Him while He's near. But as you're striving to meet project deadlines, get your chores done, pick up the kids, volunteer at church, and so much more, prayer seems to fall by the wayside. You begin worrying God sees you as a slacker. How can you pray without ceasing when you barely have time to fit in a shower?

God didn't devise prayer to be just one more to-do. So perhaps it's time to change your perspective of prayer. See God in everything that surrounds you, and lift up your thanks as you live in His wonderland.

Reveal Yourself to me, Lord, in all I do and see.

MORNING
SOUL HARMONY

Let the peace (soul harmony which comes) from Christ rule (act as umpire continually) in your hearts [deciding and settling with finality all questions that arise in your minds, in that peaceful state].

COLOSSIANS 3:15 AMPC

Does the peace of Christ rule over your heart? Or does worry have full sway? Perhaps it's a toss-up, depending on what's going on in your life.

It's easy to have a calm demeanor if everything's going just the way you want it to. The challenge comes when God pulls you out of your comfort zone or things beyond your control begin going haywire.

Yet if you trust God no matter what's happening in your life, you'll not only have peace within but be radiating it without. And that's what will make you a great witness for your faith!

Lord, may Your peace rule over my heart.

EVENING
A GOOD MEASURE

"Give, and it will be given to you. Good measure, pressed down, shaken together, running over, will be put into your lap. For with the measure you use it will be measured back to you."

LUKE 6:38 ESV

Jesus wants you to treat others well, for when you bless them, God will bless you back. Yet it may be difficult to give of yourself or your resources when you're worried you won't "have enough" for yourself.

It's time to change up that mindset. Let your worries of lack fall by the wayside, and start making this world a better place. Begin by doing one little thing for someone you know or even a complete stranger. Write down what you've done, including how you were rewarded in return, and soon your worries around lack will be a dim memory.

Show me what I can do this week, Jesus, to bless the life of another.

MORNING
ALL YOU NEED

I give thanks to Him Who has granted me [the needed] strength and made me able [for this], Christ Jesus our Lord, because He has judged and counted me faithful and trustworthy, appointing me to [this stewardship of] the ministry.
1 TIMOTHY 1:12 AMPC

God has definite plans for you. And Jesus is the one who gives you the strength to do what you're called to do. So before you say yes to anything new or remain where you are, go to Him in prayer. Ask if this is where He wants you to begin or continue. Then serve Him well, confident that He'll give you all the supernatural power and ability you need—and more.

Lord, thank You for giving me the direction, power, and ability I need to serve You well!

EVENING
BEAMING WITH LOVE

Neither death nor life, neither messenger of Heaven nor monarch of earth, neither what happens today nor what may happen tomorrow, neither a power from on high nor a power from below, nor anything else in God's whole world has any power to separate us from the love of God in Jesus Christ our Lord!
ROMANS 8:38–39 PHILLIPS

People may come against you. They may even walk out of your life or stop loving you. But you need not worry that you will ever be separated from God's love, for His love is unconditional. No matter what happens, He will love you. His love is an unbreakable cord between you and Him.

Pray that God will open your heart to His love. That you will feel that joyful love beaming down into you, surrounding you, cushioning you, holding you, blessing you, warming you, feeding you every moment of this day.

Abba God, beam Your love into my heart as I rest in You.

MORNING
A PLACE FOR YOU

*"You must not let yourselves be distressed—you must hold on to your faith in God and
to your faith in me. There are many rooms in my Father's House. . . . I am going away
to prepare a place for you. . . . I am coming again to welcome you into my own home."*
JOHN 14:1–3 PHILLIPS

Jesus doesn't want you to worry about anything. Instead, He tells you to hold on to
your faith in God and in Him! Even though He has physically left this earth, He's left
you a Helper (the Holy Spirit). Meanwhile He, Jesus, has gone ahead to get your room
ready—in His house, no less!

So set your worries aside. Hold on to your faith in Jesus and Father God. Live
without a care as you follow the Way, the Truth, and the Life in Him, looking forward
to the room awaiting you in His home sweet home.

You, Jesus, are already my home away from home.

EVENING
THE WOMAN WHO STICKS WITH GOD

*"Blessed is the man who trusts me, GOD, the woman who sticks with GOD. They're
like trees. . .putting down roots near the rivers—never a worry through the
hottest of summers, never dropping a leaf, serene and calm through droughts."*
JEREMIAH 17:7–8 MSG

Not only does worry sap your strength and energy, it also keeps you from creating,
from being productive. That's why God tells you that you're blessed when you trust in
Him, stick with Him and His plan, and believe His promises.

When you trust in God, He says you're like a tree whose roots have access to His
river of life. Even through the hottest drought, you'll still be fresh.

Trust God. And you'll be blessed in all things, at all times, and in all ways.

I'm sticking with You, Lord, refusing to let winds of worry have any sway over me.

MORNING
STANDING FIRM

"Say to him, 'Be careful, be quiet, do not fear, and do not let your heart be faint. . . . Because Syria, with Ephraim and the son of Remaliah, has devised evil against you. . .'" thus says the Lord God: "It shall not stand, and it shall not come to pass."
ISAIAH 7:4–5, 7 ESV

Some countries had threatened Judah. So God told Isaiah to tell King Ahaz "to stop worrying. Tell him he doesn't need to fear" (Isaiah 7:4 NLT). Even though others had planned evil against him, it would never take place—it wouldn't come to pass.

When worries come ready to attack you, listen to what God says: *"Stop worrying. You don't need to fear."* Besides, most of what you worry about will never happen! And even if it does, God will work it out for good.

I'm standing firm in my faith, Lord, trusting in You—no matter what comes!

EVENING
YOUR BEST DEFENSE

"Don't be afraid! Stand still, and see what the Lord will do to save you today. You will never see these Egyptians again. The Lord is fighting for you! So be still!"
EXODUS 14:13–14 GW

God had taken His people out of their comfort zone, and their worry grew into panic. They began thinking it would be better if they were slaves back in Egypt instead of being between the Egyptian army and the Red Sea. But Moses told them not to worry or be afraid, to merely stand still and watch what God was going to do.

And God won the day! He parted the sea for His people and brought the waters back to drown the attackers.

You're God's daughter, one of His people. He'll defend you no matter what. Your job is to stand still and watch Him work!

You, Lord, are my best and most powerful defense.

MORNING
THE ROAD MAP TO A CAREFREE LIFE

*Godliness with contentment is great gain, for we brought nothing
into the world, and we cannot take anything out of the world.
But if we have food and clothing, with these we will be content.*

1 TIMOTHY 6:6–8 ESV

The apostle Paul says that being right with God and happy with what you have is what really satisfies. As long as you have food in your belly and clothing on your being, you should and can be content.

So don't worry about getting more stuff if it's going to put you into debt or keep you chained to something you don't really need. Instead, look to please God and follow Jesus. That's the road map to a carefree life!

Help me live more simply, Lord, so I can live with less worry—and less stuff!

EVENING
TRUST IN THE LORD

*Don't worry about the wicked or envy those who do wrong. For like grass,
they soon fade away. Like spring flowers, they soon wither. Trust in the
LORD and do good. Then you will live safely in the land and prosper.*

PSALM 37:1–3 NLT

Sometimes it seems those who get all the breaks are the people who don't believe in God. In fact, the more they lie and cheat, going against all rules and laws, the more they seem to prosper! Yet here you are, doing the right thing, at least most of the time, and you can't seem to get ahead.

God tells you not to worry about those who are walking down the dark path. It's *you* who's truly prospering. You're on the road to eternal life and storing up treasures in heaven!

*Lord, help me keep my eyes on You and what
You'd have me do—for in You I truly prosper!*

MORNING
DELIGHT IN GOD

Delight yourself also in the Lord, and He will give you the desires and secret petitions of your heart.

PSALM 37:4 AMPC

You've had a secret desire for ages, a dream that you've wanted to pursue since you were a child, but the timing has never seemed to be right. Now you're worried, wondering if you'll ever get to realize your dream. Perhaps it's too late!

Rest easy. As long as you keep coming to God, spending time with Him, delighting in His presence and Word, "He will give you the desires and secret petitions of your heart." With God, it's never too late.

Here I am, Lord, delighting in Your Word, finding joy and peace in Your presence. Where would You have me go? What would You have me do?

EVENING
COMMIT YOUR WAY TO GOD

Commit your way to the Lord [roll and repose each care of your load on Him]; trust (lean on, rely on, and be confident) also in Him and He will bring it to pass. And He will make your uprightness and right standing with God go forth as the light.

PSALM 37:5–6 AMPC

Wondering about where to go, what to do? Worried you might have taken a wrong turn somewhere? Relax. Let God know all your concerns.

God hasn't left you alone. He, His Son Jesus, and the Holy Spirit are here to watch over and look out for you. They know the past, present, and future, hold all wisdom, and wield supernatural power. They see what you're doing, where you're going, what you're thinking, and where your heart is. Open yourself to them, be responsive to their prompts, and you will never lose your way.

Show me the way, Lord, as I shine for You!

MORNING
BE PATIENT

*Be still and rest in the Lord; wait for Him and
patiently lean yourself upon Him; fret not yourself.*
PSALM 37:7 AMPC

*When will God act? How long do I need to wait? Maybe I should be doing something to
help speed things along. . .but what?*

Have you ever had these thoughts while you anxiously waited for God to do something—or just *anything*? If so, you may have been getting dangerously close to doing something out of God's will for you, which rarely, if ever, turns out well.

Rather than worry about when God will move, just be still and rest in His presence. Wait patiently for Him to act. He has the perfect timing.

*Help me, Lord, to be still and at peace and to wait for You to move
before I step out of line. I know You have the perfect timing.*

EVENING
BY GOD'S POWER

*"They will pass safely through the sea of distress, for the waves of the sea will be held
back, and the waters. . .will dry up. . . . By my power I will make my people strong,
and by my authority they will go wherever they wish. I, the LORD, have spoken!"*
ZECHARIAH 10:11–12 NLT

When you feel as if you're drowning in troubles, don't worry. Instead, pray. Ask God to remind you He's more powerful than any other being and that He'll make sure you get safely through that sea of distress. He'll hold back the waves that threaten your life and dry up the deepest parts of the water. Your Father can do all that because He's God! Because when He speaks, things happen!

Listen: God has spoken! Believe, and you will conquer!

*Thank You, Lord, for being with me in the depths and heights of this life.
Hold back the waves when they threaten to overwhelm. Keep me strong in You!*

MORNING
GOOD TALKS

Let no corrupting talk come out of your mouths, but only such as is good for building up, as fits the occasion, that it may give grace to those who hear.
EPHESIANS 4:29 ESV

Your words have power, affecting those around you. That's why you must be careful not to pollute another person's thoughts with your worries. By voicing them, you may cause others to take on your worries as their own, and you may end up reinforcing your concerns in your own mind.

Instead of voicing worries, consider saying uplifting things to yourself and others, such as, "We can do all things with Christ's strength" (see Philippians 4:13). Or "God will make a way" (see Isaiah 43:16, 19). Or "I believe I'll see the goodness of the Lord in this world" (see Psalm 27:13).

In saying good things, you'll be building up the faith of others as well as your own!

Lord, help me speak words of Your wisdom instead of voicing my worries. Make me a builder, not a wrecker.

EVENING
WAITING ON GOD

Those who wait for the Lord [who expect, look for, and hope in Him] shall change and renew their strength and power; they shall lift their wings and mount up [close to God] as eagles [mount up to the sun]; they shall run and not be weary, they shall walk and not faint or become tired.
ISAIAH 40:31 AMPC

Rather than worry, wait on God. Expect Him to work in your life. Look for Him everywhere, smiling when you see evidence of His love, power, and compassion. Put all your hope in Him alone.

When you do, you'll find yourself refreshed, able to take on whatever comes your way. You'll be renewed in strength and power, mounting up higher and ever closer to the Son. You'll run and not get tired. You'll walk and not faint.

Wait in—and on—God. He'll keep you strong.

I'm waiting, Lord, lifting myself up to You in heavenly flight.

MORNING
A FAITH-FILLED WOMAN

*I am calling up memories of your sincere and unqualified faith (the
leaning of your entire personality on God in Christ in absolute trust and
confidence in His power, wisdom, and goodness), [a faith] that first lived
permanently in [the heart of] your grandmother Lois and your mother
Eunice and now, I am [fully] persuaded, [dwells] in you also.*
2 TIMOTHY 1:5 AMPC

How you live out your faith makes an impression on young minds. When your children
and grandchildren or someone else's children look at your life, will they see you as a
female fretter or a woman warrior?

May you, like Timothy's mother and grandmother, become much more of a prayer
warrior than a worrier, a peace- and faith-filled woman whom others can look to and
emulate.

Dear Lord, make me a prayerful woman, full of peace and strong in faith.

EVENING
LIVING GOD'S TRUTH

*"Do not be afraid, for I have ransomed you. I have called you by name;
you are mine. When you go through deep waters, I will be with you.
When you go through rivers of difficulty, you will not drown. When you
walk through the fire of oppression, you will not be burned up."*
ISAIAH 43:1–2 NLT

When you're going through tough times, you needn't give in to worry because God is
with you. As you go through a torrent of troubles, you won't drown. And when you
walk through the flames of cruelty, you won't get burned.

You'll be saved because you're God's precious daughter! He honors and loves you!
Even if you wander off, God says, "I will say to the north, 'Give them up,' and to the
south, 'Do not keep them.' Bring. . .my daughters from the ends of the earth" (Isaiah
43:6 GW).

I want to live Your truth, Father God. Walk with me as I grow in You.

MORNING
SOMETHING NEW

The LORD makes a path through the sea and a road through the strong currents. . . .
Forget what happened in the past, and do not dwell on events from long ago.
I am going to do something new. It is already happening. Don't you recognize it?
ISAIAH 43:16, 18–19 GW

God is the only being powerful enough to actually make a path through the sea, a road through the riptide. But you'll never see that new path or road if you're spending your time today ruminating over what happened yesterday.

God wants you living in the present moment, expecting the unexpected. He's going to do something totally new in your life. In fact, He's already doing it! Do you see it? He's going to "clear a way in the desert," to "make rivers on dry land" (Isaiah 43:19 GW).

Lord, I'm ready to expect the unexpected! My eyes are
focused on the new road You've already paved ahead!

EVENING
TAKE HEED

Take heed to yourselves and be on your guard, lest your hearts be
overburdened and depressed (weighed down) with the. . .worldly
worries and cares pertaining to [the business of] this life.
LUKE 21:34 AMPC

First one little worry creeps into your mind. Sometime later, a "what if" joins the first one. Then another, and another, and another come. Soon, you can barely breathe.

Jesus wants you to stay on your guard and to be alert to when the cares of this world come creeping in. When the first fret tries to gain access to you, go to God. Ask Him to relieve you, to give you a Bible verse to ward off that particular worry. As you make this a habit, you'll find yourself filled with the blessings of God's wisdom and truth rather than the curses of the evil one's worries and lies.

Help me be more vigilant, Lord, and replace my worries with Your wisdom.

MORNING
THE SPIRIT OF FREEDOM

Those who trust God's action in them find that God's Spirit is in them—
living and breathing God! Obsession with self in these matters is a dead end;
attention to God leads us out into the open, into a spacious, free life.
ROMANS 8:6–7 MSG

Every moment you have a choice as to what kind of life you want to live—in the spirit or in the flesh.

It comes down to where your focus is. The Message puts it this way: "Focusing on the self is the opposite of focusing on God. Anyone completely absorbed in self ignores God, ends up thinking more about self than God. That person ignores who God is and what he is doing" (Romans 8:8).

Today choose to trust in God and be a free woman warrior.

Lord, lead me out of myself and into You, where I'll find the peace and freedom I crave.

EVENING
SING ALONG

The Lord your God is in the midst of you, a Mighty One, a Savior [Who saves]!
He will rejoice over you with joy; He will rest [in silent satisfaction] and in His
love He will be silent and make no mention [of past sins, or even recall them].
ZEPHANIAH 3:17 AMPC

When you're writing an email, it's easy enough to fix and forget your mistakes by hitting the DELETE button. If you're using a pencil to work out a math problem, an eraser rectifies any errors. But you may find it more difficult to fix and forget the mistakes you make in what you say or do in your life.

Yet God wants you to know that when you've misstepped and asked Him for forgiveness, He not only doesn't bring up your errors but forgets all about them! And He "exult[s] over you with singing" (Zephaniah 3:17 AMPC)!

Thank You for always forgiving me when I mess up, Lord.

MORNING
GOD QUIETS POUNDING WAVES

You faithfully answer our prayers with awesome deeds, O God our savior. You are the hope of everyone on earth. . . . You formed the mountains by your power and armed yourself with mighty strength. You quieted the raging oceans with their pounding waves.
PSALM 65:5–7 NLT

You may have some worries that are deeply rooted. They're old and full of power, keeping you from easily being freed of them. That's when you need to reach out and call on God, the Master of awesome deeds.

God has not only formed all that you see around you—including you—but all that lies beyond you in this world and the next. He is a supernatural being with more power than you can even begin to imagine. Trust Him to quiet those waves of worries deep within you.

Pray, and God will faithfully answer with awesome deeds.

Lord, free me of the power of this worry. . . . My hope lies in You alone.

EVENING
BUILDING HOPE

Oh! May the God of green hope fill you up with joy, fill you up with peace, so that your believing lives, filled with the life-giving energy of the Holy Spirit, will brim over with hope!
ROMANS 15:13 MSG

Make it your aim to build up your hope in God. Scour the Bible for verses about hope. Memorize them, perhaps beginning with tonight's verse. Or maybe Psalm 42:5 (ESV): "Why are you cast down, O my soul, and why are you in turmoil within me? Hope in God; for I shall again praise him."

Remember, you are the daughter of the King, the Master, the Creator who has "plans to give you a future filled with hope" (Jeremiah 29:11 GW).

God of hope, fill me up with Your joy and peace so that I'll be brimming over with hope!

MORNING
OUT OF THE PIT

*"I called out your name, O God, called from the bottom of the pit. You
listened when I called out, 'Don't shut your ears! Get me out of here! Save me!'
You came close when I called out. You said, 'It's going to be all right.'"*
LAMENTATIONS 3:56–57 MSG

When your worries have you feeling as if you're at the bottom of a dark pit, your avenue back into the light is to call out from the depths. Call God by one of the many names that describe His character and fit your need—God Almighty, Defender, Strong Tower, the God Who Watches Over Me, Refuge, Shield, the Lord My Rock, Lord of Light.

Know that God *will* hear you and listen to what you say. He *will* get you out of the depths of darkness and into His Light.

Lord of Light and Life, free me from this pit of worry! Come close when I call!

EVENING
GOD PLANS GOOD

*"Even though you planned evil against me, God planned good to come
out of it. This was to keep many people alive, as he is doing now."*
GENESIS 50:20 GW

One day, out of jealousy, Joseph's brothers threw him into a pit then sold him to traders. He was bought by an officer of Pharaoh of Egypt, unjustly accused of rape, and thrown into a dungeon. Yet through all these things, Joseph never worried but trusted in God. No matter what happened or where he landed, "The LORD was with Joseph, so he became a successful man" (Genesis 39:2 GW) and eventually was made the number two man in Egypt. As such, he was able to save his family.

Even though you may be going through some tough times, trust that God has a purpose for you. No matter what happens, have faith that God is planning good to come out of it. And you too will be successful.

*Thank You, Lord, for loving me. I'm trusting in Your purposes,
knowing You're planning something good.*

MORNING
A HOME BUILDER

*A wise woman builds her home, but a foolish
woman tears it down with her own hands.*

PROVERBS 14:1 NLT

Worry has a domino effect. If you start fretting over something that has caught your attention and then voice it or act panic stricken, chances are others around you will fall in with your anxiety.

Better to be a wise woman who builds up her home and her fellow travelers with a steady life of prayer and encouragement as well as an evident faith in God. When worries enter your thoughts, seek Jesus' face immediately. Ask Him to take on your troubles as you pick up His peace. Trust that He will see you through no matter what lies ahead or behind.

*Lord, help me be a wise woman, building up my home
by giving You my worries and taking on Your peace.*

EVENING
RIGHT INTENTIONS

*Aim at and pursue righteousness (all that is virtuous and good,
right living, conformity to the will of God in thought, word,
and deed); [and aim at and pursue] faith, love, [and] peace.*

2 TIMOTHY 2:22 AMPC

Setting your aims or intentions for the day (or your life) before your feet hit the floor may keep you from easily slipping into worry. So, you *can* intend to not worry. But rather than going with a negative, why not set a positive intention that will leave no room for fretting.

Tonight, make it your intention to live right, the way God would have you live. Make up your mind to pursue faith, love, and peace, and worry will lose its foothold. The intentions you set are usually met.

Today, Lord, my intention is to pursue faith, love, and peace with You by my side!

MORNING
YOUR GUIDE AND GUARDIAN

*"He found them in a. . .howling wasteland. He surrounded them and
watched over them; he guarded them as he would guard his own eyes.
Like an eagle that. . .hovers over her young, so he spread his wings
to take them up and carried them safely on his pinions."*

DEUTERONOMY 32:10–11 NLT

Sometimes you may feel as if you're all alone in a desert, lost and unprotected, the wind howling all around you.

Rest easy. God is with you. He's surrounding you, watching over you. He's guarding you as if you were the apple or pupil of His eyes. He knows how fragile you can be and promises to protect you. Like a mother eagle, He's spreading His wings over you. He'll take you up and carry you, leading you to a better place where His promises will override your worries.

Thank You, Lord, for coming to meet me where I am.

EVENING
THE DEFENSE

*The Lord is my Rock, my Fortress, and my Deliverer; my God, my
keen and firm Strength in Whom I will trust and take refuge, my
Shield, and the Horn of my salvation, my High Tower.*

PSALM 18:2 AMPC

If you're looking for a defense against worry, look no further than your Lord.

In Psalm 18, David begins by telling God how much he loves Him (see v. 1). Then he describes what God is to him—his Rock, Fortress, Deliverer, Strength, Shield, Horn (power), and High Tower. Then he sings, "I will call upon the Lord, Who is to be praised; so shall I be saved from my enemies" (Psalm 18:3 AMPC).

When worry gets out of hand, keeping you from doing what God would have you do, sing a song of praise to Him. Remind yourself of who He is, and He will save you!

My Rock and Deliverer, save me from my worries as I sing a song of praise to You!

MORNING
BLESSED IN ASTONISHING WAYS

God can pour on the blessings in astonishing ways so that you're ready for
anything and everything, more than just ready to do what needs to be done.
2 CORINTHIANS 9:8 MSG

George Müller ran an orphanage in England in the 1800s. One morning, there was no money, and the children's breakfast bowls and cups were empty. Müller prayed, "Dear Father, we thank Thee for what Thou art going to give us to eat."

Then a baker, prompted by God, knocked on the door. His arms were filled with bread for the children. He was followed by a milkman whose cart had broken down in front of the orphanage. He wanted to give the kids cans of milk so he could empty and repair his wagon.

Transform your worries about want into prayers for provisions, and you'll be blessed "in astonishing ways."

Lord, bless me in astonishing ways so that I may bless others in return.

EVENING
KINGDOM-OF-HEAVEN BLESSING

Even if you suffer for doing what is right, God will reward you for it. So don't worry
or be afraid of their threats. Instead, you must worship Christ as Lord of your life.
1 PETER 3:14–15 NLT

Tonight's verse, which says you're not to worry or be afraid when you're threatened, was written by the disciple Peter, who'd been both worried and afraid when Jesus was arrested. In fact, he went so far as to deny even knowing Jesus! But in the end, Peter was more devoted to Jesus than ever.

When you feel threatened by what others say and do as you live for Jesus, just keep Him and His words set in your mind and heart. Worship instead of worry, assured of your reward and God's kingdom-of-heaven blessing (see Matthew 5:10).

With You as my Lord and fortress, I need not worry or fear the words of others.

MORNING
CHIN UP, WOMAN!

Energize the limp hands, strengthen the rubbery knees. Tell fearful souls,
"Courage! Take heart! God is here, right here, on his way to put things
right and redress all wrongs. He's on his way! He'll save you!"
ISAIAH 35:3–4 MSG

It's good to have some Bible verses memorized, ones you can just call up during times of worry, stress, fear, or crises. Isaiah 35:3–4 are two of these verses. Find a Bible version of them that really speaks to your heart. Then use it when you start feeling anxious, when your hands are weak and your knees are about to give way.

Speak Isaiah's words into your soul to strengthen your body, mind, and spirit, re-phrasing them if you need to. Say to yourself, "Chin up, woman. Be brave. Take heart. God is right here with you. He's going to put things right. He's on His way to save you!"

Thank God You're with me, Jesus! With You
heading my way, I know You'll put things right!

EVENING
NEVER SHAKEN

I will bless the LORD who guides me; even at night my heart instructs me. I know
the LORD is always with me. I will not be shaken, for he is right beside me.
PSALM 16:7–8 NLT

These days, lots of businesses are open 24-7. But God has been open and available to His people day and night since they were created.

See things through God's eternal perspective. Your days are like a moment to Him. So live life to the fullest with no worries, fears, or anxieties to distract you or to keep you from the joy and peace that is yours in Christ.

God is with you. You will never be shaken. Let that stir your spirit into moving in rhythm with Him, filled with courage, peace, and joy, all the days of your life.

I bless You, Lord, for guiding me, teaching me, and always being with me.

MORNING
PARTNERING WITH GOD

We are assured and know that [God being a partner in their labor] all things work together and are [fitting into a plan] for good to and for those who love God and are called according to [His] design and purpose.

ROMANS 8:28 AMPC

Romans 8:28 says that everything that happens in your life—whether good or bad, within or out of your control—happens for a reason and according to God's plan and that He will make everything work out for your good.

That can be hard to accept sometimes, yet that doesn't mean it isn't true. After all, it was true for Joseph, who'd been put in a pit by loved ones, sold as a slave, sent to the dungeon, and yet ended up the number two man in Egypt!

Instead of worrying about what may or may not happen, rest in the assurance that no matter what happens, God will work it out for good. Remember, God can do anything!

Lord, with You as my partner, I know all things will work out for good.

EVENING
IN GOD'S HANDS

God is our refuge and strength, always ready to help in times of trouble. So we will not fear when earthquakes come and the mountains crumble into the sea. Let the oceans roar and foam. Let the mountains tremble as the waters surge!

PSALM 46:1–3 NLT

Because you're a daughter of the Most High God, you don't have to be anxious or fear anything because you can go to God for refuge. In Him you will find all the strength and help you need to get through anything and everything.

So rest easy. Pray to God. Tell Him you know He's in control and somehow everything will be all right. You don't need to know the details. Leave them—and everything else that's on your mind—in His hands.

Thank You, Lord, for always being there, ready to shield, strengthen, and help me.

MORNING
PULLED BY PROMISES

*With promises like this to pull us on, dear friends, let's make a clean break
with everything that defiles or distracts us, both within and without.
Let's make our entire lives fit and holy temples for the worship of God.*
2 CORINTHIANS 7:1 MSG

God has a plan for your life. He wants you to live for Him, to trust Him, to base your words and actions on His promises, to expect good to come out of all things.

God wants you, His darling daughter, to be strong and fit. For that, you need "a calm and undisturbed mind and heart," which are "the life and health of the body" (Proverbs 14:30 AMPC).

For God's pleasure and your own health and welfare, make a clean break from the worries that distract you. Go to God, trusting Him with your concerns.

Help me be a fit temple for You, Lord. Give me the calm mind I yearn for in You.

EVENING
COOL IT!

*Whoever is patient has great understanding,
but one who is quick-tempered displays folly.*
PROVERBS 14:29 NIV

Unchecked anger can blow things up in a hurry, and there's often a mess after the fact that someone (likely you) will need to clean up. There's a reason people take deep breaths and count to ten when they're worked up. Those few seconds give you time to refocus your heart and to remind yourself that it's not worth it. But don't worry! If you do blow up, the Lord has a way of reminding you of that, all the same. How much better would it be to "temper" yourself ahead of time? What chaos you could avoid!

*Thank You for tempering me, Father. Help me
keep my cool, no matter what I'm facing.*

MORNING
SERVANT-MINDED

Let this mind be in you which was also in Christ Jesus, who, being in the form of God, did not consider it robbery to be equal with God, but made Himself of no reputation, taking the form of a bondservant, and coming in the likeness of men.

PHILIPPIANS 2:5–7 NKJV

If Christ, fully God and fully man, did not consider equality with God a thing to be obtained, why do we? Christ's humility is astounding! He is God, but He became a servant. How effective is a servant who continually wishes to be the master? Until we realize that we—our sinful nature—is what prevents us from entering into a relationship with the Lord and living for His glory, then walking with our Savior is not a thing to be grasped.

Father, forgive me for trying to be You. Though I don't want to admit it, my pride is a great and daily struggle. Lord, help me to wait, listen, and obey. Amen.

EVENING
LOOKING ON THE HEART

But the LORD said unto Samuel, Look not on his countenance, or on the height of his stature; because I have refused him: for the LORD seeth not as man seeth; for man looketh on the outward appearance, but the LORD looketh on the heart.

1 SAMUEL 16:7 KJV

In our pursuit of improving our appearance, it's best if we first make sure our hearts are clean. We might look good on the outside, but if our hearts aren't pure before God, then we aren't pleasing to Him. Before we jump on the bandwagon and spend a lot of money on cosmetics, maybe we should ask God about our hearts and make sure He approves. It's far more important to please Him than to please the world.

Lord, give me a pure heart. Help me to desire Your approval over man's approval. Amen.

MORNING
PEACE WHILE YOU WORK

You will keep in perfect peace those whose minds
are steadfast, because they trust in you.
ISAIAH 26:3 NIV

There are some women who balance the demands of work or their calling with extraordinary grace. They calmly endure crises with joy, they patiently wait for God to act when things go awry, and they confidently navigate numerous daily pressures. Then there are those of us who panic, burn ourselves out trying to control the future, strive while we work, and worry ourselves into fitful nights without sleep.

Internal rest is found in belief and trust in God (see Hebrews 3:18–19)—even while we work. Do you want to experience internal rest and peace while you work? Choose to trust God and believe that all that concerns you is under His control. Let Him carry your burdens.

Lord, thank You that I can trust You with all that happens to me today.

EVENING
WHAT OTHERS THINK

Fear of man will prove to be a snare,
but whoever trusts in the LORD is kept safe.
PROVERBS 29:25 NIV

In the original Hebrew language, the word *snare* in Proverbs 29:25 is the word *mokashe*, and it means "trap." No one wants to fall into a trap, but that is exactly what allowing the fear of people to rule us will do. Fearing what they think. Fearing their retribution. Fearing their shame. Fearing their judgment. Fear gives others the ability to control us.

When we trust God instead of allowing the fear of others to rule us, then we will be able to say with confidence, "If God is my salvation, I will trust and not be afraid."

Lord, help me to live for an audience of one. . .You!

MORNING
STRONG HANDS

"Do not fear. . .let not your hands be weak. The Lord your God in your midst, the Mighty One, will save; He will rejoice over you with gladness, He will quiet you with His love, He will rejoice over you with singing."
ZEPHANIAH 3:16–17 NKJV

Sometimes we find ourselves heading in the wrong direction. And whatever the cause, the result is always the same: we become fearful, anxious, worried. That's when we need to let God get ahold of us again. He is the One who will bring us back to Him, saving us from whatever is leading us away. And then He'll rejoice over our return! He'll calm our worries with His amazing love and light. And we'll once again have the courage we so desperately need to live this life to which He has called us.

Only You can quiet my fears with Your love, Lord. To You, I lift my hands in praise!

EVENING
A LIMITLESS GOD

Show me your ways, Lord, teach me your paths. Guide me in your truth and teach me, for you are God my Savior, and my hope is in you all day long. . . . My eyes are ever on the Lord.
PSALM 25:4–5, 15 NIV

God has plans for our lives. But oftentimes we find ourselves standing in His way. And in so doing, we limit His power and blind ourselves to what He is looking to create in our lives. The solution is to make Him your number one Adviser. Search out His Word for your direction and path. Know that He is holding your hand as you walk, step by step. Amazing things are happening; the possibilities are limitless, and His blessings abundant. Just rest, knowing He has got you. He will never let you go. And everything is going according to His plan.

My hope is in You, dear Lord, for I know You have the best plan for my life.

MORNING
FORGET ABOUT IT!

"Forget about what's happened; don't keep going over old history. Be alert,
be present. I'm about to do something brand-new. It's bursting out! Don't you
see it? There it is! I'm making a road through the desert, rivers in the badlands."
ISAIAH 43:16–21 MSG

Sometimes we get so stuck on something that happened in the past. We tell ourselves, *Get over it already*, but it still keeps coming up. Meanwhile, we miss the new things that God is doing. To get unstuck, follow the example of the apostle Paul, who wrote, "But one thing I do: Forgetting what is behind and straining toward what is ahead, I press on" (Philippians 3:13–14 NIV). Lift your feet out of the quicksand of old history and move forward to see what new thing God is doing for and revealing to you before you miss it!

I'm ready for something new. Speak to me, Lord!
I'm listening! In Jesus' name I pray, amen.

EVENING
HEART STRENGTH

I would have lost heart, unless I had believed that I would see the
goodness of the LORD in the land of the living. Wait on the LORD;
be of good courage, and He shall strengthen your heart.
PSALM 27:13–14 NKJV

When things don't seem to be going our way, it's easy to lose heart. And when we're still reeling, having difficulty finding our feet, it's hard to stand up to even the littlest of daily challenges. But you *can* find a rainbow in the middle of these storms. It comes with the power of God and the belief that you will one day see His amazing goodness in your life. All you need to do is take courage and wait on Him. He will not only see you through but also give you whatever strength you need to find your feet and walk on stronger than ever before.

Lord, I'm hanging on to Your promise that I'll one day see
Your goodness come streaming through. I'm waiting on You.

MORNING
THE-GOD-WHO-SEES

Now the Angel of the Lord found her. . . [and] said to her, "Return to your mistress, and submit yourself under her hand." . . . Then she called the name of the Lord who spoke to her, You-Are-the-God-Who-Sees.

GENESIS 16:7, 9, 13 NKJV

Like Hagar, who was running away from her abusive mistress, Sarai, we sometimes think we can run from our troubles. But when we come to the end of ourselves, God is there, ready to give us the wisdom we need but may not want.

Even today, this God-Who-Sees sees you and your situation. He is ready to reveal Himself to you and share His wisdom. He may not remove you from your circumstances, but He will give you the word you need to get through them. Afterward, you'll see your situation in a new light, with a new hope for your future, step by step.

Lord, be with me now. Show me where You want me to submit. Remind me that You have a plan and vision for my life—and that it is all meant for my good.

EVENING
OPEN UP!

Who is the King of glory? The Lord, strong and mighty; the Lord, invincible in battle. Open up, ancient gates! Open up, ancient doors, and let the King of glory enter.

PSALM 24:8–9 NLT

Jesus is outside the gate of your heart, waiting for you to open up your total being— mind, emotions, and will—to His saving presence. He, strong and mighty, invincible, is knocking at the door of *your* heart. He wants you, His temple, to open up your gates so He can spend time with you. Do you hear His knock? Are you willing to let Him into not just a small corner of your life but your *entire* life? He will not force His way in, for it must be your decision. He will be gentle and loving, only wanting the best for you. Will you open up?

Jesus, my heart is open! Please come in! In Your sweet name I play, pray, live, love, and breathe now and evermore! Amen.

MORNING
A WOMAN REBORN

"No one can enter the kingdom of God unless they are born of water and the Spirit. Flesh gives birth to flesh, but the Spirit gives birth to spirit. You should not be surprised at my saying, 'You must be born again.'"

JOHN 3:5–7 NIV

God once breathed life into you when you were born physically, but now you have been reborn spiritually, brought to life by the breath of the Holy Spirit. You are a new creation (see 2 Corinthians 5:17). Repeat this truth from God's Word: *I am a new creation in Christ, a daughter of God. With my Father, anything is possible because I can do all things through my Brother who strengthens me.* It's the new improved you, a woman reborn, now a sister of all, courtesy of heaven above.

God, thank You for this new life in Christ!

EVENING
FREEDOM FROM GUILT

If we confess our sins, he is faithful and just and will forgive us our sins and purify us from all unrighteousness.

1 JOHN 1:9 NIV

Sin leaves a spot—an indelible mark—on us. We can't hide it. We can't scrub it away. We can't disguise it with a lovely scarf. It marks us for life. Until Jesus. When we encounter Jesus, when we take Him at His word and ask for His forgiveness, He performs in an instant what we could not perform in years of trying. The sin—all that ugliness of the past—is gone. Poof. No guilt. No condemnation. No doubt. When we make Him Lord of our lives, we get the best "laundering" job of our lives. What a joy, to be spot-free!

Father, thank You for removing not only my sin but the lingering guilt as well. I'm so grateful!

MORNING
TRUST

*"But blessed is the one who trusts in the LORD, whose confidence is in him.
They will be like a tree planted by the water that sends out its roots by the
stream. It does not fear when heat comes; its leaves are always green.
It has no worries in a year of drought and never fails to bear fruit."*
JEREMIAH 17:7–8 NIV

Have you ever been asked to place your trust in the hands of a surgeon? That moment, just before the anesthesia kicks in, is one of complete surrender. You drift off to sleep, anxieties lifted, cares behind you. He does his best work when you're completely submitted to the process. The same is true when it comes to trusting God. We have to relax. Submit. Lay ourselves at His feet, trusting that He will do His very best work. We can't look to ourselves or others for answers. They come from Him alone.

*So many times I've put my trust in others, Lord, only to be let down. How
grateful I am to know that You will remain faithful, no matter what.*

EVENING
STARTING OVER

*Then Peter came to Jesus and asked, "Lord, how many times shall I forgive
my brother or sister who sins against me? Up to seven times?" Jesus
answered, "I tell you, not seven times, but seventy-seven times."*
MATTHEW 18:21–22 NIV

Words stick. At times, you really wish you could have a do-over. If only you could hit the REWIND button! The good news is, you can. With God's help, you can have countless do-overs. Sure, there will still be a mess to clean up, but He's pretty good at that part too! Why else do you think He told Peter there would be so many opportunities to forgive?

Ah, new beginnings! I'm so grateful for them, Lord!

MORNING
MY HELP COMES FROM ABOVE

*Commit everything you do to the L*ORD*. Trust him, and he will*
help you. He will make your innocence radiate like the dawn,
and the justice of your cause will shine like the noonday sun.

PSALM 37:5–6 NLT

Have you ever been on a quest to find the right doctor to cure a particular ill? Maybe you go to your primary care physician, and he sends you to a specialist. Perhaps that specialist sends you to a subspecialist. At every step along the way you groan and say, "I just want someone who can help me!" Aren't you glad to hear that you have a straight shot to your heavenly Father? You don't need a referral. You don't need to wait in line. And He's got the solution to any problem you might be facing.

How wonderful to know that I don't have to go looking for help. You're standing nearby,
Lord, ready to plead my case and to bring about justice when I face unjust situations.

EVENING
LET ALL THINGS BE SILENT

*"And the L*ORD *will take possession of Judah as His inheritance in*
the Holy Land, and will again choose Jerusalem. Be silent, all flesh,
*before the L*ORD*, for He is aroused from His holy habitation!"*

ZECHARIAH 2:12–13 NKJV

Throughout scripture we see the command to "be silent" or "be still." Why silence? In silence there is self-control, awareness, focus, wonder, awe, and deference. The God of the universe, all powerful (omnipotent), all knowing (omniscient), and all being (omnipresent) deserves our thoughts and meditation. When we take the time to focus and listen, we glorify Him. No, there may not be a resounding voice that echoes in your soul, but when you dwell on God's character and His promises, you become more aware of and intimate with Him.

Father, I pray that I can draw closer to You. Help me to seek You each day.

MORNING
LIGHT OF THE MORNING

"The God of Israel said, the Rock of Israel spoke to me: 'He who rules over men must be just, ruling in the fear of God. And he shall be like the light of the morning when the sun rises, a morning without clouds, like the tender grass springing out of the earth, by clear shining after rain.'"

2 SAMUEL 23:3–4 NKJV

Our God is just. We as followers of Christ and children of God must know and pursue God as He is revealed in the scriptures. His justice is like the light of the morning. The rising sun is constant; our Savior is constant. The same justice He gave to the Israelites is the same justice He gives to us. Know that there will be darkness, there will be night, but morning comes.

Lord, thank You for the beauty of Your creation. Thank You that it reminds me of Your promises that, though seemingly dormant, spring forth overnight.

EVENING
WOE BE GONE

How long, O LORD? Will You forget me forever? How long will You hide Your face from me? . . . But I have trusted in Your mercy; my heart shall rejoice in Your salvation. I will sing to the LORD, because He has dealt bountifully with me.

PSALM 13:1, 5–6 NKJV

In Psalms, David asks the Lord many times if He has forsaken him. We watch David question the Lord, then explain his troubles, pain, and circumstances. Always near the end of a psalm, David revisits God's great character and works. Loving-kindness, salvation, bountiful. . .he reflects, remembers, and trusts in God. We must do the same when God appears distant. Reflect on the God of the scriptures and the wonders He has done in your life.

Father, You never said it would be easy following You. Thank You for not lying, and thank You for life in Christ.

MORNING
STRONG SHEPHERD

Behold, the Lord GOD shall come with a strong hand, and His arm shall rule
for Him; behold, His reward is with Him, and His work before Him. He will
feed His flock like a shepherd; He will gather the lambs with His arm, and
carry them in His bosom, and gently lead those who are with young.

ISAIAH 40:10–11 NKJV

God's is not a passive shepherding. Throughout the verses, we see Him come with might; we see Him rule, tend, gather, carry, and lead. He is our Protector. Why would we ever want to stray from this Shepherd? Unlike man, God does not abuse His power. Throughout scripture and history, we see dictators rise and fall, kings and queens take advantage of the poor; yet our God is just. He rules and leads His flock, and *nothing* is outside His control.

Father, thank You for being a diligent and mighty Shepherd.

EVENING
UNSHAKABLE CHARACTER

The LORD is my shepherd; I shall not want. He makes me to lie
down in green pastures; He leads me beside the still waters.

PSALM 23:1–2 NKJV

When we follow our Shepherd, where does He lead us? He leads us beside still waters, a place where things are calm and in His control. This is not to say being one of the flock is an easy lifestyle. We know that later on in Psalm 23, we "walk through the valley of the shadow of death," but we will fear nothing, because our Shepherd controls all (v. 4 NKJV). When we follow our Shepherd, it may be by quiet streams or tumultuous chasms, but with Him we walk *through*. We won't be trapped or lost, because we walk with Him.

Father, thank You for rest in You. Thank You for being my Shepherd.

MORNING
A SOUND MIND

For God hath not given us the spirit of fear;
but of power, and of love, and of a sound mind.
2 TIMOTHY 1:7 KJV

We must allow God's Spirit to rule our thinking process. We must accept the love He has shown to us and embrace the sound mind He has given us.

As we read God's Word and spend time in prayer with Him, He plants within our minds those things we need to have a sound mind. A sound mind is one the devil can try to attack, but his efforts will be futile. We must be on guard every day to preserve the mind God has given us. Fertilize it with good ideas that glorify God and His purpose.

Father, I accept the power, love, and sound mind You have
given me. Help me to preserve it diligently.

EVENING
HOLD ME UP, LORD

Hold up my goings in thy paths, that my footsteps slip not.
PSALM 17:5 KJV

We can't dwell on past failures and allow them to drag us down. Satan would like nothing better than to discourage us and get us off track. The important thing is to correct those mistakes by admitting we were wrong and asking God to forgive us. He offers grace to those who want and need it.

The psalmist prayed that the Lord would hold him up as he walked so his feet wouldn't slip on the path, a good prayer for anyone who wants to follow Christ and please Him. We can't do it alone. We need His assistance.

Lord, You know I'm human. I need Your help.
Hold me up. Keep me going in the right direction. Amen.

MORNING
BE FILLED WITH JOY

Now the God of hope fill you with all joy and peace in believing,
that ye may abound in hope, through the power of the Holy Ghost.
ROMANS 15:13 KJV

Are you fighting a battle that seems futile? Have you lost hope of seeing a resolution? Take heart; you're not alone. Look at what Paul wrote:

1. We serve a God of hope. Trust Him to supply you with hope to make it during dark days.

2. God is your source. Rely on Him to fill you with joy and give you peace in the time of trouble.

3. Believe that God is who He says He is, that He has made a way for you through His Son, Jesus.

4. Allow the Holy Spirit to empower you to abound in hope. We are often powerless to conquer our problems, but God's Spirit can arise within us to make us overcomers.

Push the darkness away. God is on your side. Allow Him to work for you.

Father, fill me with Your joy and peace through the Holy Spirit.

EVENING
FREE THROUGH CHRIST

Stand fast therefore in the liberty wherewith Christ hath made
us free, and be not entangled again with the yoke of bondage.
GALATIANS 5:1 KJV

No matter what our past or present, Christ can set us free. There is no bondage that He cannot break, no power that can defeat Him. We become new creations in Christ when we surrender our lives to Him. The danger lies in our taking control and becoming entangled in the bondage of sin once again. We must allow Christ to be in complete control and then stand fast in the liberty through which He has set us free.

Jesus, I surrender my life to You.

MORNING
A STRONG TOWER

The name of the LORD is a strong tower:
the righteous runneth into it, and is safe.
PROVERBS 18:10 KJV

Everyone has felt fear at one time or another. Fear can paralyze us and keep us from feeling secure and confident. The name of the Lord is a place of safety for His people. We can't stop bad things from happening to us, but when they do, we can call on His name. He provides a haven of safety for us, both physically and mentally. The next time you feel afraid, run to Jesus. His name is the Strong Tower you need.

Lord, help me to remember that You are my Strong
Tower. I can run to You with every problem.

EVENING
TOUCHING JESUS

When she had heard of Jesus, [she] came in the press behind, and touched
his garment. For she said, If I may touch but his clothes, I shall be whole.
MARK 5:27–28 KJV

The woman with the issue of blood suffered for twelve years. She must have felt she was at the end of her rope. But then she heard about Jesus. The crowd surrounding Him may not have wanted to give way to her, but she pressed in; and when she reached Jesus, she touched His clothes and received healing.

The secret to solving any problem is to touch Jesus. We can't see Him in the flesh, but we can touch Him through prayer and His Word. Like the woman in this story, we must press through whatever may hinder us. Don't give up! Touching Jesus is all that matters.

Jesus, give me the determination to press through the
crowd until I touch You and receive the answer I need.

SING A LITTLE SONG

Is anyone among you in trouble? Let them pray.
Is anyone happy? Let them sing songs of praise.
JAMES 5:13 NIV

James teaches us how to respond to life's experiences. He says if you're in trouble, pray about it. We're much better off when we pray about what's bothering us, no matter what the problem, than to let it show for the world to see. Likewise, if we're happy, we can let those around us know it by singing. When we pray about our troubles, we feel better and can then sing that song we feel in our hearts. Are you facing a problem today? Take it to God in prayer, and let Him take care of it for you. Are you happy? Then sing that little song you feel coming on.

Lord, help me to rely on You in times of trouble and sing Your praises when I'm happy.

EVENING
KEEPING OUR TESTIMONY

And the LORD was with Joseph, and he was a prosperous man; and he was in the house of his master, the Egyptian. And his master saw that the LORD was with him.
GENESIS 39:2–3 KJV

Against incredible odds, Joseph proved himself a trustworthy servant, and his master took note of it, making Joseph his overseer. God was with him.

You may be living in a home or working at a job where you are the only Christian, but no matter where you are, God is able to bless you and direct your life if you allow Him to. No matter what environment you find yourself in, God will be there. Your situation may be painful, you may be fearful, the people around you may abuse you in some way, but like Joseph, God will be with you. Trust Him to take care of you.

Lord, help me to trust You in my situation.
Give me the strength to live a life pleasing to You.

MORNING
CHRIST GIVES STRENGTH

I can do all things through Christ which strengtheneth me.
PHILIPPIANS 4:13 KJV

God doesn't want us to take on so many responsibilities that we can't be our best for Him and our families. We're all going to get tired sometimes, but when we do, Philippians 4:13 tells us that Christ gives us strength and we can do all things through Him. Maybe it's time we decided what is most important. Try making a list of priorities with Jesus at the top, then pray about what He would have you to do in order to please Him. Chances are, some things will be deleted from your life that you thought were necessary, and you'll find yourself less stressed. Then rest in Christ, and He will give you strength to do all you need to do.

Jesus, give me wisdom as I make my choices in life.

EVENING
ASK GOD FIRST

The Israelites sampled their provisions but did not inquire of the LORD.
JOSHUA 9:14 NIV

Asking for God's guidance doesn't mean everything will go the way we expect. But when we ask, the events of our lives do go according to God's plan. Jesus inquired of God before choosing the twelve disciples. Judas was among the twelve. God intentionally allowed Jesus to pick a man who would betray Him so God's plan for our redemption would be accomplished.

Asking God puts the burden on Him to reveal to us His will. In what area of your life have you been handling things on your own? Where do you need to seek God's will?

Heavenly Father, thank You for loving us enough
to care deeply about the details of our lives.

MORNING
GOD IS IN THE MESS

*"This is what we will do to them: We will let them live, so that God's
wrath will not fall on us for breaking the oath we swore to them."*

JOSHUA 9:20 NIV

God can be glorified in the messiness of life. Paul tells us that the Gospel can be preached
even if from wrong motives. The original sin isn't justified, but it doesn't hamper God's
ability to work.

It can be hard to see God at work in the midst of difficult things, but He is there
the whole time. Even when the sin is being committed, He is planting the seed of
redemption. He does not abandon us to our sins or the sins of others.

*God, thank You for never leaving me, for always being
by my side no matter how messy my life is.*

EVENING
OBEDIENCE BRINGS PEACE

*So Joshua took the entire land, just as the LORD had directed
Moses, and he gave it as an inheritance to Israel according to
their tribal divisions. Then the land had rest from war.*

JOSHUA 11:23 NIV

Obedience can take a long time. It's a daily choice, not a onetime act. Faithful obedience
keeps our hearts soft before the Lord and keeps us out of a pattern of disobedience that
leads to a hard heart that cannot hear God's voice.

Ultimately, obedience brings peace. We can't control our circumstances, but when
we obey God, we will find peace in the midst of them. If you don't have peace, look for
where you're not obeying. What are you trying to control that you should give to God?

*Lord, open our eyes to the lie of control.
Show us that next step You want us to take. Amen.*

MORNING
THE LORD IS OUR INHERITANCE

But to the tribe of Levi he gave no inheritance, since the food offerings presented to the Lord, the God of Israel, are their inheritance, as he promised them.
JOSHUA 13:14 NIV

Many verses in the Old Testament talk about what it means for the Lord to be our portion:
Psalm 16:5 says He gives us provision, security, and His presence.
Psalm 73:26 says God is our advocate and with us always.
Psalm 142:5 says He is our refuge. He hears us. He protects us and gives us freedom. He is good to us.
Lamentations 3:19–33 says His mercies are new every morning. His love is great.
Isn't it amazing to think that God belongs to us? He resides within us and is with us in everything we do.

Heavenly Father, thank You for the gift of Your Son that allows us to have You as our inheritance.

EVENING
THE DEFINITION OF FAITH

Now faith is confidence in what we hope for and assurance about what we do not see.
HEBREWS 11:1 NIV

In whom or what do you place your faith? God's character and His promises are faithful. Faith is the pathway to our relationship with God. We have faith to please God, to earnestly seek Him and believe in His reward, even when we can't see it with earthly eyes. We need to cultivate our eyes of faith, knowing that most of our reward for a faithful life will not be found in this life but in the next.

Ask God to help you exercise your eyes of faith so you can see Him working. If you can't see Him, ask Him to reveal Himself to you.

Heavenly Father, thank You for making a relationship with You possible.

MORNING
FOLLOW YOUR PATH

*[F]ixing our eyes on Jesus, the pioneer and perfecter of faith. For
the joy set before him he endured the cross, scorning its shame,
and sat down at the right hand of the throne of God.*

HEBREWS 12:2 NIV

When we follow our path by faith, we please God, just as Jesus pleased Him with His sacrifice. And all those believers who have gone before us are cheering us on. The stories of their journeys are meant to encourage us, just as your journey can encourage others. So share with others what God is doing on your path.

We need to accept the path God has given to each of us—not with reluctance or annoyance but with faith and grace and trust, acknowledging that He knows best.

*Father God, thank You for never leaving us. Help us
to take that next step, even when it's hard. Amen.*

EVENING
GOD HAS A PLAN

*"Here is a boy with five small barley loaves and two small
fish, but how far will they go among so many?"*

JOHN 6:9 NIV

So often in life we want to know the whole plan up front. And if God doesn't give us the plan, we start making it up on our own.

Spiritually, Jesus gives us everything we need to be satisfied and then even more, so it spills over onto others. When we seek God and put His kingdom first, He provides for our physical and spiritual needs. He is our satisfaction. He is the ultimate answer.

Surrender to Him, and see how He works beyond your limited thinking. He always exceeds our expectations.

Dear Jesus, thank You that You are not limited by what we can see or do.

MORNING
GOD ISN'T SURPRISED

*A strong wind was blowing and the waters grew rough. When they
had rowed about three or four miles, they saw Jesus approaching
the boat, walking on the water; and they were frightened.*
JOHN 6:18–19 NIV

When we pray during life's storms, we tend to think God is going to make things the
way we want, with ease, comfort, lack of conflict, and prosperity. But those things are
not the things that draw us closer to Him and grow our faith. He promises to never
leave us and to give us His peace, not the world's peace. His ways are different from
ours, and we can't see the whole plan.

It can be hard to see God in the struggles of life. But we should be expecting Him.

Lord Jesus, thank You for never leaving us to handle the storms of life by ourselves.

EVENING
REDUCING LOVE TO FEELINGS

*Now that you have purified yourselves by obeying the truth so that you
have sincere love for each other, love one another deeply, from the heart.*
1 PETER 1:22 NIV

A wise woman chooses love by doing love. And while she is doing love out of commitment, she does not fear because she knows that as sure as the tide rolls in and out, the
pleasant feelings of love will return again too.

Don't be deceived by reducing love to feelings. If you do, your relationships will
be tossed by the winds of every circumstance. But when you make love a choice, you
will steady yourself and choose for yourself a firm foundation whereby the most difficult challenges cannot destroy love.

*Lord, please forgive me for those times when I allow my emotions to drive my
reactions in relationships. Please help me to pursue love by serving my loved ones.*

MORNING
FILLING IN THE BLANKS OF GOD'S PROMISES

Your love, Lord, reaches to the heavens, your faithfulness to the skies.
PSALM 36:5 NIV

Sometimes we fill in the blanks with God. Maybe He reveals something He is going to accomplish in our lives, such as a new job or the birth of a child. We then make the mistake of filling in the blanks of what He said with details He never gave us.

We need to be careful not to add on to what God said lest we become discouraged and blame Him for being unfaithful. When life doesn't make sense, we can hold firmly to the certain promises He has given. He will always do what is absolutely best for us according to His agape love, and His perfect character and love demand the perfect handling of all that concerns us.

Lord, please help me to trust You when I don't understand all that You are doing.

EVENING
WHEN YOU FEEL LIKE YOU DON'T MEASURE UP

For the word of God is alive and active. Sharper than any double-edged sword, it penetrates even to dividing soul and spirit, joints and marrow; it judges the thoughts and attitudes of the heart. Nothing in all creation is hidden from God's sight. Everything is uncovered and laid bare before the eyes of him to whom we must give account.
HEBREWS 4:12–13 NIV

Have you ever had a sense when you read the Bible that you just weren't measuring up? That you were totally blowing it?

It's never God's desire to burden us with guilt that leads to death, but to reveal our sin so we can experience life! It's to show us where our thoughts and intentions are wrong so He can lead us to what is right.

Ah! Joyous liberty!

*Thank You, Lord, that my soul and spirit are laid bare
and exposed before You. You know everything about me.*

MORNING
GOD IS BIGGER THAN THE WRONG DONE TO YOU

"But if you do not forgive others their sins, your Father will not forgive your sins."
MATTHEW 6:15 NIV

It can be tough to forgive. It presses us to the edge of ourselves where we are forced to acknowledge that God is greater than the wrong that has been done to us. When we choose to forgive, it keeps God's power in perspective.

Think about something someone has done to you that has demanded forgiveness. Do you believe God is bigger than the wrong? Are you convinced His love and His rule are redemptive? If so, let the person who has wronged you off the hook. Stop thinking that he or she has ruined your life and that you will never recover—because God is a Redeemer.

Lord, help me to remember that there is nothing that will happen
to me that You cannot redeem for my good and Your glory.

EVENING
TRUTH IN PLAIN SIGHT

"Then you will know the truth, and the truth will set you free."
JOHN 8:32 NIV

God tells us who He is; we doubt it. He confesses His love for us in scripture; we ignore it. He tells us how to live; we do things our own way. And so it is with us like it was with the disciples when Jesus asked them, "Do you not yet see or understand? Do you have a hardened heart?" We see, but we don't see. We hear, but we don't listen. We know it, but we don't understand. All of this means that we miss the Truth that is right in front of our eyes; we remain bound when we could be set free. It's not the person who just intellectually knows the truth who is set free; it's the person who knows and believes who is set free.

Lord, help me to believe You so that I can see You at work.

MORNING
THE GUARANTEE OF FINDING HIM

"You will seek me and find me when you seek me with all your heart."
JEREMIAH 29:13 NIV

There are few guarantees in life, but this scripture provides one: when you seek God with all your heart, you will find Him. There's no wondering if you'll find Him, if you'll be able to make your way to Him, or if you will be allowed to find Him. There's no question. He will show Himself to you when you genuinely search for Him through prayer and worship.

Lord, sometimes You seem elusive and sometimes I can't sense Your presence, but I stand on the promise that You have said I can find You when I seek You.

EVENING
HOW YOU CAN KEEP BELIEVING

For we live by faith, not by sight.
2 CORINTHIANS 5:7 NIV

This is what faith does. . .

It believes. In spite of what we can't see. In spite of what we don't understand. Faith always bends its knee to the God who made everything and knows everything. And faith remembers that this is not heaven, that this current life is a dot on the timeline of eternity. And faith is confident that in time God will make all things right. Maybe not this moment, maybe not next week, and maybe not next year. But when Christ returns, justice will be served, every wrong will receive its recompense, everything will be made beautiful, and everything will be made new.

Will you choose to believe God despite your circumstances?

Lord, give me the faith to follow You no matter what happens in my life. Amen.

MORNING
PRACTICING GOOD BOUNDARIES

The righteous choose their friends carefully.
PROVERBS 12:26 NIV

It's understandable that when we become hurt, we may want to protect ourselves by becoming cynical rather than trusting God with our pain. But this is unwise. A better idea is to practice discernment.

Even Jesus, who knew the evil intent of men's hearts, wasn't jaded or overly self-protective. He was not cynical but discerning. Because He was in communion with His Father, He knew who was on His team and who wasn't. He did not make the mistake of being overly self-protective or nasty. He was tender when needed and firm when necessary. When we practice discernment by listening to the Holy Spirit and receiving wise counsel, we can become empowered to practice good boundaries.

Lord, thank You that I don't have to become cynical or overly self-protective in relationships. Please give me Your wisdom.

EVENING
EVERY DAY OF THE YEAR

This is the day the LORD has made; we will rejoice and be glad in it.
PSALM 118:24 NKJV

Interestingly, while Sunday is seen as the last day of the weekend, it is actually the first day of a new week. Yet since Monday brings work and responsibility, we like to put it off as long as possible. But if our lives are grounded in Christ, then we need to ask Him for an uplifted outlook whether we face scorching hot August days or blustery winter winds. We cannot stop the progress of the week nor the parade of the seasons. Would we want to? Heaven is the only place where a continual "now" will be good for us. On this earth, God is at work in us throughout every day, every month, and every season of life. That's good news!

Lord, make me willing to submit to Your work in me on every slot in my calendar. Amen.

MORNING
THE RIGHT ASSURANCE

And we know that all things work together for good to them that
love God, to them who are the called according to his purpose.
ROMANS 8:28 KJV

Only the ones who are following Christ can lay claim to the promise that God will work all things together for good. Those who trust and obey can rest in the assurance that everything (the good and the bad) fits together in the pattern He has laid out for them.

Lord, thank You for helping me bear my burdens and for keeping track of
the things in my life. I know You are working all things for my good.

EVENING
TRADING COMPLAINTS FOR PRAISE

Praise the LORD, for the LORD is good;
sing praises to His name, for it is pleasant.
PSALM 135:3 NKJV

God knows that we become what we focus on. He desires that we be people of praise. Remember the Hebrews in the wilderness and how they complained and murmured every time something went wrong? Eventually, it affected their faith, and they did not believe they could defeat the giants in Canaan, and God let them wander around for forty years until they were all dead. No doubt, many of them saw their sin, but it was too late to change the consequences.

The antidote for complaining is praising. Praise is the language of Christians. When we are praising, we are focusing not on ourselves but on Christ and His glory. And of course, this is where we find the most happiness.

Dear Lord, remind me to praise when I feel like complaining. Show me
how to switch gears and keep an attitude of praise to You all day long.

MORNING
MORE THAN A PIECE OF FRUIT

Thank you for making me so wonderfully complex!
Your workmanship is marvelous—how well I know it.
PSALM 139:14 NLT

A woman is much more intricately designed than a piece of fruit. And the basic shape of our bodies is something over which we have no control; genetics handles that. We do have a say in what we eat and how we dress and whether we put much effort into exercise and upkeep.

Women were designed by God to be beautiful. And He likes variety. If we're speaking about the plant world, think about the many species of flowers around the globe. They come in every imaginable shape and color and petal dimension. And each of them has its own unique glory. Maybe we should be more like the flowers—stay connected to the Source of our being, accept the sunshine and rain, and reflect His glory in how we grow.

Lord, give me the right perspective of my body
and beauty; may I honor You with my being.

EVENING
WINNING BIG

"He who is faithful in what is least is faithful also in much."
LUKE 16:10 NKJV

All the earth's resources belong to God, and He will give them to us if we need them to fulfill His will. ("The earth is the LORD's, and the fulness thereof" [Psalm 24:1 KJV]; "The silver is mine, and the gold is mine" [Haggai 2:8 KJV]; "Every beast of the forest is mine, and the cattle upon a thousand hills" [Psalm 50:10 KJV].)

Accumulating wealth is not to be our focus. (Matthew 6:19–24)

Coveting is a sin. (Luke 12:15; 2 Timothy 3:2; Colossians 3:5; Exodus 20:17)

Moneymaking schemes are like traps and usually lead to sin. (1 Timothy 6:9)

We are to trust Him, not in "uncertain riches." (1 Timothy 6:17; Proverbs 11:28)

God will take care of our needs if we honor Him. (Matthew 6:31–33)

Lord, help me be wise in how I use the money
I am given. I want to be a faithful steward.

MORNING
STAY CONNECTED

Give all your worries and cares to God, for he cares about you.
1 Peter 5:7 nlt

At its simplest, prayer is talking to God. And when we don't talk to Him, we shut Him out of the details of our lives. Of course, being omniscient, He is aware of what is going on anyway, but He wants us to invite Him in, to want to share our days with Him.

Have you prayed today? Don't see it as an obligation or a guilt inducer but as a chance to communicate with the One who loves you more than anyone else and who can do more about your situation than anyone else.

Lord, thank You for being interested in everything that concerns me today. Amen.

EVENING
AN EXCLUSIVE PLACE

But now they desire a better, that is, a heavenly country. Therefore God is not ashamed to be called their God, for He has prepared a city for them.
Hebrews 11:16 nkjv

Think about the joy of arriving home for Christmas or coming to a family reunion, that moment when you walk in the front door to warm hugs and happy cries of welcome— that's the delight of every moment of eternity. Isn't it a comfort to know that we have this place waiting for us when this life is over?

Heaven is prepared for those who are in relationship with God. The only way to get there is by accepting the sacrifice of Jesus Christ's work on the cross. Salvation is an inclusive invitation to an exclusive place. Have you made plans to go?

Heavenly Father, thank You for preparing a heavenly city where I can live for eternity.

MORNING
SOLID AND UNFADING

No prophecy of Scripture is of any private interpretation, for prophecy never came by the will of man, but holy men of God spoke as they were moved by the Holy Spirit.

2 PETER 1:20–21 NKJV

God has preserved His Word. He inspired holy men of old to write. He guided those who did the copying and the translating. And He guided those who agonized over which books should be included in the canon, the sixty-six books that have been handed down to us.

Remember, "The grass withers, the flower fades, but the word of our God stands forever" (Isaiah 40:8 NKJV); "All Scripture is given by inspiration of God, and is profitable for doctrine, for reproof, for correction, for instruction in righteousness" (2 Timothy 3:16 NKJV).

Lord, You have given us Your Word. Thank You for it.
Use it to light my path and guide my steps.

EVENING
LOVING THE LOST THINGS

"For the Son of Man came to seek and save those who are lost."

LUKE 19:10 NLT

When it comes to people, God loves each of us, no matter our pedigree or "breed," our size or our temperament. And He goes after the ones no one else wants. He loves the castoffs and misfits, the oddballs and the eccentrics. He has a place for each one. He sees the uniqueness of each individual life.

God cares about the animals too. He wants us to care for them and enjoy them. But people are worth so much more. And any day is a great time for people to be rescued and celebrated and made part of His big family.

Lord, You made the animals for our pleasure and use; I'm glad of that. But I'm most thankful for Your love for each of us and the privilege of being part of Your family.

MORNING
GOD IS GOOD

Praise the Lord, for the Lord is good;
sing praises to His name, for it is pleasant.
PSALM 135:3 NKJV

We hear it in church. We say it to others. We want to believe it. God is good. All the time. The Bible says it, so we know it is true.

And when disease or tragedy or hardship enters our lives, we can rest assured that God is not the author of these destructive things and that someday He will cleanse this globe of its misery and set everything right. Until then, He has given us His strength, His hope, and His promise. That is enough to keep us going.

Father God, I praise You. You are good. Your works are wonderful. I
know You love me. Help me to trust Your plan and purpose for me.

EVENING
THE GIFT OF SLEEP

In peace I will lie down and sleep.
PSALM 4:8 NLT

No matter the rhythm of one's internal clock, all of us need sleep. Our bodies require sleep to renew themselves and recharge for the next day.

And when you think about it, God did plan the nighttime for our benefit, right? In the beginning, He separated the darkness and light and gave each a place in the cycle of a twenty-four-hour day. And though He never needs to rest, we do. We cannot do the 24-7 thing; we weren't meant to. And as long as God sustains the earth, there will always be tomorrow in which to work.

Lord, let me praise You by getting the proper rest for my body so that I
may be at my optimum level of energy and creativity for Your glory.

MORNING
THE WORKERS ARE FEW

*The Spirit who lives in you is greater
than the spirit who lives in the world.*

1 JOHN 4:4 NLT

So many Christians avoid serving the church because they feel inadequate, uneducated, and unworthy. Jesus said, "The harvest is plentiful but the workers are few" (Matthew 9:37 NIV).

The truth is we are no longer enslaved to sin. Through the Holy Spirit, we have the power to overcome and carry on. Romans 8:37 (NIV) says, "We are more than conquerors through him who loved us." The Holy Spirit is always full of grace for the believer. Every conviction is for growth, sharpening, and disciplining, never guilt and shame.

Our confidence is in Christ, not ourselves. And He has set us free!

*Lord, thank You for setting me free. Speak into my heart and continually
remind me that I am clean in Your sight because of Your work, not mine.*

EVENING
BY THE POWER OF YOUR TESTIMONY

I will speak to kings about your laws, and I will not be ashamed.

PSALM 119:46 NLT

Your story may not be dramatic or emotional, but it bears witness to Christ, no matter how simple.

Satan will whisper that your story isn't important, that no one wants to hear it. He'll bring up all your failings and hypocrisy. He'll quiet you any way he can.

Peter admonishes us, "If someone asks about your hope as a believer, always be ready to explain it" (1 Peter 3:15 NLT). Written, spoken, or videoed—your personal testimony is one of the most powerful tools you have for the kingdom, and no one can take that away.

*Jesus, give me boldness, and let the whole world
hear from my lips Your wonderful works in my life.*

MORNING
THE RELUCTANT SERVANT

He will also keep you firm to the end, so that you will be blameless.
1 CORINTHIANS 1:8 NIV

Moses and Jonah were both examples of men who were reluctant to accept God's call. Moses was insecure—slow of speech and unassertive. Jonah was simply rebellious. Yet both men eventually fulfilled God's purposes.

Philippians 1:6 (NKJV) says, "He who has begun a good work in you will complete it." God does the work, and for some amazing, beautiful reason, He wants to include us!

No matter how incompetent we feel, we can rest assured that God will not let us fail. He will provide us with everything we need to accomplish His perfect plans.

Lord, thank You that I can trust You to bring about Your purposes in me. Even though I am an imperfect person, my incompetence does not hinder Your outcomes.

EVENING
THE WANT FOR WONDER

Praise the LORD God, the God of Israel, who alone does such wonderful things.
PSALM 72:18 NLT

In the early days of the apostles, many Jews repented and were baptized. They devoted themselves to teaching and fellowship, and "a deep sense of awe came over them all" (Acts 2:43 NLT). They were amazed by God!

We can regain our wonderment through reading God's Word. The more we learn about Him and our own condition, the more we can appreciate His love. Proverbs 25:2 (KJV) says, "It is the glory of God to conceal a thing: but the honour of kings is to search out a matter."

Is it time for you to examine the character of God in a fresh way? Pray today that He would open your eyes to His wonderful mysteries.

Father, restore in me the wonder of who You are.

MORNING
STRIVING NOT STRUGGLING

In all these things we are more than conquerors through Him who loved us.
ROMANS 8:37 NKJV

Don't struggle or strive. Instead, abide.

How much sweeter would our own Christian lives be if we took the same advice and applied it to everything we do?

Stop striving in marriage. Stop trying to create perfect children. Stop trying to control every situation, and instead abide in Christ. Let the love of God flow through you, and trust Him to shine.

The Christian life will be filled with obstacles and struggles, but the Holy Spirit has given us the power to overcome. When we abide in Christ, those struggles become the fertilizer that brings about the fruit of the Spirit.

Lord, You promised that we are more than conquerors through You.
Help me to embrace the truth and live in confidence of those promises.

EVENING
ARE YOUR HANDS TOO FULL?

Trust in the LORD with all your heart.
PROVERBS 3:5 NKJV

It's wonderful that we fiercely love our families and favorite causes, but has our affection manifested into a self-appointed queenship, in which we see ourselves as co-magistrate with God, where we sort of consult with Him instead of submit to Him?

Submission requires trust, and that can be difficult, especially if you've been disappointed before. But God has proven His faithfulness. Jesus said, "You believe because you have seen me. Blessed are those who believe without seeing me" (John 20:29 NLT).

Will you empty your hands? Let go of control and receive peace, joy, contentment, satisfaction, and confidence in its stead.

Jesus, give me the courage to give You control of my life.
You already have it. Now teach me to rest in that.

MORNING
SUFFERING CHANGES YOU. . .FOR THE BETTER

After you have suffered a little while, [God] will himself restore you.
1 PETER 5:10 NIV

Don't despair in the dark places of suffering, but rather consider the ways God has used it to enrich your character. As the apostle Paul explained, "We also glory in tribulations, knowing that tribulation produces perseverance; and perseverance, character; and character, hope. Now hope does not disappoint" (Romans 5:3–5 NKJV).

In times of travail, watch as the Lord conforms you to His image, and consider yourself blessed.

Jesus, show me the value of my suffering, and make me more like You through it all.

EVENING
IN HIS PRESENCE

In Your presence is fullness of joy; at Your right hand are pleasures forevermore.
PSALM 16:11 NKJV

We should long to enter through the secret door of our souls and spend time with the ultimate Restorer. No wonder so many Christians have shallow roots and withering leaves—they spend no time with God!

Bible study and congregational worship may sustain you temporarily, but without the nutrients and connectedness to the Vine, death is the ultimate destination—like cut flowers in a shop.

God is personal. He doesn't just want your work. He wants *you*, and that requires meeting with Him, talking with Him, gleaning from Him. In His presence, we are refreshed.

Lord, I say that I love You, but it has been so long since I have spent time in Your presence. Forgive me, and let us come together right now.

MORNING
GOD'S SYSTEM OF JUSTICE

Yet the LORD longs to be gracious to you; therefore he will rise up to show you compassion. For the LORD is a God of justice. Blessed are all who wait for him!
ISAIAH 30:18 NIV

The world's justice tells us we don't deserve God's graciousness—we've made too many mistakes—but God's justice is wrapped in love and mercy. Instead of pointing to our failures and telling us we're worthless, He forgives our sins and totally forgets them. They're as far from His thoughts as the east is from the west (see Psalm 103:12).

When we run into His arms of love and let His grace overwhelm us, we will long for more of Him. He's too magnificent to ignore. It's impossible to turn our backs on all He does for us. The natural response is to accept His compassion. He longs to give it and waits patiently until we're ready to receive.

Dear Lord, I long to receive Your gracious compassion. I yearn for more of You!

EVENING
THE KING'S TEMPLE

You realize, don't you, that you are the temple of God, and God himself is present in you?
1 CORINTHIANS 3:16–17 MSG

We take Jesus with us all the time. Wherever we are, He is there. We may feel His presence more some times and places than others, but we have the assurance that He will never leave us. Whether we're climbing majestic mountains, working at a desk in an office, or standing in the checkout line at a grocery store, He is there. We can depend on Him to provide everything we need to thrive.

Heavenly Father, I'm absolutely in awe, knowing You want to dwell in me.
Nothing can separate us, and nothing is impossible when You are within me. Amen.

MORNING
HARVESTTIME

"You know the saying, 'Four months between planting and harvest.' But I say, wake up and look around. The fields are already ripe for harvest."

When we notice a task that needs to be done, could it be a nudge from God? It's easy to think someone else will take care of it—whatever *it* is. We may believe we're not qualified or our schedule is too full, or we might even think it's beneath us.

But the only way our work will matter eternally is to allow God to direct our plans every day and ask Him to show us exactly what will touch someone's life. Most often, He will tell us simply to show His love in some uncomplicated way that comes naturally. Obeying in those effortless situations prepares us for the times when the Lord directs us to do something that requires total dependence on Him to accomplish.

Lord God, I choose to be available to work however You want me to, as You harvest the ripe fields.

EVENING
OUR STRONGHOLD

The LORD is good, a strong hold in the day of trouble; and he knoweth them that trust in him.

Our enemy, Satan, comes against us with doubts and fears and disasters. He wants to destroy everyone, especially those who put their trust in Jesus for salvation.

But God is our supernatural Stronghold, mightier than any fortress built by men. The Lord will protect us in times of trouble; He knows those who depend on Him for shelter and refuge. Nothing can destroy us when He wraps us in His loving strength. What a comfort in the face of adversity.

Father, thank You for providing a safe place, reserved for those who put our trust in You. Let me stay there forever.

MORNING
MY GOOD SHEPHERD

*"You are my flock, the sheep of my pasture. You are my people,
and I am your God. I, the Sovereign LORD, have spoken!"*

EZEKIEL 34:31 NLT

Jesus told a parable about the lost sheep. Though ninety-nine were safe, the shepherd searched until he found the one that was missing. Our Good Shepherd rejoices when He finds one sheep that strayed from the flock. He reminds us of the joy in heaven each time a sinner repents—when the Shepherd brings him safely from the wilderness to the sheepfold.

How desperately we need a Shepherd to care for us. God sets pastors over us to carry out His plans, but above them, the perfect Shepherd leads each of us into our eternal home. Even though sometimes we act like willful sheep, He cherishes and protects us with every step we take.

Heavenly Shepherd, no matter how far I stray, I know You will find me and carry me home. Thank You that You never give up, no matter how obnoxious I behave.

EVENING
BEST FRIENDS FOREVER

*"You are my friends when you do the things I command you. I'm no
longer calling you servants because servants don't understand what
their master is thinking and planning. No, I've named you friends
because I've let you in on everything I've heard from the Father."*

JOHN 15:14–15 MSG

I'm so glad the Bible never gives the impression that people have to be superspiritual to be Christ followers. Look at Peter, the disciple many of us can identify with because he seemed to speak before he thought. When we read about the disappointing acts of Jesus' friends, we don't have to despair when our own lives don't measure up.

Yes, they failed sometimes, but they repented and never gave up. Because they kept trying, Jesus called them friends. He is the same now as He was then, so we can be assured we are His friends too.

Precious Friend, I long to be close to You forever.

MORNING
FOREVER THE SAME

*"I am the LORD, and I do not change. That is why you
descendants of Jacob are not already destroyed."*
MALACHI 3:6 NLT

God won't throw us away because of the dumb things humans do. He hasn't resorted to stripping us of our free will, even though that would make things easier for Him. He didn't decide we aren't worth saving. He still invites us to work with Him.

And because He doesn't change, He will never destroy His people.

Jesus promised, "I am with you always, even to the end of the age" (Matthew 28:20 NKJV). And the writer of Hebrews 13:8 (NKJV) said, "Jesus Christ is the same yesterday, today, and forever."

Because He doesn't change, we can look forward to eternity with Him. Just because of who He is.

Dear Lord, I praise You for being changeless.

EVENING
GLORIOUS FREEDOM

*So Christ has truly set us free. Now make sure that you stay
free, and don't get tied up again in slavery to the law.*
GALATIANS 5:1 NLT

Our Lord endured undeserved torture, brutal beatings, and the agony of crucifixion. Yet as He died, He asked God to forgive the very people who did unspeakable things to Him. If anyone ever had a reason to pray, "Father, they aren't worthy of forgiveness," it would have been Jesus. Instead, He forgave.

He knew from the beginning the path He was to follow. He realized He would have to endure excruciating pain and humiliation, but He willingly faced it to free us from the bondage of the Law. He liberated us to live lives of forgiveness.

*Praise You, Lord Jesus, for the wondrous miracle of salvation. Give me grace
to understand that as I receive forgiveness, I'm free to offer it to others.*

MORNING
HE WILL LIFT US UP

The LORD upholds all who fall,
and raises up all who are bowed down.
PSALM 145:14 NKJV

In our daily lives, the Lord is the One who picks us up when we fall. Our falls may not be the kind that lead to broken bones, but we plunge into sin or slip on some stupid temptation or collapse into a pit of depression. Through everything that comes our way, He teaches us to depend on Him to lift us up and encourage us to go on. Always.

Precious Lord, I cannot fall so low You won't rescue me.
I rejoice in Your faithfulness, my Redeemer. You rescue me.

EVENING
GOD'S COMMAND

You made me; you created me. Now give
me the sense to follow your commands.
PSALM 119:73 NLT

Many scriptures tell us He is slow to anger. He abounds in loving-kindness. He doesn't punish us as we deserve. Yet we tend to whine and feel abused when anything bad happens.

All God expects is obedience, and His rules are simple. He knows we will break His commandments, so He only asks that we love and trust Jesus. We can't just go through the motions or follow rituals, trying to get what we want. Our deep, genuine love and an intimate relationship are what He yearns for. The more we know Him, the easier it is to worship Him, to adore Him—to give back to Him the love He freely gives to us.

Heavenly Father, following Your commands is so simple.
You loved me first. And now I love You.

MORNING
THE LIGHT OF JESUS

For you were once darkness, but now you are light in the Lord. Live as children of light.
EPHESIANS 5:8 NIV

Even as adults, darkness can envelop us, leaving us with unreasonable fears. But Jesus doesn't let us fumble and stumble through the dark places on our own. He became one of us and brought light into our lives. He wants to shine divine light into every dark situation.

Colossians 1:13 (NIV) assures us, "For he has rescued us from the dominion of darkness and brought us into the kingdom of the Son he loves." When we belong to Jesus, we're part of His kingdom. We become children of light, and the darkness dissipates.

*Thank You, Lord, that darkness can't overshadow Your light. And
because I belong to You, I can shine light into other dark lives.*

EVENING
A FIRM FOUNDATION

*When the whirlwind passes by, the wicked is no more,
but the righteous has an everlasting foundation.*
PROVERBS 10:25 NKJV

God wants us to build our lives on a strong foundation that will withstand storms—sickness, broken relationships, financial losses, or actual destruction from a natural disaster. Jesus said, "Therefore whoever hears these sayings of Mine, and does them, I will liken him to a wise man who built his house on the rock" (Matthew 7:24 NKJV).

Jesus is our everlasting foundation, our Rock when troubles come. He is eager for us to run to Him.

When we cling to Him, we have assurance that He will hold us safely in His tender care. That doesn't mean no storms will come, but when they do, we know that nothing can separate us from His love.

*Dear Lord, when the storms of life approach,
keep me safe in the strong foundation of Your love.*

MORNING
LIVE IN HOLY LIGHT

*"If you are generous with the hungry and start giving yourselves
to the down-and-out, your lives will begin to glow in the darkness,
your shadowed lives will be bathed in sunlight."*

ISAIAH 58:10 MSG

Jesus wants us to live an abundant life, and when we do—when we are full of His Spirit—we have plenty to share with the people He puts in our lives. That abundant overflow comes from spending time with God. When we pray, listen, read the Bible, meditate on His magnificence, and enjoy fellowship with other believers, we get filled to the brim. Whether we have material wealth or not, we will have spiritual riches to share with others.

We will "glow in the darkness" of the world. People will be drawn to the light they see in us. Our lives will be bathed in the Son's light, like noon on a clear, bright day.

*Father, may I feed Your Word to those who are hungry and satisfy their
need to know You. I long to shine Your light and joy in dark places.*

EVENING
NO CONDEMNATION

*Who is he who condemns? It is Christ who died, and furthermore is also risen,
who is even at the right hand of God, who also makes intercession for us.*

ROMANS 8:34 NKJV

God the Father sees us through His Son. Jesus is eager to forgive the worst sinner. When we turn to Him, all our sins are washed away in His blood; we're spotless. And there's a glorious celebration in heaven whenever a sinner turns to Jesus.

No matter how filthy we feel, we're never more than a prayer away from being clean, as pure as if we never sinned.

*Thank You, Lord, for setting me free from the sin and guilt that try to trap me.
I praise You because even though I don't deserve it, You intercede for me continually.*

MORNING
LEAD MY HEART

*May the Lord lead your hearts into a full understanding and expression of
the love of God and the patient endurance that comes from Christ.*
2 THESSALONIANS 3:5 NLT

If we try to control our own destiny, we flounder, and our lives are full of confusion.
We search for love in the things of this world and find broken hearts. We seek joy, only
to face emptiness. We convince ourselves there is no truth, because we ignore reality.
We waste time searching for things that bring no satisfaction.

When we bow our hearts and minds to the Creator and follow Him, we can bask
in the calm of His unwavering peace. He leads us into a full understanding of true love
and abundant life.

*Dear Father, I ask You to continually fill me with Your love. Please lead me into
a full understanding of Your love, and keep me from choosing the wrong path.*

EVENING
A LIFE OF THANKS

*Rejoice always, pray continually, give thanks in all circumstances;
for this is God's will for you in Christ Jesus.*
1 THESSALONIANS 5:16–18 NIV

Have you ever wondered what God's will is for your life? Here is the answer! First
Thessalonians tells us exactly what God's will is for each of us: rejoice and pray always,
and give thanks no matter the circumstances. Simple? Yes! Easy? No way!

How is it possible to pray and give thanks always? It is not possible on our own.
But the great news is that we have the Spirit of God living inside of us, reminding us of
God's truth and leading us each step of the way. Are you walking in the Spirit of God?

*God, I trust my life and my decisions to You. I am
thankful for Your great and abiding love for me.*

MORNING
NO WORRIES

Do not be anxious about anything, but in every situation, by prayer and petition, with thanksgiving, present your requests to God. And the peace of God, which transcends all understanding, will guard your hearts and your minds in Christ Jesus.
PHILIPPIANS 4:6–7 NIV

How can you shut off the anxiety and worry to make room for the abundant life God has for you right here and now? Our gracious God has given us a game plan:

Whenever you find yourself worried or anxious, stop to pray.

Give thanks! Tell God your worries, and ask Him to fill you with joy in His presence (see Psalm 16:11).

When you do those things, the very peace of God—which doesn't make any sense to our human minds—will guard your heart and mind through Christ.

If you are struggling with an uncertain future, find rest and peace in Christ alone.

God, I'm worried and afraid. Please fill me with Your peace. Thank You for Your unfailing love!

EVENING
A GOOD DAD

Give thanks to the LORD, for he is good; his love endures forever.
PSALM 107:1 NIV

In Luke 11:13 (NIV), Jesus says, "If you then, though you are evil, know how to give good gifts to your children, how much more will your Father in heaven give the Holy Spirit to those who ask him!"

God is a good Dad who gives us His Spirit to live in us and teach us in each moment. We are never alone. We have a constant, perfect, loving parent and friend with us at all times and in every situation.

What an amazing gift to be thankful for always!

God, You are a good and loving Dad. The love I feel for others doesn't even come close to the love and graciousness You have for me. Thank You!

MORNING
HIS LOVE NEVER QUITS

Give thanks to God—he is good and his love never quits. Say, "Save us, Savior God, round us up and get us out of these godless places, so we can give thanks to your holy Name, and bask in your life of praise."

1 CHRONICLES 16:34–35 MSG

You may have had a parent, friend, or spouse abandon you at some point in your life. God won't do that. You may feel alone and fearful. God won't leave you. You may feel sad and crushed. God says He is close to the brokenhearted and saves those who are crushed in spirit (see Psalm 34:18).

God, I trust that You love me and that You will be with me always.

EVENING
COMMON DAYS

And so, dear brothers and sisters, I plead with you to give your bodies to God because of all he has done for you. Let them be a living and holy sacrifice—the kind he will find acceptable. This is truly the way to worship him. Don't copy the behavior and customs of this world, but let God transform you into a new person by changing the way you think. Then you will learn to know God's will for you, which is good and pleasing and perfect.

ROMANS 12:1–2 NLT

God tells us that He wants us to live a life of everyday worship. He wants to transform us from the inside out. This isn't about trying harder to please God or going to church more and giving more money. . . . It's about letting the Spirit of God lead you in every moment and thanking Him along the way. It's about listening for His still, small voice and following Him no matter what everyone else is doing.

God, show me how to live a life of everyday worship.

MORNING
THANK GOD

Hallelujah! Thank GOD! And why? Because he's good, because his love lasts. But who on earth can do it—declaim GOD's mighty acts, broadcast all his praises? You're one happy man when you do what's right, one happy woman when you form the habit of justice.

PSALM 106:1–3 MSG

You are the only one in charge of your attitude. Many things will happen today. Some good, some maybe not so good, but all are outside of your control. You can control how you respond to everything that happens this day. Why not thank God no matter what? Think that might change how well your day goes? Why not give it a try and see what happens!

God, please remind me in this moment of Your goodness and Your great love for me! Help me thank You in every circumstance.

EVENING
WITH ALL MY HEART

I will give thanks to you, LORD, with all my heart; I will tell of all your wonderful deeds.

PSALM 9:1 NIV

God, your Creator, is the only One capable of healing your heart and making you whole again. He heals broken hearts and binds up wounds (see Psalm 147:3). It's also been said that God can heal your broken heart, but first you must give Him all the pieces.

When you build walls to protect your heart, you end up keeping out the bad. . . but you also keep out the good. Allow God to break down the walls of your heart so He can start putting the pieces back together. Then you'll be able to give thanks with all your heart.

God, I want You to have my whole heart. . .all the pieces! Please break down my walls and reveal Yourself to me.

MORNING
BRIMMING WITH WORSHIP

Do you see what we've got? An unshakable kingdom! And do you see how thankful we must be? Not only thankful, but brimming with worship, deeply reverent before God.
HEBREWS 12:28–29 MSG

If you aren't brimming with worship, ask God to wake you up and change you from the inside out! Remember, God's Word tells us that we have not because we ask not (see James 4:2). . .so why not ask? If our prayers are in line with God's will, He longs to give us the desires of our hearts (see Psalm 37:4).

The presence and power of God in your daily life will change you. Even if you're in the middle of a dark time, God wants to give you His peace that goes beyond your understanding. He will. . .if only you will let Him!

God, I want to be brimming with worship for You. Please wake me up so that I can know and love You more!

EVENING
A SACRIFICE OF PRAISE

"Spread for me a banquet of praise, serve High God a feast of kept promises, and call for help when you're in trouble—I'll help you, and you'll honor me."
PSALM 50:14–15 MSG

In Hebrews 13:15 (NIV), God's Word tells us, "Through Jesus, therefore, let us continually offer to God a sacrifice of praise—the fruit of lips that openly profess his name." To sacrifice in worship means to have faith in God even when you don't feel like it. Even when you can't see Him anymore. The only way we can do that is through the power of Christ working in our lives in each moment. Because of the cross, we can rise above our circumstances and trust that the God of heaven has purpose for everything that comes our way. We are able to look at situations from God's perspective and trust Him no matter what.

God, please increase my faith so that I can trust You and worship You despite my circumstances.

MORNING
MY EYES HAVE SEEN

*"He alone is your God, the only one who is worthy of your praise, the one who
has done these mighty miracles that you have seen with your own eyes."*
DEUTERONOMY 10:21 NLT

God is not only the great Creator of all things; He is a personal God actively alive in every moment of your life. He knows your words before you even speak them. He wants you to know Him intimately (see Psalm 139). When that miraculous moment occurs—the head knowledge turning into heart knowledge—God begins to open your eyes to see Him in everything.

Suddenly, hard times begin to make sense. God is working them all out for good in your life (see Romans 8:28). You start to notice God's hand at work in all areas of your life.

*God, please open my eyes to see You at work in my life. Move in my
heart to see things from Your perspective and great purpose.*

EVENING
SAFE AND SAVED

I sing to GOD, the Praise-Lofty, and find myself safe and saved.
PSALM 18:3 MSG

God gives us His Word so that we won't be afraid. He is closer to us than we think. Whenever you feel afraid or lonely, call on His name. Ask Him to make Himself known to you. Copy these scripture verses on note cards, and read them again and again. God's Word is living and active, and the Spirit of God will remind you of these truths when you need them most. Don't be ashamed when you feel afraid. . .just take your fears straight to the only One who can free you from them. He will comfort you and cover you with His loving-kindness.

God, please hide me in Your shelter and cover me with Your truth and love.

MORNING
I WILL PRAISE HIM AGAIN

*Why am I discouraged? Why is my heart so sad? I will put my
hope in God! I will praise him again—my Savior and my God!*

PSALM 42:5–6 NLT

A life of faith is marked by an authentic, loving relationship with God. You tell Him
your burdens, and He carries them for you.

What God wants from you is this: Instead of telling every person but God your
troubles, go to Him first. He will lovingly restore you and meet your every need. He
will bring resources to you and show you the way! If you let go of trying to manipulate
your circumstances and allow God to come to your rescue, He will!

*God, forgive me for going to everyone but You for help. I give You
my needs and desires. Please fill my heart with hope.*

EVENING
GREAT EXPECTATION

*All praise to God, the Father of our Lord Jesus Christ. It is by his great mercy that
we have been born again, because God raised Jesus Christ from the dead. Now we
live with great expectation, and we have a priceless inheritance—an inheritance that
is kept in heaven for you, pure and undefiled, beyond the reach of change and decay.*

1 PETER 1:3–4 NLT

If heartache and trials have marked your life, it's time for a new beginning. Take heart
from Isaiah 43:19 (NLT): "For I am about to do something new. See, I have already
begun! Do you not see it? I will make a pathway through the wilderness. I will create
rivers in the dry wasteland."

If you are weary and burdened, take those burdens straight to the cross of Christ and
allow Him to give you new life. Then be on the lookout—with great expectation—for
the amazing ways that God shows up in your everyday life.

*God, I give You praise tonight. I will watch with great
expectation as You make Yourself known in my life.*

MORNING
SPIRITUAL MEDICINE

*"The virgin will conceive and give birth to a son, and they
will call him Immanuel" (which means "God with us").*
MATTHEW 1:23 NIV

Neediness has a solution. The One who will never leave us or forsake us gives mercy and grace when we enter His throne room. He can redeem our losses, compensate our loneliness, understand our emotions, and satisfy our longings. How? By filling us with Himself. We have the fruit of the Holy Spirit when we focus on God. Colossians 3 gives practical steps for focusing our minds: put on love, let peace rule our hearts, fill our lives with the Word of Christ, sing to the Lord, and give thanks in all things. That is God's prescription for what ails us.

*God of mercy and grace, as You have ministered to me when I am broken,
give me sensitivity to others who are hurting, so I can point them to You.*

EVENING
BIBLE BOOKENDS

*"Look, I am coming soon. . . . I am the Alpha and the Omega,
the First and the Last, the Beginning and the End."*
REVELATION 22:12–13 NLT

God often used literary structure in His Word to call attention to something important. For example, the Bible has "bookends," showing that history (His-story) will go full circle and accomplish His purposes. These bookends are the first two and last two chapters of the Bible.

Right now, we are in the "between" chapters. Corruption and evil abound. Society grows increasingly godless and immoral. Families are fragmented; relationships are disposable. But Revelation 21–22 will come. Everyone who has accepted the redemption Jesus provided will live with Him forever because He said, "Let anyone who is thirsty come. Let anyone who desires drink freely from the water of life" (Revelation 22:17 NLT).

*Until You come again or I go to You, Lord, help me
to abide in You and depend on Your Word.*

MORNING
A JOY FOCUS

For the joy set before him he endured the cross. . . . Consider him who endured
such opposition from sinners, so that you will not grow weary and lose heart.
HEBREWS 12:2–3 NIV

What if God does not deliver *from* a trial? Then He will sustain us *through* the trial by bearing our burdens with us every day.

When we "grow weary" and find ourselves "losing heart," focus on God our Savior, our sovereign Lord, our Burden Bearer. If the joy of the Lord is our focus, then it will also be our strength (see Nehemiah 8:10).

God of my salvation, I look forward to spending eternity with You.
Until then, thank You for bearing my burdens and giving me escapes
from death. Help me stay joyful because I'm focused on You.

EVENING
JUST FOLLOWING GOD

"I will make your descendants as the dust of the earth; so that if a man could
number the dust of the earth, then your descendants also could be numbered.
Arise, walk in the land through its length and its width, for I give it to you."
GENESIS 13:16–17 NKJV

Sarai and Abram, just ordinary people, trusted God for something bigger than they ever could have imagined. They just stepped out, confident God would deliver all He promised.

Although Sarai at some later crossroads had her moments of doubt, struggled to believe that God's promises included her, and battled her earthly circumstances and thoughts, she continued to follow the Lord.

Like Sarai, God has called you to walk with Him. He has set *you* apart to follow Him and live according to His way. Choose to do so right now.

God, I choose to walk with You. No matter what the earthly circumstances
are surrounding me, I trust You to lead me on the right path.

MORNING
UNITY WITH THE FATHER

"Love your enemies and pray for those who persecute you, that you may be children of your Father in heaven. . . . Be perfect, therefore, as your heavenly Father is perfect."
MATTHEW 5:44–45, 48 NIV

It's easy to get caught up in the drama when someone pushes your buttons or you feel used, abandoned, mistreated, or hurt. Society is full of people looking for revenge and a way to make someone pay for wrongs done to them. As a child of God, you can choose another way—your heavenly Father's way.

He responds with grace and forgiveness to both good and evil people. He is the calm in the middle of the storm. He desires to put His love, poured out lavishly upon you, to work *in* you and let it operate *through* you. You can rest in His peace, knowing He chose a perfect way for you.

Father, I desire to walk in unity with You, allowing Your love to flow through me and responding in peace to all.

EVENING
LOVINGLY CONNECTED

I look up at your macro-skies, dark and enormous, your handmade sky-jewelry, moon and stars mounted in their settings. Then I look at my micro-self and wonder, Why do you bother with us? Why take a second look our way? Yet we've so narrowly missed being gods, bright with Eden's dawn light. You put us in charge of your handcrafted world.
PSALM 8:3–6 MSG

As God's creation, you are in His thoughts. He longs for a relationship with you. He wants to visit you and spend time with you. He is always with you, even when your thoughts are not on Him.

God holds you close. You are precious and valuable to Him. His relationship with you runs deeper than even the tie you share with friends and family. You are lovingly connected to the Lord of the world without end.

God, I am Yours and You are mine. Thank You for loving me unconditionally.

MORNING
FAITHFUL FRIEND

*The LORD kept his word and did for Sarah exactly what he had promised.
She became pregnant, and she gave birth to a son for Abraham in his
old age. This happened at just the time God had said it would.*
GENESIS 21:1–2 NLT

What promises has God made to you? Do you remember times when He proved Himself faithful?

Regardless of what you are going through today, God is your faithful friend. Remind yourself of His presence and His promise to walk with you and never leave you nor forsake you. Hold fast to Him and His promises!

*Lord, You are my closest, most faithful friend. I trust
You to keep every promise You have made to me.*

EVENING
WHISPERS OF LOVE

*I am praying to you because I know you will answer, O God. Bend down
and listen as I pray. Show me your unfailing love in wonderful ways.*
PSALM 17:6–7 NLT

Like the psalmist David, you probably have a day now and then when you feel empty or alone. Maybe you struggle to keep nagging, negative thoughts at bay. In many of his psalms, David shared his challenges to keep his negative thoughts from imprisoning him. At first, he would give in, but then as he remembered God's faithfulness, he was able to break the tentacles of doubt.

Remind yourself of God's Word just as David did, and doing so will bring you back to your spiritual senses. As the light of God's truth makes its way in, you will begin to break free.

God is there—as He has always been. Listen quietly for the gentle whispers of His unfailing love.

Thank You, God, for Your whispers of love.

MORNING
SECRETS OF THE KINGDOM

He replied, "You are permitted to understand the secrets of the Kingdom of Heaven, but others are not. To those who listen to my teaching, more understanding will be given, and they will have an abundance of knowledge. But for those who are not listening, even what little understanding they have will be taken away from them."

MATTHEW 13:11–12 NLT

Jesus told stories to crowds, but His disciples, who were also listening, were given more knowledge than those who saw Jesus only on the surface. When you live in Christ and walk closely with Him, when you go deep with Him, you too will see and experience more than those who know Him superficially.

Lord, I want to know the secrets of the kingdom. Give me ears to hear, eyes to see, and a heart that understands.

EVENING
LET YOUR SOUL RETURN

The law of the LORD is perfect, converting the soul; the testimony of the LORD is sure, making wise the simple; the statutes of the LORD are right, rejoicing the heart; the commandment of the LORD is pure, enlightening the eyes.

PSALM 19:7 –8 NKJV

You grow in relationship with your heavenly Father as you come to understand Him and His ways through the Bible. As you live and breathe in the wisdom and knowledge God has revealed to you through His words, your soul is made new in Him.

Just as the sun restores a darkened earth's light, the Word of God restores your entire person, bringing your mind, will, and emotions back to that divine connection for which you were created—a relationship with Him.

Jesus, I desire Your truth found in the holy scriptures as much as I desire sunlight.

MORNING
THE STRENGTH THAT DOES NOT FAIL

But [Joseph's] bow remained strong and steady and rested in the Strength that does not fail him, for the arms of his hands were made strong and active by the hands of the Mighty God of Jacob, by the name of the Shepherd, the Rock of Israel.
GENESIS 49:24 AMPC

Joseph endured great adversity, starting with his older brothers selling him into slavery as a young boy. Each battle Joseph faced required courage and faith in God to rescue him and provide him with strength. Joseph's bow remained strong because he relied on God's strength. God's hands supported Joseph as he used his weapon against his enemies.

As you endure difficulties, burdens, and persecution, remember that you don't have to fight alone. God is with you and has provided you with the strength that does not fail.

God, I believe that as I follow You, I cannot fail. You will fight for me. All I have to do is invite You in.

EVENING
LET GO AND LET GOD

And Moses said to God, Who am I, that I should go to Pharaoh and bring the Israelites out of Egypt? God said, I will surely be with you.
EXODUS 3:11–12 AMPC

When the Jews were slaves in Egypt, Pharaoh ordered all their male children to be murdered. Moses' mother, Jochebed, knew she couldn't hide him anymore, so she gave him to God, trusting Him to take care of her son (see Exodus 2:3).

As Jochebed released the basket that held her baby boy, she didn't know what would happen. She didn't know God's plan, but she trusted God to go with, protect, and keep her baby.

What has God asked you to entrust to Him?

God, I've held tightly to some things. You know what they are. Tonight, I release them to you, trusting You to do a greater work than I can ever imagine.

MORNING
REVELATION JUST FOR YOU

Jesus replied, "Blessed are you, Simon son of Jonah, for this was not revealed to you by flesh and blood, but by my Father in heaven."
MATTHEW 16:17 NIV

Do you ever just have a sort of knowing in your heart about something?

God often gives you insight and revelation to walk out your journey with Him. He is always there, ready to show you the path to take, the word to say, or the move to make. His job is to speak into your life. Your job is to listen and obey.

Heavenly Father, I want to hear Your voice. I will listen quietly to what You are revealing to me today. Give me insight into Your plan, and help me follow Your instructions.

EVENING
QUIET MOMENTS

The LORD is my shepherd; I shall not want. He makes me to lie down in green pastures; He leads me beside the still waters. He restores my soul. . . . Yea, though I walk through the valley of the shadow of death, I will fear no evil; for You are with me.
PSALM 23:1–4 NKJV

If you are not intentional about spending time with God, before you know it, you have become distant or have detoured away from Him. You find your soul is hungry for His presence and peace.

God is calling you to reconnect. No matter where you are, when you recognize your need for Him, stop whatever you are doing and step away from others. Once you are alone with Him, establish a reconnection. Allow His presence to wash over you and restore your soul.

Lord, when life begins to consume me, speak to my heart and draw me to You. Help me to disconnect from the busyness of this world and reconnect with Yours.

MORNING
SPRING EVENTUALLY COMES

"The LORD is my strength and my song; he has given me victory. This is my God, and I will praise him—my father's God, and I will exalt him!"
EXODUS 15:2 NLT

Wouldn't it be nice if something or someone would predict your future? Will the figurative storms in your life continue to rage or cease? How long will a season of hardship and suffering continue? Regardless of today's shadow, spring will inevitably come in your own life. The cold, dark, bitter challenges you might be facing will eventually end. As you cling to the promises found in scripture, you will find hope. Blossoms will bloom!

Father, whether I'm walking through heavy snowdrifts or dancing in a field of lilies, I'll praise You because I believe that spring is on its way or has already come!

EVENING
GRACE GIVEN

So the last shall be first, and the first last: for many be called, but few chosen.
MATTHEW 20:16 KJV

The parable of the workers in the vineyard, found in Matthew 20:1–16, is about God's grace in your life. Sometimes it doesn't feel fair when grace is given to others. You might want justice. Yet when the tables are turned, it may be hard for you to receive unmerited favor.

Why some people are given their fair share, others less, and some more doesn't always seem to make sense. What is clear is that God loves you no matter what! Even when circumstances in your life don't make sense, abide in Him. As you do, watch the barricade in your life come tumbling down because you are open to the grace He gives.

Lord Jesus, I choose to receive Your grace and extend it to others.

MORNING
TO SERVE OR NOT TO SERVE?

"You must serve only the LORD your God."
EXODUS 23:25 NLT

As you go about the day, be mindful of who you are serving—Jesus Christ—and how you can serve others out of the love you have for Him. Focus on serving God and leading by His example. Doing so will be more fruitful and satisfying than anything this world has to offer.

Jesus, I need to remain connected to You by serving and leading in the ways that glorify You. May my life be an instrument—a reflection—of You.

EVENING
FIRST THINGS FIRST

" 'Love the Lord your God with all your heart and with all your soul and with all your mind.' This is the first and greatest commandment. And the second is like it: 'Love your neighbor as yourself.' "
MATTHEW 22:37–39 NIV

Take a moment now to love God with your whole being. Then do some self-reflecting. See if there's something for which you need to forgive yourself—and do so. Then extend that same love and forgiveness toward others. Ah, how freeing! Like David, you can now say to God, "You are my hiding place; you will protect me from trouble and surround me with songs of deliverance" (Psalm 32:7 NIV).

Jesus, You are the greatest thing in my life! I revel in the love You have for me, the love I have for others and myself, and the love I have for You.

MORNING
SING A NEW SONG

He has given me a new song to sing, a hymn of praise to our God. Many will see what he has done and be amazed. They will put their trust in the LORD.
PSALM 40:3 NLT

Sing a song of praise for what Jesus has done in *your* life, how He heals and restores you! David wrote, "O LORD my God, you have performed many wonders for us. Your plans for us are too numerous to list. You have no equal. If I tried to recite all your wonderful deeds, I would never come to the end of them" (Psalm 40:5 NLT).

How wonderful to sing a never-ending song about all the amazing things Jesus has done in your life, how He turns all your sorrow into joy!

Lord, whatever physical condition I might struggle with, help me to have an endless supply of praise for You. Your never-ending wonders give me hope.

EVENING
CALMER OF SOULS AND STORMS

[Jesus' disciples in the boat] all saw Him and were agitated (troubled and filled with fear and dread). But immediately He talked with them and said, Take heart! I AM! Stop being alarmed and afraid.
MARK 6:50 AMPC

Remember who Jesus is and the amazing things He has done for you. Never think He's overlooking you. Take courage that you will recognize His voice, His presence, and His power when He is near. Be assured He's looking out for you. He will never pass you by. He has words to calm your spirit. He's ready to get into your boat and still your storms. Simply allow Him into your vessel.

Lord, come to me now. Speak to me. Calm my inner and outer storms.

MORNING
CONSTANT HELP

Lord, I believe! [Constantly] help my weakness of faith!
MARK 9:24 AMPC

Jesus has one request when you ask for help with your own issues: Take the *if* out of the equation when it comes to believing in His power. Have faith that *He can do* anything in your life, that for Him *nothing is impossible.*

But when (and *if*) you do fall short in faith, know that the Lord will constantly help you, pouring on you more than a sufficient amount of grace, enabling Him to work even through your weakness.

No matter what your level of faith, constantly call on Jesus. He will come, grip your hand, and lift you up into a life of seemingly impossible miracles.

Jesus, everything is possible with You in my heart.
Help me to believe this more and more each day.

EVENING
YOUR FOREVER GOD

We pondered your love-in-action, God. . . . Your name, God, evokes a train
of Hallelujahs wherever it is spoken, near and far; your arms are heaped with
goodness-in-action. . . . Our God forever, who guides us till the end of time.
PSALM 48:9–10, 14 MSG

It seems almost impossible to imagine that God is with you now, surrounding you with His protection and strength. That He will be with you when it's time for you to cross over to heaven. And that He will be with you for all eternity, when there will be no more sorrow, pain, war, or death itself.

Although this constant presence of a living Lord may seem impossible, Jesus assures you that "all things are possible with God" (Mark 10:27 AMPC). So rest easy every moment of every day, knowing you will be forever guided by the One who loves you with all of His being.

Just thinking of Your constant presence, Lord,
fills me with such awe and comfort, peace and strength.

MORNING
CONSTANT AND CONTINUAL

Jesus, replying, said to them, Have faith in God [constantly].
MARK 11:22 AMPC

God has created you to be with Him, so abide in Him. He has given you His Son, Jesus, to guide you in all things, so follow Him. He has left behind His Spirit to comfort you, so cling to Him. This faith is fed and fueled by your actively spending time with the greatest of beings—Father, Son, and Spirit. Do your part (He is already doing His), and you will have a constant, living faith and a continual, abiding peace.

Here I am, God. Let's talk.

EVENING
IN GOD'S MIND

I know and am acquainted with all the birds of the mountains, and the wild animals of the field are Mine and are with Me, in My mind.
PSALM 50:11 AMPC

In the same way that God knows His birds and animals, He knows you. He sees your struggles, has memorized your features, and knows the number of hairs on your head.

No matter where you go or what you do, you are with Him. You are in God's mind. There is nothing you can hide from your Master, your Creator.

Allow His Word, His voice, to speak to you. Meld your mind with His. Seek the wisdom He is bursting to share. Know Him as He knows you. Love Him as He loves you.

For when you become one with the great I AM, nothing He has will ever be out of your reach.

I want to know You, Lord, as You know me. I come to You now, opening myself to You. Enter into my heart and mind.

MORNING
YOUR INMOST HEART

Behold, You desire truth in the inner being; make me
therefore to know wisdom in my inmost heart.
PSALM 51:6 AMPC

Proverbs 4:23–27 (MSG) gives some ideas of how to keep our hearts in check: "Keep vigilant watch over your heart; that's where life starts. Don't talk out of both sides of your mouth; avoid careless banter, white lies, and gossip. Keep your eyes straight ahead; ignore all sideshow distractions. Watch your step, and the road will stretch out smooth before you. Look neither right nor left; leave evil in the dust."

When you are honest with yourself and God, true in your innermost heart of hearts, you will not stumble. But if or when you do, go to God. Ask His forgiveness and ask Him to make you a wiser woman.

Lord, help me to keep my eyes on You. Deep within, I long
for Your truth. Make me "heart smart" as I walk in Your way.

EVENING
PROMPTINGS OF THE SPIRIT

Now there was a man in Jerusalem whose name was Simeon. . . . And
prompted by the [Holy] Spirit, he came into the temple [enclosure].
LUKE 2:25, 27 AMPC

When you are close to God, you too are in tune with the Holy Spirit. You too can feel His nudges and promptings. You too can hear His leadings.

Take some time tonight to draw close to God. "Seek the LORD while He may be found, call upon Him while He is near" (Isaiah 55:6 NKJV). Be open to His Spirit's leadings. Follow His promptings. If you don't, you will always be wondering what God did not want you to miss.

Lord, keep me open to Your Spirit's nudges. I don't want to
miss anything You may have in store for me. I want to see
Jesus and His power in my life! In His name I pray, amen.

MORNING
YOUR MISSION

*Let all that I am wait quietly before God, for my hope is in him. He alone
is my rock and my salvation, my fortress where I will not be shaken.*

PSALM 62:5–6 NLT

Amid all the hubbub of busy days, how can you wait silently before the Lord? In fact, how can you even sit still for one minute?

It takes commitment to make sitting silently before the Lord a priority. But only when you do so will you be able to, at all other times, step into the fortress where you cannot be shaken.

Make it your mission to seek the Lord in silence. Expect Him to be there to refill and refuel you. Make your motto the words "I wait quietly before God, for my victory comes from him" (Psalm 62:1 NLT).

*Lord, all I need can be found in You. So here I am, Lord, seeking
Your presence, hoping in You alone, my Rock and my Refuge.*

EVENING
JESUS DOES THE UNEXPECTED

When the Lord saw her, his heart overflowed with compassion. "Don't cry!" he said.

LUKE 7:13 NLT

Know that Jesus sees what you are going through. That His heart overflows with compassion for you.

So don't cry. Don't be discouraged. Don't despair. Don't grieve. Only believe. At the last minute, Jesus just may surprise you beyond anything you ever imagined or expected and turn your entire life around by doing the impossible.

*Jesus, You never cease to amaze me. Thank You for the reminder that I
need never despair. For You see what is happening in my life. I feel Your
love and compassion surround me! I will not grieve—only believe.*

MORNING
SOFT SHOWERS

You care for the land and water it; you enrich it abundantly.
PSALM 65:9 NIV

You, just like all other women, experience dry spells in your life—times when the creative juices will not come, when productivity hits an all-time low, when no one wants what you have to offer. You most likely hit spiritual dry spells as well—when God's voice is hard to hear, when your prayers seem to go nowhere and your faith feels so small.

All you have to do in those times is hold out your empty, dry hands to God. Even if the only word you can manage to speak is "Help," it is enough. Even if you cannot speak at all. God will answer your silent cries with living water—water that leads to eternal life. Water that leaves you wanting more of Him.

Lord, water my dry land and enrich my life. Amen.

EVENING
TRUE LIGHT

"See to it, then, that the light within you is not darkness."
LUKE 11:35 NIV

In Luke 11, Jesus is talking to His disciples about the kind of light they have. He says, "When your eyes are healthy, your whole body also is full of light" (v. 34). And He warns them to make sure the light they think they're carrying is not really darkness in disguise.

How many times have you felt a surge of happiness or a thrill of purpose only to later realize that what you thought was a solid change in your heart was really created by a fleeting emotion or an artificial cause? The light of Jesus won't leave you wanting. It won't come in a moment and leave you in the next. It'll stay and grow and give warmth and banish every bit of darkness.

Lord, help me to discern true light from darkness.

MORNING
THE CONFESSION

You, God, know my folly; my guilt is not hidden from you.
PSALM 69:5 NIV

David could have pointed the finger at his haters. Instead, he admitted his own guilt. He confessed to God his own foolish choices. And he asked God not to let those who hoped in Him be shamed due to his disgrace.

This is the beauty of knowing and living with God. When your eyes are on Him, you can see your own faults more clearly. But also you have hope that He will not leave you sinking under the weight of those faults. He will reach down into your sorrow and your sorry-ness and lift you up into His grace.

Dear Lord who sees me, help my eyes stay trained on You.

EVENING
BIRD BUSINESS

"How much more valuable you are than birds!"
LUKE 12:24 NIV

It's not a bad thing to make plans—it's just a stifling thing to *live* for those plans. God wants you instead to keep going about the business He has created you to do—to love one another, to tell others about Jesus, and to love God with all your heart, soul, mind, and strength. To seek His kingdom first, and then all the rest will fall into place. That is His promise! And if this God of yours, who created such beautiful little feathered creatures, sees fit to take care of their needs, then do you really believe He will neglect yours?

Father God, teach me not to fret about tomorrow.

MORNING
FROM BIRTH ON UP

*From birth I have relied on you; you brought me forth
from my mother's womb. I will ever praise you.*

PSALM 71:6 NIV

From the moment you were born (and even before that), whether you know it or not, you began relying on God every minute of your life. He gave you the parents you have. He knitted your body into the particular shape it would be, along with molding your particular set of abilities and challenges.

So praise Him today for being there for you from day one. Praise Him for providing capable hands to care for you. Praise Him for making you who you are today!

God, I praise You for making me, me.

EVENING
JESUS' PLEA

*"Jerusalem, Jerusalem, you who kill the prophets and stone those sent to
you, how often I have longed to gather your children together, as a hen
gathers her chicks under her wings, and you were not willing."*

LUKE 13:34 NIV

So many times you turn Jesus away without even realizing it. You choose to ignore your own sin issues, weave webs of deceit that even fool yourself, and turn to other comforts that only seek to destroy you. Jesus calls out to you then: *"Daughter, you who run away from the only One who can save you, I just want to love you. Please turn and let Me give you forgiveness and peace."*

Open your ears to this heart cry of Jesus. If you have been running, turn around. Let Him love you. If you haven't, just rest in Him tonight.

Lord, let me stay under Your wing.

MORNING
PROMISES FULFILLED

Not one of all the LORD's good promises to Israel failed; every one was fulfilled.
JOSHUA 21:45 NIV

Do you know what promises God has made to you? Read His Word. Search for the promises of love and compassion, forgiveness and grace, reward and suffering. He does not just promise good things will come. He also tells you that you will have trouble. You will be tempted. You will suffer for His name. But like the Israelites who had struggled for so long and spent so much time fighting their way into the Promised Land, you will also find rest on every side. If you stay with Him, He will rescue you and bring you to a land of peace. It's a promise.

God, I want to remember Your promises. Help me too to keep my word.

EVENING
BE FREE

"You cannot serve God and be enslaved to money."
LUKE 16:13 NLT

It's easy to be enslaved to money when you are wealthy and feel the need to keep up appearances. There's so much pressure, once you have risen to the top level of society, to do all that's needed to stay there.

But followers of Jesus can be free from these concerns. Jesus has told you not to worry—God will provide your needs. And He has told you that everyone is equal in His eyes—there's no need to hang on to a certain placement in society. God won't love you more for wearing the latest shoe style.

Lord, help me to let go of the hold money has on me.

MORNING
THE GUEST LIST

"He has gone to be the guest of a sinner."
LUKE 19:7 NIV

Zacchaeus needed Jesus. He needed Him so much, he was willing to make a spectacle of himself just to get a glimpse of the Man. He climbed up into that sycamore fig tree, high above the crowd who wanted to put him down. And it worked—Jesus saw him.

What are you willing to do to see Jesus? What would you risk? How silly would you allow yourself to look?

No matter what you could give up, Jesus gave up more—and He did it for you. So, if you get a chance to sit at His table—even if your invitation is addressed to the Biggest Sinner of All—make sure you don't miss it. Be His guest.

Lord, have mercy on me, a sinner.

EVENING
HE IS FAITHFUL

But then I recall all you have done, O LORD;
I remember your wonderful deeds of long ago.
PSALM 77:11 NLT

God is as faithful today as He was in the past. He provides. He sustains. He shows up.

When you question your Father's love, look back. Recall altars of remembrance in your own life, those constructed at places of His provision. Can you see them in your mind's eye? They are there, standing as strong as the stone monuments by which the Israelites remembered Him.

Thank God in your weakest hour for the way He came through the last time and the time before. He is the God who sees you (see Genesis 16:13), who never changes (see James 1:17), the one whose faithfulness to you endures forever.

Thank You, heavenly Father, for Your faithfulness.
You are the same yesterday, today, and forever.

AN UNSEEN PATHWAY

*Your road led through the sea, your pathway through the
mighty waters—a pathway no one knew was there!*

PSALM 77:19 NLT

When you find yourself between a rock and a hard place, cry out to God. When circumstances lead you to a dead end, lift your eyes toward heaven. God is the "great I AM," meaning that He is what you need in each moment. At times of anxiety or fear, you need the Prince of Peace. Other times, when filled with gratitude, you sing praises to the King of Glory.

Then there are Red Sea moments. At such crossroads, rely on Yahweh, the Lord who provides unseen pathways, who makes a way where there seems to be no way (see Isaiah 43:16–20)!

*God, remind me that You are truly a God of miracles. In my
Red Sea moments, I trust You to make a way.*

MIRACLE WORKER

*This miraculous sign at Cana in Galilee was the first time Jesus
revealed his glory. And his disciples believed in him.*

JOHN 2:11 NLT

On the day Jesus turned water into wine, Mary must have smiled to herself. Now others knew what she had known all along. This was no ordinary wedding guest. This was the Messiah, whose ministry had now begun.

Do you recognize Him? When Jesus shows up in your everyday life, do you watch in expectation as Mary watched that day at the wedding feast? Expect the unbelievable. You serve a miracle-working Savior.

Jesus, I want to believe in miracles. Strengthen my faith, I ask.

MORNING
EVERLASTING WATER

*The woman left her water jar beside the well and ran back to
the village, telling everyone, "Come and see a man who told me
everything I ever did! Could he possibly be the Messiah?"*
JOHN 4:28–29 NLT

When the woman at the well met Jesus, truly met Him, she tossed her water jar aside. She did not walk but ran into the town to tell everyone about the Messiah.

Imagine her: skirt flying, arms flailing, a smile spread full across her sun-scorched face. The head that had once hung in shame now turned upward to heaven, a changed countenance mirroring a new heart.

What are you clinging to today? What stands between you and reckless abandon for Christ? What could you toss aside today and never miss as you instead soak up the goodness of everlasting water and never, ever thirst again?

Jesus, may I be like this woman who left the well, experiencing reckless abandon for You!

EVENING
LESS IS MORE

*Another of his disciples, Andrew, Simon Peter's brother,
spoke up, "Here is a boy with five small barley loaves and
two small fish, but how far will they go among so many?"*
JOHN 6:8–9 NIV

At times the crowds were so overpowering that Christ would gather His closest twelve and withdraw. But on this day, He taught the people and decided to feed them. All of them. He did so by multiplying one child's small lunch! And ended up with leftovers!

Never wonder if your Savior has forgotten your need. He sees your longing just as He saw the hunger of more than five thousand gathered on that hillside. Never wonder if He's going to come through for you. He may not do it the way you imagine, but He will provide, and it will always be His best for you.

Miracle-working Jesus, help me remember that nothing is impossible with You. Amen.

MORNING
SET FREE

"I removed the burden from their shoulders;
their hands were set free from the basket."
PSALM 81:6 NIV

Your God is a burden remover. He does not desire for you to remain enslaved to addiction or abuse. He wants to part the waters before you and provide safe passage. He may calm the storm and beckon you to walk on the water, or He may hold you close and calm you in spite of the storm that causes destruction all around you.

If you are downcast, look up today! Find God there, ready to call you His child, ready to loosen the chains of that which binds you. Find Him faithful. Release your burden to the One who has the power to cast it out of your life.

Burden-removing Father, free me from that which plagues me today.

EVENING
LIFE VS. DEATH

"The thief does not come except to steal, and to kill, and to destroy. I have
come that they may have life, and that they may have it more abundantly."
JOHN 10:10 NKJV

When you consider the difference between the father of lies and the Father of Lights, note this: Satan kills. Christ gives life. Satan destroys. Christ builds and rebuilds. Satan steals. Christ gives good gifts.

Live the abundant life that is offered to you as a believer. Reject the temptations of the devil. Run to Jesus. In Him there is life abundant and free.

Jesus, You are the Giver of all good gifts. Bind Satan
from my life that I might follow You always.

MORNING
CALL ON GOD

In the day of my trouble I will call upon You, for You will answer me.
PSALM 86:7 NKJV

God is there for you night and day. His Word tells you He never sleeps. When you are depressed or lonely, He's there. When you don't know what to do, He's there. There's no trouble you could encounter that would cause God to turn His back on you. He's ready and waiting for you, His daughter, to call out to Him.

Think about the best earthly father you know. Would that daddy desert his children in a time of need? Would he ever be too busy to come running? How much more does your heavenly Father long to attend to the needs of His own?

God, I know that You are always ready to help.
May You be the first one I turn to with my troubles.

EVENING
JESUS IS ALWAYS RIGHT ON TIME

When Mary came where Jesus was, and saw Him, she fell down at His feet,
saying to Him, "Lord, if You had been here, my brother would not have died."
JOHN 11:32 NKJV

Lazarus had been dead four days, yet Jesus asked that the stone blocking the entrance to the tomb be moved. An unusual request. But that's because something unusual was about to happen.

Jesus called for Lazarus to "come forth" (John 11:43 NKJV), and Lazarus did! The Savior had shown up and given life back to a dead man.

"Trust in the LORD with all your heart and lean not on your own understanding" (Proverbs 3:5 NIV). Looking for a miracle in your life? Hold on. Jesus is never late.

Jesus, thank You for this reminder that Your power and timing are always perfect.

MORNING
TRIED AND TRUE

As for God, his way is perfect; the word of the LORD is tried:
he is a buckler to all them that trust in him.

2 SAMUEL 22:31 KJV

If you feel like you are forever waiting and praying for God's promises to be fulfilled in your life, David would understand completely. The psalms show how David wrestled through many bleak days to keep his hope fixed on the Lord. But finally, after being on the run from Saul and fighting numerous enemies, David assumed the throne and sang today's song of praise!

Today, no matter what you are up against, spend some time with David's song of praise, recounting the victories and grace the Lord has given you. Reminding yourself of His goodness and His help in the past will give you hope for the waiting—just as it did for one famous shepherd-king.

Lord, I praise You for being tried and true!

EVENING
PLAN TO TRUST

The LORD knows all human plans; he knows that they are futile.

PSALM 94:11 NIV

Certainly you have made plans for a secure life: working toward a full savings account or keeping your family healthy or other good goals. But what's driving your plans—fear of the future or faith that God's grace will be there for you in the future? Every Christian struggles with this. But relying on anything for security apart from God never ends well. . .and it puts distance between you and Him. Where is fear steering your way? Pour out your worries to Him, and He will restore your heart with His abiding peace (see John 16:33).

Jesus, help me plan to trust You; teach my heart to expect Your grace in what's ahead.

MORNING
RESTORING THE KINGDOM

"You shall receive power when the Holy Spirit has come upon you;
and you shall be witnesses to Me in Jerusalem, and in all
Judea and Samaria, and to the end of the earth."
ACTS 1:8 NKJV

You may feel powerless when you see the brokenness in your community, but you are not; God has given you His Spirit to empower your work in His plan to restore the world, and He has prepared the work for you to do (see Ephesians 2:10). As you lean on His power to serve your community, ask Him to give you wisdom and courage to bear witness to His hope to everyone around you—with your words, your hands, your life.

Father, I want to give Your hope to my community!
Show me my part in Your plan to bring restoration.

EVENING
HELP IN DOUBT

For the LORD is great and greatly to be praised;
He is to be feared above all gods.
PSALM 96:4 NKJV

Maybe pain is running rampant in your life or you are looking at what's happening in the world and wondering where God even is. But He's here, and He's powerful—the God who brought the widow's boy back from the dead also raised your Savior. . .and resurrected your heart to new life.

When doubt strikes and death seems triumphant, immerse yourself in His truth. Don't fear your doubt, for God doesn't; abiding in Christ sometimes looks more like clawing to catch hold of Him. Seek Him; He will show you the truth the widow knew—that He is present and mighty—and fill your heart with what it needs.

Father, thank You that You will help me when doubt strikes.

MORNING
WILDERNESS DAYS

*So he said, "I have been very zealous for the L*ORD* God of hosts; for the children
of Israel have forsaken Your covenant, torn down Your altars, and killed Your
prophets with the sword. I alone am left; and they seek to take my life."*
1 KINGS 19:10 NKJV

Instead of God giving Elijah a pep talk—"Remember all My miracles? My ravens feeding
you by the brook? Get back in the game, Elijah!"—God sent an angel to sustain him
in his grief. At the end of the forty days, God showed His servant His nearness in the
still, small voice after the earthquakes and the wind and fire.

Maybe you have beaten yourself up for not doing more or being more for God. Or
maybe you feel like your efforts go unseen or your resources are exhausted. But during
your wilderness days, your compassionate God is by your side too, and He always has
more grace than you expect.

Lord, thank You that You are near on my wilderness days.

EVENING
SHINING BRIGHTLY

Light is sown for the righteous, and gladness for the upright in heart.
PSALM 97:11 KJV

Until heaven comes and God's light fills the Holy City, making the sun and moon obso-
lete (see Revelation 22:3, 5), be confident that Jesus, the Light of the World, is lighting
your way. As you spend time in the Word and prayer, He will help you cultivate joy in
the midst of uncertain bends in the path. As the season of summer blooms—months
of bustle and fruitfulness, of gardens and relationships growing in the sunshine—may
you reap a harvest of irrepressible joy as you grow closer with your faithful God who
lights your pathway through any darkness, through any valley (see Psalm 23:4).

Father, fill me with Jesus' joy so I may shine just as brightly!

MORNING
"HIS EYE IS ON THE SPARROW," PART 1

I am like a pelican of the wilderness; I am like an owl of the desert.
I lie awake, and am like a sparrow alone on the housetop.
PSALM 102:6–7 NKJV

God sees every sparrow, and His children are worth much more than the birds of the air (see Matthew 10:29–31). You are seen; your pain does not go unnoticed.

As tempting as it is to put on a brave front and swallow your pain, don't withhold your lament from the Lord. Lamenting is different from complaining—it's not blaming God but crying out for His mercy. Follow the psalmists' example: there are more psalms of lament than any other type. Lamenting is part of abiding—for it is waiting patiently through your tears, waiting in expectant hope for the help of the One who hears, the One who will answer.

I sing of Your truth, Father, trusting You: Your eye is on
the sparrow, and I know You are watching me.

EVENING
"HIS EYE IS ON THE SPARROW," PART 2

He shall regard the prayer of the destitute, and shall not despise their prayer.
PSALM 102:17 NKJV

Endurance in trials comes not from an immediate alleviation of your circumstances but the expectation that you will see the character of the One who holds you fast; that you will see His mercy and favor (see v. 13), His glory—beheld by all the nations of the earth (see vv. 15–16); that you will witness those things in your own life as you entrust your life to His care.

Whether you feel destitute—of inspiration, willpower, love, physical strength, holiness—He hears you. He doesn't despise you in your weakness but draws near to you, for nothing can separate you from His love (see Romans 8:38–39). Keep holding on—He will give you strength in the prayer-filled wait for restoration.

Father, when I feel I have little to offer, thank You that You always hear my prayer!

MORNING
NOTHING IS WASTED

At that time a great persecution arose against the church which was at Jerusalem; and they were all scattered throughout the regions of Judea and Samaria, except the apostles.
ACTS 8:1 NKJV

God's Word promises that whatever happens, your story fits perfectly into the big picture of His plan (see John 9:1–3; Romans 8:28). Nothing is wasted, neither your victories and hard work nor your sins or pain or attacks from others. He fashions every part of your life for your good and His glory. Whatever you endure now, God will not waste it.

Will you open your pain to Your heavenly Father, trusting that He will use it beautifully as a conduit for His glory? Rest in and be empowered by His promise of working all things together "for good" (Romans 8:28), knowing that "He who promised is faithful" (Hebrews 10:23 NKJV).

Father, thank You for being the Author of my story and that You are in charge of it all!

EVENING
SOMETHING LIKE SCALES

Immediately, something like scales fell from Saul's eyes, and he could see again. He got up and was baptized.
ACTS 9:18 NIV

Ponder for a moment the "Saul" in your life. Who is the least likely candidate to become a Christian? Think about that coworker or friend who scoffs at you for being so "religious." The world has its claws dug deeply into this individual who is wearing spiritual blinders.

Pray for this person now. Ask God to remove the scales covering the eyes of your "soul." He's done it before, and He can do it again. You serve a miracle-working God!

God, please open the eyes of _____. Draw _____ to yourself by the power of the Holy Spirit. In Jesus' name, amen.

MORNING
BOUNDARY LINES

You have set a boundary that they may not pass over,
that they may not return to cover the earth.

PSALM 104:9 NKJV

After the flood, God put a rainbow in the sky as a promise. He made a covenant with humans that He would never again flood the earth. He told the waves they would never come forth with such a vengeance again.

God sets forth boundaries in your life as well. Those "boundary lines" fall for you in "pleasant places" (Psalm 16:6 NIV).

Even if you are facing your own "flood" in life—unemployment, loss, disappointment, or depression—God is your portion. Your joy is found in Him, not your circumstances. He will never give you more than you can bear and will draw the lines for you. He is always with you and always has your best interests at heart.

God, thank You for being all I need.

EVENING
ATTITUDE MAKES THE DIFFERENCE

I will sing to the LORD all my life; I will sing praise to my God as long as I live.

PSALM 104:33 NIV

If you determine to sing to the Lord all the days of your life, as the psalmist did, you will have a hard time listing off all your troubles to everyone who will listen. It's pretty tough to sing praises to Jesus while whining about what aches.

Happiness is a choice. If you have the joy of the Lord planted deep within your soul, you will be able to shine for Him, regardless of your circumstances. Commit to praise Him all the days of your life. It will make all the difference in the world!

Heavenly Father, You are so good. You are my Provider and my
Companion. Whether I have plenty or am in need, whether I am
among others or on my own, You are my God and I will praise You.

MORNING
PRAISE THE LORD

Give praise to the LORD, proclaim his name;
make known among the nations what he has done.
PSALM 105:1 NIV

When you receive a blessing, rather than just being happy, discipline yourself to immediately thank God. Praising the Father for who He is and thanking Him for all that He does go hand in hand. And gratitude, as it turns out, increases your sense of well-being! It's a win-win!

You are called to make God's name known throughout the nations. This starts by praising Him in your own home, workplace, and community. Wherever you are, whatever you do, remember the importance of praising God!

Father, I praise Your holy name. May I always remember to worship You. Amen.

EVENING
GOD OF MIRACLES

He listened to Paul as he was speaking. Paul looked directly at him,
saw that he had faith to be healed and called out, "Stand up on
your feet!" At that, the man jumped up and began to walk.
ACTS 14:9–10 NIV

Do you believe as this man did? Do you wake up each day expecting the Lord to do great things? Or have you given up and laid to rest a big dream in your life?

You serve a God who is powerful enough to make a lame man stand up and walk! Believe in Jesus. He's above and beyond all you can imagine. He can bring beauty from ashes in your life. He can make dry bones live again.

God, give me hope again where I am hopeless. You are a God who still works miracles in Your children's lives. Help me to believe. Help me to stand up on my feet again!

MORNING
OUT OF NOWHERE

He opened the rock, and water gushed out; it flowed like a river in the desert.
PSALM 105:41 NIV

Abide in Christ. Read His Word. Stand on His promises. He has called you more than a conqueror (see Romans 8:37), has promised you hope and a future (see Jeremiah 29:11), and will never leave nor forsake you (see Hebrews 13:5).

You may never see water flood out of a rock, but get ready. There are blessings ahead of you that will seem to come out of nowhere! God has a bright future in store for you and is able to do above and beyond what you can imagine in your wildest dreams.

Father, help me to believe in miracles. I know You have a good future for me.

EVENING
FREE FROM DEPRESSION

He brought them out of darkness, the utter darkness, and broke away their chains.
PSALM 107:14 NIV

When you are in the abyss, when all you can see is the darkness, God will provide you with a helper, for you were never meant to live life in your own power. God has created physicians, psychologists, counselors, and even friends and family members to help you. So reach out to someone standing outside of the pit, someone in the light, who can lift you up and out.

If you are not in such a dark place, take inventory of those around you. Reach out to one who may need help in loosing his or her own chains.

Heavenly Father, thank You for Your promise to rescue those
who are in darkness. You are glorious, everlasting Light.

MORNING
GOD-CENTERED REQUEST

*Solomon son of David established himself firmly over his kingdom,
for the LORD his God was with him and made him exceedingly great.*

2 CHRONICLES 1:1 NIV

Because what Solomon asks for is coming from the bottom of his heart and is a selfless request, a very pleased God grants his request for wisdom—and grants him great wealth as well!

Solomon was a person totally devoted to God, who stuck close to and sought God while He was near (see Isaiah 55:6–7), a great example for any human to follow!

What would you like to ask God for? If your request is heart centered, God serving, and selfless, God will surely grant it—and more besides!

*God, help me to search my heart, to find the request I want to make
of You, that would further Your kingdom. May it please You.*

EVENING
YOU ARE LOVED

*For great is your love, higher than the heavens;
your faithfulness reaches to the skies.*

PSALM 108:4 NIV

Know this: God loves you. He is your true husband, father, brother, and friend. He has your name written on the palms of His hands (see Isaiah 49:16). And He will love you from here to eternity. For "He is good; his love endures forever" (2 Chronicles 5:13 NIV).

With God, there is no time or space. He is not limited by feelings or circumstances. He has no earthly constraints. He promises in His Word that He will never leave you. Bank on it. Start living like a daughter of the King. Hold your head high. You are dearly and infinitely loved.

Thank You, Father, for Your great love for me.

MORNING
WHAT SHALL I DO, LORD?

"What shall I do, Lord?" I asked. "Get up," the Lord said, "and go into Damascus. There you will be told all that you have been assigned to do."
ACTS 22:10 NIV

In a moment, Paul's life and mission changed. What had it taken? A personal encounter with Christ.

Do you have a personal encounter with Christ each day? Do you go before Him asking, "What shall I do today, Jesus?" If not, start today. See where the Lord takes you. But be as pliable as Paul. Be ready to carry out whatever mission Christ may set before you.

Savior, what would You have me do today? If You need to stop me in my tracks as you did Saul on the road to Damascus, please take that liberty in my life.

EVENING
JESUS STANDS NEAR

The following night the Lord stood near Paul and said, "Take courage! As you have testified about me in Jerusalem, so you must also testify in Rome."
ACTS 23:11 NIV

Christ stands with you every single day of your life. Listen. Do you hear Him now? He whispers words of affirmation, which He spoke over your ancestors, words He will speak to your descendants. Be still now. Hear Him:

"You are Mine. You are a beloved sheep of My pasture, and I am your Good Shepherd. Be bold in My name, for I have declared you more than a conqueror. I've breathed new life into you. You are cherished. Be strong and courageous because I go with you into battle. I'll help you share your story. Your testimony will draw others to My side so that I may stand near to them as well!"

Father, help me to remember that You are always standing near me. Amen.

MORNING
NO FEAR OF BAD NEWS

They will have no fear of bad news; their hearts are steadfast, trusting in the Lord.
PSALM 112:7 NIV

Scripture does not say you will not face trouble. It does not claim that bad—*really bad*—things cannot touch your life. What it does promise is that you, Christian sister, will never go it alone. God is at—and on—your side.

Stay true to Him. Put your faith in the One who will hold you tight and walk with you when bad news does come. Trust He knows what's best for you. He's got this.

Thank You, God, that I need have no fear of bad news.

EVENING
FIGHTING FOR US

"With him is only the arm of flesh, but with us is the Lord our God to help us and to fight our battles."
2 CHRONICLES 32:8 NIV

Hezekiah and Isaiah prayed, and the Lord sent an angel "who annihilated all the fighting men" (v. 21 NIV) of Assyria. So the Lord saved Hezekiah and Jerusalem, just as He had saved His people before and just as He would do again and again.

This same God is continuing to fight for you—answering your prayers and giving you confidence to do battle against any kind of power that seeks to control your heart. You may not ever have to fight off kings and armies, but you can count on your Lord to give you strength to defend your peace.

Lord, thank You for helping me to fight my battles.

MORNING
BE GLAD

The Lord has done it this very day; let us rejoice today and be glad.
PSALM 118:24 NIV

What has God done for you already this day? Open your eyes and see the works He has performed. Maybe He kept you safe on your commute to work. Maybe He sent rain to water dry fields. Maybe He cleared the clouds and gave you a bit of sunshine to start your morning. God shows His love and care for you every day all day long in both big and small ways. Don't forget to look around and see what God is doing for you and for others today. Then rejoice and be glad!

God, I'm so glad You love me! Thank You!

EVENING
ACCESS DOOR

Therefore, since we have been justified through faith, we have peace with God through our Lord Jesus Christ, through whom we have gained access by faith into this grace in which we now stand.
ROMANS 5:1–2 NIV

Accepting Jesus as your Lord and Savior gives you special access to the center stage of God's theater. You don't have to stay in the shadows watching a more joy-filled life go by. God invites you to step into His light and live boldly in the scenes He has written just for you. He is your Director and Guide, your Manager and your adoring Audience. And He is the Author of your life, the Gifter of grace.

Though you may sometimes get butterflies in your stomach, you don't have to be afraid to use your voice. You can find peace in the certainty that God will be with you every minute.

God, thank You for the grace in which I stand.

MORNING
DEAD OR ALIVE?

Count yourselves dead to sin but alive to God in Christ Jesus.
ROMANS 6:11 NIV

Does dying to sin mean you will never sin again? Never make a mistake? Never choose to do wrong? No. Accepting Christ does not make you perfect—at least not all at once. It does, however, give you purpose. And that purpose becomes the driving force behind your choices and actions. What is that purpose? To love the Lord our God with all your heart, mind, soul, and strength and to love others as you love yourself. That's really living!

God, thank You for making me alive in You.

EVENING
UNDER CONSTRUCTION

Do not interfere with the work on this temple of God.
EZRA 6:7 NIV

Don't you wish sometimes that someone could send out a decree on your behalf? "I hereby decree that everyone leave [insert your name here] alone while she gets her life together."

These days you don't go to one temple to talk with God, but God does live inside you, and you are under construction—a work in progress, so to speak. He's busy every day building you up into the person He created you to be, making you into a temple of the Holy Spirit.

Make sure you don't let anyone or anything—even you!—interfere with this work.

God, thank You for working on me. Help me not get in the way!

MORNING
WORTHLESS THINGS

Turn my eyes from worthless things, and give me life through your word.
PSALM 119:37 NLT

The thousands of amusing, alarming, and even admirable articles you find on the Internet can be harmless diversions, but they are still diversions. They divert you from your connection to God through prayer and reading His Word. They divert you into accepting a virtual life instead of really living.

How much better might your days be if you started the morning off by listening to what God has to say to you, dwelling in His Word, and memorizing some scripture that might help you get through your days?

Don't miss your chance to hear what God has to say to you today.

Lord, help me to remember to look in Your Word before I go out in the world today.

EVENING
IN ALL THINGS

We know that in all things God works for the good of those who
love him, who have been called according to his purpose.
ROMANS 8:28 NIV

God is always at work. He doesn't take vacation days. He doesn't ever stop knitting you together and unfolding His grand story. Even at the times when you feel your weakest, when you don't even know what to pray for and can't find the words to say, the Spirit helps you and speaks for you. No matter how you feel, where you are, what you are doing, or who you are with—God is working for your good.

God, I want to join You in Your work. Teach me to be a good servant for You.

MORNING
ARTIST AND AUTHOR

Your hands made me and formed me;
give me understanding to learn your commands.
PSALM 119:73 NIV

The same Artist who shapes a newborn's elbows and carved out mountains is the Author who is writing the story of your life and laid out plans to guide you along the way. You may spend several hours wondering at the hand of the Artist but then skip right over the words of the Author.

You need to pray the prayer of the psalmist: "Give me understanding to learn your commands." This understanding doesn't come along with those tiny toes and sweet cheeks—you have to seek it out, to ask for it. Sometimes you might even have to start by asking God to grant you the spirit to want to understand.

God, who made every part of me, help me learn every part of Your Word.

EVENING
THE SACRED MUNDANE

Take your everyday, ordinary life—your sleeping, eating, going-to-work,
and walking-around life—and place it before God as an offering.
ROMANS 12:1 MSG

If you are giving every moment of your day to God, it will be easier for you to stay set apart from this world—and "be transformed by the renewing of your mind" (Romans 12:2 NIV). Instead of just following the same old routine that everyone else does, if you actively gave over your schedule to God, praying through your day and committing to honor Him in your actions, then how do you think that might change you? What might happen to your day if you offered every piece of it to God?

Lord, take my body and my time—I offer them to You.
Please show me Your will, and I will serve You all my days.

MORNING
COME AND FIND ME

I have wandered away like a lost sheep; come and find me.

PSALM 119:176 NLT

Face it. There's no good argument for leaving the Shepherd. He knows you. He's the only One who knows every thought you have ever had, every word you have ever said or left unsaid. And He still loves you and wants you to be with Him. Can you really think of a good reason to leave Him?

But undoubtedly you will. Everyone will stray. Everyone will turn their backs again and again.

"Come and find me," you will pray. And He will. Your Shepherd will come with grace and mercy. He will come and pick you up and take you back to the flock again. Maybe this time you will stay.

Lord, help me to understand that my best safe place is with You.

EVENING
AWAKE

He who watches over you will not slumber.

PSALM 121:3 NIV

If you have ever taken care of a small child who is sick in the night, you know what it's like not to slumber. Even when you get so tired that your eyelids won't stay open, you can't really get into a deep sleep. A small sound—a sniffle, a cough, raspy breathing—wakes you.

God watches over you like a parent watching over a sick child in the night. Except God's eyes never shut, and He never tires. He is always there to comfort you, guide you, and hold you in His strong arms.

God, thank You for watching over me even when I don't realize You are.

MORNING
A HOPE TO BE HEARD

"Though he slay me, yet will I hope in him."
JOB 13:15 NIV

Job had suffered the loss of almost everything he valued, and he couldn't understand why.

Job was a man of God. Job knew God.

So Job proclaims that he wants to argue his case before God. He wants his day in God's court. He wants to hear God's testimony against him and understand why everything has been taken from him.

And even though he knows God could crush him, Job still wants to come before God because he trusts Him. His hope is in God. His understanding is that God is good. His experience is that God is truth.

May you yourself aspire to have the faith of Job—the faith that will keep you turning to God even in the darkest times.

God, let my hope always rest in You.

EVENING
LET YOUR LIFE BE A SONG FOR HIM

I will praise You with my whole heart; before the gods I will sing praises to You. I will worship toward Your holy temple, and praise Your name for Your lovingkindness and Your truth; for You have magnified Your word above all Your name.
PSALM 138:1–2 NKJV

You were born to worship—to live, to move in God. You were created to be an instrument of praise. Worship from your lips ushers you into His presence and brings Him pleasure.

One of the greatest gifts you can give God—aside from your heart through salvation—is worship. Take time to fully express your adoration of Him. Invite Him to show you who He has created you to be. As you become one with Him, your life becomes a song sung for Him.

Lord, I praise You. Thank You for Your loving-kindness and truth. I want to be an instrument of praise to You. May my life bring You pleasure in all I do.

MORNING
EVEN WHEN YOU DON'T SEE, BELIEVE

Yet God has made everything beautiful for its own time. He has planted eternity in the human heart, but even so, people cannot see the whole scope of God's work from beginning to end.

ECCLESIASTES 3:11 NLT

The concern you, as a woman, have for others can almost consume you. You imagine a thousand things that could come from the current situation and another thousand ways you could possibly fix things. You find yourself wanting to wrap your arms around your loved one and tell him it's going to be okay. But deep down, you know it's going to hurt for a while.

Chin up. You know God is at work behind the scenes. He makes all things beautiful in His time. He is there to heal your loved one—and you. Yes, God will make it beautiful again.

God, You are making all things beautiful in Your time. Amid the turmoil in my life and the lives of those I love, I will trust You.

EVENING
GOD IS ALWAYS THINKING ABOUT YOU

You saw me before I was born. Every day of my life was recorded in your book. Every moment was laid out before a single day had passed. How precious are your thoughts about me, O God. They cannot be numbered!

PSALM 139:16–17 NLT

Have you ever wondered what God thinks about you? Not a moment passes that you are not in His thoughts. From the very beginning of time, your Father's thoughts for you compelled Him to send His Son, Jesus, to the cross so you could have an eternal relationship with Him.

What a powerful revelation to know you are on God's mind. Take time tonight to contemplate this news from a novel perspective. Let this truth sink into your heart as you begin to understand how God thinks about you.

God, thank You for reminding me that because every day of my life is recorded in Your book, nothing about my life catches You off guard.

MORNING
DRINK OF HIS GLORY

I saw the Lord sitting on a throne, high and lifted up, and the train of His robe filled the temple. Above it stood seraphim; each one had six wings: with two he covered his face, with two he covered his feet, and with two he flew. And one cried to another and said: "Holy, holy, holy is the LORD of hosts; the whole earth is full of His glory!"
ISAIAH 6:1–3 NKJV

The earth truly is full of God's glory. In the busyness of life, so filled with distractions, it's easy to miss the wonder and majesty of His glory.

Consider the works of His hands—the beauty and variety of flowers growing wildly, the powerful crashes of the ocean's waves, the majestic heights of a mountain range.

He wants you to step outside of the everyday chaos that tries to hem you in to experience His presence and His glory. He speaks to you in the little and big things found in His creation.

Heavenly Father, thank You for filling the earth with Your glory.

EVENING
THIS IS THE WAY

The heart of the wise inclines to the right, but the heart of the fool to the left.
ECCLESIASTES 10:2 NIV

Perhaps you are tired of all the confusion life presents. You lie in bed wide awake, unable to sleep, thoughts spinning around and around.

Perhaps the best place to start is with prayer.

You sit and have a chat with the One who has loved you since the beginning of time and longs to hear your voice. And suddenly you feel snug and warm in the once chilly house. You feel God's familiar embrace and hear a soft whisper: "I've always been with you." Your eyes open. Then you spy your Bible and, with a smile, pull it out from underneath a stack of books and begin reading.

God, thank You for sticking with me all the way. Help me keep my feet on Your path.

MORNING
MADE NEW

Therefore if any person is [ingrafted] in Christ (the Messiah) he is a new creation (a new creature altogether); the old [previous moral and spiritual condition] has passed away. Behold, the fresh and new has come!

2 CORINTHIANS 5:17 AMPC

Some days everything seems to go wrong, and you just want to sit down and cry. Maybe you need a good cry. Just don't forget to follow it up with prayer. Let God know you need more of Him. That your focus has been elsewhere. You have let too many things get in the way. Ask Him to wash away the old and tired and bring back the new—the dedication and love you experienced when you first came to know Him.

Then take a deep breath. Feel His embrace. He will help you make a clean start.

God, life fills up so fast. Help me continue to experience the newness of who You have created me to be.

EVENING
A QUIET CONFIDENCE

For thus said the Lord God, the Holy One of Israel: In returning [to Me] and resting [in Me] you shall be saved; in quietness and in [trusting] confidence shall be your strength.

ISAIAH 30:15 AMPC

You may go through some very difficult times. And your life may look very different from what you expected. But you also know that God has been and will be faithful through all the health challenges, financial obstacles, relationship difficulties, job losses, heartbreaks—everything you have faced and may still be facing in life.

So make it a point to return to God daily. Rest in Him. Be still and know that He is God (see Psalm 46:10). In so doing, you will be saved.

Lord, thank You for a quiet confidence in times of waiting.

MORNING
WHISPERS WITH GOD

"Come and listen to my counsel. I'll share my heart with you and make you wise."
PROVERBS 1:23 NLT

God called to Moses from a burning bush in the desert and gave him the assignment of his life. God whispered to Samuel in the middle of the night while he was just a child to warn him of things to come in the prophet Eli's house. And Jesus questioned a Christian-persecuting Saul, who soon became the apostle Paul.

As you build your relationship with God and grow in knowing His voice, you learn to follow His lead. There are no perfect prayers or right ways of talking to God. He is ready and willing to hear your heart and answer the big and small questions in life.

God, thank You for Your gentle nudges and whispers of love.

EVENING
GOD'S GRACE THROUGH THE DETOUR

But he said to me, "My grace is sufficient for you, for my power is made perfect in weakness." Therefore I will boast all the more gladly about my weaknesses, so that Christ's power may rest on me.
2 CORINTHIANS 12:9 NIV

Right now you may feel as though God interrupted your life. But here's the thing: God always has permission to interrupt. And even though you may be having a hard time understanding what it all means, rest assured that you are just on a detour right now—and you cannot detour out of the reach of God's grace.

So there's no need to worry. Your job is just to take this time to relax and enjoy the scenery.

God Almighty, when You interrupt my life with a detour, help me to embrace it. I choose to trust You to take care of the details.

MORNING
ISOLATED BUT NOT ALONE

*"Can a mother forget the baby at her breast and have no compassion
on the child she has borne? Though she may forget, I will not forget
you! See, I have engraved you on the palms of my hands."*
ISAIAH 49:15–16 NIV

As Jesus' captors dragged Him away, He saw no supportive, familiar faces in the crowd. Isolated, He held tight to God. Even when the Father turned away, Jesus called to Him for assurance. Jesus gave up His life and died, fully committed to the Father's plan. He faced death, burial, and resurrection—isolated but not alone. His faith remained unshaken because He knew God would never abandon Him.

No matter what circumstances you are facing today, God has not forgotten you. When you feel isolated, remember that you are never alone.

Heavenly Father, just as You were with Jesus, I know You are with me.

EVENING
HEALTHY HEART

*Pay attention to what I say; turn your ear to my words. Do not let
them out of your sight, keep them within your heart; for they are
life to those who find them and health to one's whole body.*
PROVERBS 4:20–22 NIV

God stresses the importance of guarding well your heart where His truths are stored, truths that bring you life and healing. When you hear the voice in your head, the one that says you are a failure, stupid, too much or not enough, raise your shield and grab your sword. Meditate on what God says about you. You are holy, without blame, more than a conqueror, a beloved child of God, alive in Christ.

God, help me replace my earthly thoughts with Your heavenly truths.

MORNING
DELIGHTFULLY YOU

*You [Judah] shall no more be termed Forsaken, nor shall your land be called
Desolate any more. But you shall be called Hephzibah [My delight is in
her], and your land be called Beulah [married]; for the Lord delights in you,
and your land shall be married [owned and protected by the Lord].*

ISAIAH 62:4 AMPC

Your name at birth is the first gift from your parents *and* your first identity. But no matter how you have been labeled until now, your God has given you a new name: "My Delight."

Let go of the other names you have accumulated: Too Heavy, Too Tall, Not Smart Enough, Not Pretty Enough, Too Much Trouble. You *are* enough. . .and not too much. God is not seeking perfection, beauty, or grace. He is seeking *you*. Bloom in the love of a Father who has renamed you His Delight.

*Father God, thank You for delighting in me. Help me to fully accept my
new name and live as one accepted and adored by her Father.*

EVENING
FULLNESS

*I pray that you, being rooted and established in love, may have
power. . .to know this love that surpasses knowledge—that you
may be filled to the measure of all the fullness of God.*

EPHESIANS 3:17–19 NIV

The fullness of God is like the deep pool at the base of a mountain waterfall, deep enough for you to plunge into, laughing with joy. Immerse yourself in the great incomprehensible mystery of who God is—an all-knowing and all-powerful being who *chooses* friendship with you. He is enduringly faithful but forgives all of your unfaithfulness. He is God, the mighty warrior of the Old Testament, and Christ, the gentle lamb of the New.

*Father God, help me absorb the deep and
extravagant love with which You fill me to the brim.*

MORNING
GOD'S TRADEMARKS

God's Message: "Don't let the wise brag of their wisdom. Don't let heroes brag of their exploits. Don't let the rich brag of their riches. If you brag, brag of this and this only: That you understand and know me. I'm God, and I act in loyal love. I do what's right and set things right and fair, and delight in those who do the same things. These are my trademarks."
God's Decree.
JEREMIAH 9:23–24 MSG

God sees deep inside your heart. His desire is that, out of your relationship with Him, love, righteousness, and fairness will overflow onto others, leaving small puddles that become your delightful trademark.

Busyness, volunteering, and achievements can be added to the list of things that are outer signs of worth. And you may tend to rely on those exterior things to demonstrate your worthiness. Yet your heart will be happiest when you find your worth in God.

Thank You, Lord, that Your heart desires the best of relationships with me. Help me know and understand You!

EVENING
PROTECTIVE PEACE

Do not be anxious about anything, but in every situation, by prayer and petition, with thanksgiving, present your requests to God. And the peace of God, which transcends all understanding, will guard your hearts and your minds in Christ Jesus.
PHILIPPIANS 4:6–7 NIV

When anxiety begins to push at your thoughts, when a problem is on the horizon, immediately run to God, and then pray, petition, and thank. The situation may not be resolved as you had imagined, but you will know you received the result God was looking for—and be left with God's shield of peace, a transcendent gift beyond all understanding.

God, thank You for providing peace tonight right when and where I need it. I trust You to reign in every detail. Amen.

MORNING
GATHERED UP

So spacious is he, so expansive, that everything of God finds its proper place in him without crowding. Not only that, but all the broken and dislocated pieces of the universe—people and things, animals and atoms—get properly fixed and fit together in vibrant harmonies, all because of his death, his blood that poured down from the cross.
COLOSSIANS 1:19–20 MSG

No matter how broken up or beat down you may feel, you are—in reality—gathered up, contained in Jesus. You are restored, all in one piece, all in one place in the absolute fullness of God.

When you comprehend that the scattered pieces of yourself are gathered up and redeemed, the fissures that have left you painfully cracked can heal. You can look at yourself with the word *reconciled* scripted around you in flowing circles. You are complete.

God, help me walk today as one who is gathered up, redeemed, and healed.

EVENING
AN HONEST APPROACH

Honesty lives confident and carefree, but Shifty is sure to be exposed.
PROVERBS 10:9 MSG

Confidence comes from knowing you have done your best to be trustworthy and truthful in your dealings with others. And although being honest and upfront is sometimes difficult, especially when it means others might be displeased or you might get in trouble, the effort is worth it.

Being truthful with *yourself* is just as important as being honest with others. And while you are being honest with others and yourself, be honest with God as well. Tell Him just what is going on, how you feel, what you are thinking. He knows the whole truth anyway, so you might as well come clean from the start. You will both feel better about it—and about each other.

Lord, help me have an honest approach. Remind me when I slip into anything less. Thank You for helping me walk in truth.

MORNING
BELOVED SHEEP

"I myself will gather the remnant of my flock out of all the countries where I have driven them and will bring them back to their pasture, where they will be fruitful and increase in number. I will place shepherds over them who will tend them, and they will no longer be afraid or terrified, nor will any be missing."
JEREMIAH 23:3–4 NIV

Being God's sheep means that you can reside in a peaceful pasture, green with peace and gladness at any time or place. When you feel a little beat up by life outside the pasture, you can remember that your Good Shepherd understands. He promises not to lose even one of His fold. He keeps a careful head count and goes in search of those who wander off.

Thank You, Good Shepherd, for providing what I need in a pasture. I trust You to care for us all.

EVENING
WHOLEHEARTEDNESS

"For I will set My eyes on them for good, and I will bring them back to this land; I will build them and not pull them down, and I will plant them and not pluck them up. Then I will give them a heart to know Me, that I am the LORD; and they shall be My people, and I will be their God, for they shall return to Me with their whole heart."
JEREMIAH 24:6–7 NKJV

Who else but God can rescue you from your wanderings? Who else can build you up, layer upon layer of strength and courage? Only God can plant your roots deeply in a place that becomes a lasting home.

Return to Him now. Discover the freedom of hoping in a future that is good. Find your ease in loving God with your whole heart. Grasp the deep and abiding love with which He first loved you.

God, help me grasp Your wholehearted love for me.

MORNING
HOPE

*"I will come to you and fulfill my good promise. . . . For I know the plans I
have for you," declares the LORD, ". . .plans to give you hope and a future."*
JEREMIAH 29:10–11 NIV

God declares hope over, around, and through you. He has prepared a future for you
and has plans for your well-being. A powerful as well as personal Being, God doesn't
give you someone else's future. He has made one just for you. Allow your heart to hope
in Him and whatever future He has planned.

*Father God, I thank and trust You for the future You have planned for
me. Please make my hope a constant in good times and bad.*

EVENING
HIDDEN THINGS

*"This is GOD's Message, the God who made earth, made it livable and lasting,
known everywhere as GOD: 'Call to me and I will answer you. I'll tell you
marvelous and wondrous things that you could never figure out on your own.'"*
JEREMIAH 33:2–3 MSG

God's answers are sometimes long in coming, other times quick, but He always hears
when you call Him and is not slow to speak. He unravels every single mystery as you
patiently listen for, then follow, His promptings. The beauty is in your relationship with
Him. The almighty Father God whispers into the ear of you, His beloved daughter,
telling you the wondrous things only He can impart. Listen and attend carefully. For
at times He speaks softly to your spirit. At other times He will gently nudge your soul.

*Father God, I trust You to show me marvelous and wondrous things.
Help me know when You are speaking. Quiet my soul to listen.*

MORNING
AIMING FOR LOVE

*Now the purpose of the commandment is love from a pure
heart, from a good conscience, and from sincere faith.*

1 TIMOTHY 1:5 NKJV

Pure love looks like intentional listening and seeking to understand. It believes the best despite another's mistakes. It helps quietly.

When you desire to love others exceptionally, God will direct your heart—and theirs. Be ready to set aside lesser things to fulfill your mission. And know that God, who is constantly guiding your steps by pure love, will keep your aim true.

*Father God, thank You for Your heart of love poured out over me.
Show me one way to touch someone with that same love today.*

EVENING
BUILDING WITH LOVE

*The wise woman builds her house, but with
her own hands the foolish one tears hers down.*

PROVERBS 14:1 NIV

What does a home built with love look like? It looks like connection, acceptance, forgiveness, and honest conversations. The wise woman builds her home with a balance of healthy boundaries and kindness. She builds with hugs and smiles and laughter. She constructs a home for herself and those she loves with creativity and courage and cuddling.

Loving well is not easy, and mistakes will happen. Sometimes the walls may need patching or the floors recarpeting. No problem. God is the best of home renovators and takes great pleasure in moving right in! After all, God *is* love.

God, let love reign here.

MORNING
TRAIL OF TEARS

"Walking and weeping, they'll seek me, their God. They'll ask directions
to Zion and set their faces toward Zion. They'll come and hold tight
to God, bound in a covenant eternal they'll never forget."
JEREMIAH 50:4–5 MSG

When the Israelites arrived in Jerusalem, they sought God and jumped into true worship. They hugged the invisible God with all their heart, mind, soul, and strength; and God tied them to Him with a new covenant (see Jeremiah 31:31). This covenant was eternal, unbreakable—unforgettable—and one that later, with Jesus, was extended to Gentiles as well.

Whatever your personal trail of tears, God waits for you to return, to hug Him tight. Through Christ's death on the cross, you are bound to God in a covenant of love that will never end.

Oh Lord, my Guide, when I've gone astray, bring me back as I seek
Your guidance step by step. Thank You for Your eternal embrace.

EVENING
A BALANCED LIFE

A simple life in the Fear-of-God is better than a rich life with a ton of headaches.
PROVERBS 15:16 MSG

Solomon isn't comparing wealth and poverty but using them as illustrations. Possessions may ease headaches, but the better way—the more effective, excellent way—to ease inner confusion and pain is the fear of the Lord. It's your lifeblood as a Christian, pumping from your new heart throughout your body. It activates the mind of Christ in you and moves your hands and feet as a member of Christ's body. The Holy Spirit serves as the generator, replacing the headaches of the old life with simple trust and the fear of the Lord.

Righteous God, you are all I need, whatever the balance in my bank account.
Let me live in Your shadow, my fear of You making me unafraid of anything else.

MORNING
WAITING FOR HOPE

When life is heavy and hard to take, go off by yourself. Enter the silence.
Bow in prayer. Don't ask questions: Wait for hope to appear. Don't run
from trouble. Take it full-face. The "worst" is never the worst.

LAMENTATIONS 3:28–30 MSG

Jeremiah suggests that when life is "heavy and hard," there are six steps to prepare you to "take it full-face." To get ready to fight, you must first retreat. That means to (1) go off by yourself, (2) get quiet, (3) pray, (4) be still, and (5) listen for God's voice. Let His promises sink in. And (6) wait for hope to fill your tank.

Only after you retreat are you equipped to face the problem. You won't run from it, ask questions, or try to make sense of it. You just take it head on—and realize the worst is never the worst. It can't be. God is by your side.

Heavenly Father, right now life seems heavy and hard. Let me retreat into You and wait for Your hope to appear so that I will be ready to face what lies ahead.

EVENING
MAKING PLANS

We can make our own plans, but the LORD gives the right answer. People
may be pure in their own eyes, but the LORD examines their motives.
Commit your actions to the LORD, and your plans will succeed.

PROVERBS 16:1–3 NLT

Whatever your approach to planning, tonight's passage applies. If you plan without consulting God, you are building on shaky ground.

God probes deep, looks at your blueprints, and determines what's right. He looks for what's good about your plans—and, more importantly, who is in charge of those plans.

Plans made without God will have a fatal design flaw. All plans committed to the Lord *will* succeed.

Lord, let me invite You into my plans before I start. Without You, I will fail.

GOD'S TREASURE HUNT

*The refining pot is for silver and the furnace for gold,
but the Lord tries the hearts.*
PROVERBS 17:3 AMPC

Just as the metals removed from the mine are useless until they are refined and become the beautiful elements humans crave, your heart requires a similar testing. In Christ you are holy and righteous. But to reach that reality here and now, God sends tests to remove any impurities. His standard doesn't change between you and another of His children. His holiness is absolute. His scales reveal your exact spiritual weight, and He prescribes a training regimen customized just for you.

When God is finished, you will be the rarest treasure on earth—a child of God, holy and dearly loved.

*Holy God and Judge, may I pay attention when You try my
heart. Try me and change me until I'm pure as snow.*

EVENING
HEAVEN'S ART GALLERY

*A present is a precious stone in the eyes of its
possessor; wherever he turns, he prospers.*
PROVERBS 17:8 NKJV

When God gives you a gift, He expects you to use it. Like parents who treasure their children's schoolwork, He awaits your efforts. If human parents give each picture, essay, and test a place of honor on the refrigerator, what will God do with *your* work?

When you delight in the gifts God gives to you, returning them to His use, He treats them as precious. He showers more gifts on you. He wants to fill His art gallery with your works.

*Loving Father, may I treasure Your gifts to me, polishing them, sharing them
in praise to You. May any increase flow back to You and Your kingdom.*

MORNING
AN ANCHOR IN THE SEA

Humble yourselves, therefore, under God's mighty hand, that he may lift you up in due time. Cast all your anxiety on him because he cares for you.

1 PETER 5:6–7 NIV

Casting your burdens on the Lord is often easier said than done. You might be born with a tendency to cling stubbornly to your problems, believing you alone are capable of ironing out the wrinkles and restoring control. You may think having a white-knuckled grip on your worries will somehow solve them. But in reality, only God is in control. In the stormy seas of life, He is the only thing that remains steadfast and unshakable. Unless you are holding on to Him, you will be tossed unceasingly on the waves.

So how do you let go? You can begin by humbling yourself before God, acknowledging His might and ability to care for you. You can bask in the incredible knowledge that He eagerly desires to relieve you of your burdens.

Mighty God, thank You for being my anchor.

EVENING
THE AUTHOR OF TIME

But do not forget this one thing, dear friends: With the Lord a day is like a thousand years, and a thousand years are like a day. The Lord is not slow in keeping his promise, as some understand slowness. Instead he is patient with you, not wanting anyone to perish, but everyone to come to repentance.

2 PETER 3:8–9 NIV

Often your deepest concerns and problems are resolved at what seems to be a glacial pace. You pray and lay your needs before God. And then you wait for an answer. And wait some more. Eventually, you might begin to think that God is indifferent to your daily struggles. But this couldn't be further from the truth.

His responses may seem painfully slow, but God is all knowing, and He sees the span of eternity in infinite detail—whereas all you can see is the moment before you. You can rest in the knowledge that His timing is perfect, even if it may not feel that way.

God, You are the Author of time. I place my life in Your capable hands.

MORNING
OTHERWORLDLY

*See how very much our Father loves us, for he calls us his children,
and that is what we are! But the people who belong to this world don't
recognize that we are God's children because they don't know him.*

1 JOHN 3:1 NLT

Since many people do not know or understand your heavenly Father, chances are you will be misunderstood. Your customs and behavior will seem strange and otherworldly. In one of his letters, Peter addresses Christians as sojourners and exiles. How true this is! He calls you this because you are seeking a better country to call your own. You know that your stay here is fleeting.

When the pressures of this world are overwhelming, remember that your Father has lavished His love on you. He is your Refuge. He is your home.

*Father, when I feel misplaced and alone, remind me that my hope rests
in the promise of abundant, eternal life in a better country.*

EVENING
PERFECT LOVE

*There is no fear in love. But perfect love drives out fear, because fear has to
do with punishment. The one who fears is not made perfect in love.*

1 JOHN 4:18 NIV

God designed you to experience perfect love. This kind of love fortifies and sustains. It places you on solid ground. It surrounds you and fills you up. And it sets you free from fear. Can you fathom a love so whole, so pure? It might be difficult for you to imagine such a perfect love because no one has ever offered it to you—except for the One who laid down His life for yours, who shouldered God's wrath in order to spare you. His love is perfect and utterly selfless. In it there is no fear of condemnation. No fear of unfaithfulness. No fear of separation. Death's sting has been erased.

*Jesus, how exquisite and deep Your love is for me. Turn my
heart toward it daily. With You, I have nothing to fear.*

MORNING
EVEN NOW

"Even now," declares the LORD, "return to me with all your heart, with
fasting and weeping and mourning." Rend your heart and not your garments.
Return to the LORD your God, for he is gracious and compassionate, slow
to anger and abounding in love, and he relents from sending calamity.

JOEL 2:12–13 NIV

God says, "*Even now* return to me." Even after all you have done—after all the idols you have pursued and all the commandments you have broken—come back home. All He requires is your whole heart, brimming with repentance. A heart that has been torn by the remembrance of the depth of your depravity and your deep, deep need for a Savior.

Like Israel, you also are God's treasured possession, His precious child. His gates remain open, anticipating your return.

Lord, truly You are gracious and compassionate, abounding in love. Thank You.

EVENING
THE SHADOW OF FEAR

When I saw him, I fell at his feet as if I were dead. But he laid his right hand on me
and said, "Don't be afraid! I am the First and the Last. I am the living one. I died,
but look—I am alive forever and ever! And I hold the keys of death and the grave."

REVELATION 1:17–18 NLT

When John saw the Lord and collapsed at His feet, Jesus placed His hand on His servant and told him not to fear. For though Jesus endured the wrath of God and death, He now lives forever and ever. It's impossible to fathom the breadth of eternity, but Christ will fill it. And He holds the keys of death and the grave. He has mastered them, and He promises that neither of them shall take you captive. He has rescued you.

Although there are many fearful things on this forsaken earth, remember that nothing can usurp Christ's rightful rule.

In You, Christ, I am safe. You are my King and Protector.

MORNING
WHEN ALL THE WORLD FALLS APART

The Sovereign Lord is my strength; he makes my feet like the feet of a deer, he enables me to tread on the heights.

HABAKKUK 3:19 NIV

In Habakkuk, you can see that even though the hour of trouble may come, the Lord is your strength. He will not only lift you up but will give you a lightness of spirit just like the deer. If you have ever watched a deer leap through the woods, you know that amazing nimbleness, that graceful soaring in action.

That strength and lightness are what God offers you. Rest in that knowledge. Call on the Lord, knowing His promise is meant not only for the whole world but for you.

Holy Spirit, dwell in me fully so that when trouble comes, I might know Your strength.

EVENING
BEAUTY IN TRUTH

"Every word of God is flawless."

PROVERBS 30:5 NIV

Isaiah 40:8 (NIV) says, "The grass withers and the flowers fall, but the word of our God endures forever." Even though God's creation is glorious, there is even more beauty in His Word, the flawless truth of God's living Word—the Bible. It has power to guide you. To comfort you. To challenge, illuminate, and convict you. To tell you of the mercy and grace of Christ, who has the power to set you free for all time.

Holy Spirit, please illuminate my path with the beauty of Your truth, and give me the courage to live it out in my daily life.

MORNING
GETTING TO HOME

But the Lord God called to the man, "Where are you?"
GENESIS 3:9 NIV

Shame causes us to feel bad about who we are, and it makes us forget what we know. But God calls out to us, reminding us we are His, and the reward comes when we make it home—home with Him.

As you begin a new day, remember who you are. Remember *whose* you are. Leave behind whatever shame you're hiding behind and just come home.

Lord, I don't want to be afraid to face You. Help me to make the choices I
need to make to stay on the right path. Help me make it home—to You.

EVENING
BLESSED

"Blessed are those who mourn, for they will be comforted."
MATTHEW 5:4 NIV

We have this promise: we will be comforted. There will be days that are hard and exhausting, but there will be days of hope and peace too. We may receive comfort from good friends who take care of us in practical ways—bringing us meals, taking us out, just talking, or even sitting in silence. We may receive comfort from reading God's Word and through prayer.

The point is we *will* be comforted. And through that comfort, we will become closer to the Comforter. That is where the blessing comes. If we refuse to be isolated, if we let others help us, if we let God speak to us, and if we reach out to others, we will no longer be alone in our grief.

My Comforter, I give my burdens to You.

MORNING
SURROUNDED

I lay down and slept, yet I woke up in safety, for the LORD was watching over me. I am not afraid of ten thousand enemies who surround me on every side.
PSALM 3:5–6 NLT

Our mighty God knows what it's like to be surrounded by enemy voices. He knows what it's like to have insults hurled at Him. He knows what it's like to have crowds shouting out His name—not in support but in rage.

The One who faced such hatred is watching over you. He is surrounding you too—but with His love and strength. Wake up in safety, and don't be afraid.

Lord, I know You can silence these voices that sometimes bring fear into my heart. Thank You for watching over me.

EVENING
COUNTING STARS

"Look now toward heaven, and count the stars if you are able to number them." And He said to him, "So shall your descendants be."
GENESIS 15:5 NKJV

God speaks to us in so many ways. He speaks to us through His written Word. He speaks to us through amazing natural glory. He speaks to us through music. He speaks to us through artistry. He speaks to us through hands of service. He speaks to us through hugs.

As many as the stars in the sky—that's how many ways God has of showing us His plan. All we have to do is keep our eyes and ears open and look and listen for Him.

Six, seven, eight, nine. . . Keep counting on God.

Lord God, help me keep my eyes on You.

MORNING
TRUST HIM WITH YOUR TOMORROWS

*"So don't worry about tomorrow, for tomorrow will bring
its own worries. Today's trouble is enough for today."*
MATTHEW 6:34 NLT

It's natural to want to provide for yourself and for the ones you love. There's nothing wrong with working hard. But becoming worried or anxious over things is a red flag that your life might be a little out of balance. Remember that the God who takes care of the birds in the barns will not forget you.

Lord, help me trust You more with my tomorrows.

EVENING
NEVER SHAKEN

Who may live on your holy mountain?
PSALM 15:1 NIV

The list of character qualities in Psalm 15 seems almost unattainable. But if that's what it takes to climb up the mountain—to dwell with the Lord—what should we do? We have to do what any good climber does—keep trying. And each time we climb, we get a little closer. We get a little smarter. We get a little stronger. We get a little better. And somewhere along the way, we realize that we are not climbing alone—that we have never been alone, because the whole mountain is where the Lord dwells. God is not just sitting on the peak, like the man with the white beard in the cartoons, with his head in the clouds, waiting for someone to finally reach Him. God is in the valley too. God is in the hard places. God is in the ravines. God is in the footholds. And yes, God is in the high places.

*Lord, I can never live on Your mountain on my
own merits. Please shake me with Your truth.*

MORNING
FORTRESS AND FIGHTER

The LORD is my rock, my fortress and my deliverer;
my God is my rock, in whom I take refuge,
my shield and the horn of my salvation, my stronghold.
PSALM 18:2 NIV

God is both our Fortress and our Deliverer. He is the massive wall surrounding us, protecting us from the arrows of the evil one. He is the fighter high up on the wall's edge, pushing back the enemy. And He is the comfort at the center of a community, spreading out in ripples of love and compassion and kindness.

Be secure within His walls.
Be confident in His ability to defend.
Be inspired by His love.

Mighty God, thank You for protecting me even when I didn't know I needed protection. Thank You for defeating death so I can live forever with You.

EVENING
A STORY TOLD

The heavens declare the glory of God, and the sky displays what his hands have made. One day tells a story to the next. One night shares knowledge with the next without talking, without words, without their voices being heard.
PSALM 19:1–3 GW

God's story is displayed in a million ways all throughout our world.

God tells His story again and again. When Jesus walked on the earth, He, Yeshua, told the story with His life and His words: "I will open my mouth to illustrate points. I will tell what has been hidden since the world was made" (Matthew 13:35 GW).

God keeps telling His story. All we have to do is listen, watch, follow, and realize that we are part of His story too.

God, thank You for showing me Your story.

MORNING
STUBBORN

*But when Pharaoh saw that relief had come, he became stubborn. He
refused to listen to Moses and Aaron, just as the Lord had predicted.*

EXODUS 8:15 NLT

So often we hold on tightly to the things in our possession, the relationships we are tied
up in, the emotional rides we have ridden for years—we hold on so tightly, even if it
hurts our own hands or our hearts. We just don't want to admit defeat. Or we want to
believe that we can somehow perform a miracle ourselves and change what's hurting
us into something that heals. But only God can heal. And only God can work these
kinds of miracles. If God is telling you to let go, it's time to let go.

Lord, help me to release anything that is keeping me from You.

EVENING
BE STILL AND GO

*"The Lord is fighting for you! So be still!" Then the Lord said to Moses,
"Why are you crying out to me? Tell the Israelites to start moving."*

EXODUS 14:14–15 GW

The Bible doesn't indicate how Moses expected to get the Israelites across the Red Sea.
Perhaps he was aware of the problem from his experience of fleeing Egypt forty years
earlier. Whatever the case, on their own, the Israelites couldn't cross the sea on foot
with the Egyptian army breathing down their necks.

But God knew all along. *"Trust Me. Stop wasting time, get going, and let Me deal
with the problem."*

Whether God says to go, to stand still, or to fight, He'll always win the battle.

*Mighty God, how often I waste time when a problem overtakes
me! Let me present the situation to You in prayer and act on Your
instruction, knowing I can trust You to win the battle!*

MORNING
WHEN TRUST IS SCARY

*Moses said to the people, Fear not; for God has come to prove you, so that
the [reverential] fear of Him may be before you, that you may not sin.*
EXODUS 20:20 AMPC

Trusting God isn't always comfortable—and that's a good thing. God reconciles His people to Himself through Christ, that they might have eternal life and grow in holiness.

God also prods His people to correct and teach them. The reason? Moses stated it plainly: to keep His people from sinning.

Trust God to do whatever it takes to make you holy as He is holy.

*Holy God, trusting You in Your holiness can be downright scary. Because You are
not only sinless, You are also everything sin is not. Purity. Light. Wholeness. You
call me and equip me to be as You are. Do Your work in my life, sovereign Lord.*

EVENING
TRUSTING GOD WITH THE IMPOSSIBLE

*"Absolutely everything, ranging from small to large, as you make it a
part of your believing prayer, gets included as you lay hold of God."*
MATTHEW 21:22 MSG

When God tells His people He's ready to move a mountain, they'd better start praying. That's a prayer God will honor.

Prayer is all about trust. Trusting God is listening. Trusting Him to reveal His will. Trusting Him to act according to His nature and to do as He promised.

Prayer is trust in action, even when we don't ask for a thing.

*Listening God, let me set aside my doubts and my failures and simply wait
before You in simple trust. You will take that tiny seed of faith, water it,
nourish it, and cause it to grow. Thanks for the blessing of answered prayer.*

MORNING
WHEN GOD DOESN'T ACT

*Lord, you have seen this; do not be silent. Do not be
far from me, Lord. Awake, and rise to my defense!*
PSALM 35:22–23 NIV

David's cry is as ancient as Job's, as modern as the Holocaust and beyond: "Awake, and rise to my defense!"

"Abba Daddy, wake up! I need help."

Like David, Jesus circled back to trusting faith. "Nevertheless, not as I will, but as You will" (Matthew 26:39 NKJV). His absolute surrender is an example of trust carried to the extreme.

You may not be called to such extreme tests. But whenever it seems God is taking a break, voice your fears and requests—then fall back to trust God to do what's best.

*Whenever Your silence adds confusion to the attacks of the enemy,
Father, thank You for accepting my complaints and cries. Let
praise and trust rise up in me before I see You in action.*

EVENING
BANK ON HIS GENEROSITY

*"You may ask, 'What will we eat in the seventh year if we do not
plant or harvest our crops?' I will send you such a blessing in the
sixth year that the land will yield enough for three years."*
LEVITICUS 25:20–21 NIV

Tonight's Leviticus reading gives a fascinating look at God's generosity and provision: Every seventh year, the Israelites were to leave the land fallow, a "festival year. . . .a year to honor the LORD" (Leviticus 25:4 GW). If the Israelites were obedient in this, God promised to provide extra for their needs, far beyond the bare minimum, so they and the land could rest that year.

Jehovah Jireh, our Provider, is delighted to care for His people. What have you been waiting for God to provide? All throughout His Word is evidence of His generosity and compassion. He will provide for your needs for today and for tomorrow—you can bank on it.

*Lord, You are a generous God. It's hard to wait for Your answer, but I trust in
Your promise that You take care of Your children (see Philippians 4:19).*

MORNING
COMPARISON GAME

"Well did Isaiah prophesy of you hypocrites, as it is written: 'This people honors Me with their lips, but their heart is far from Me. And in vain they worship Me, teaching as doctrines the commandments of men.'"

MARK 7:6–7 NKJV

Our standing before God has never been founded on "how well we're doing"—only grace. Even back in Leviticus 26:44–45, God promised to be faithful to the Israelites whether they were obedient or wayward. And today, our salvation rests solely on Jesus; we just humbly receive His gift.

So, when tempted to find our worth by seeing where we stack up with one another, let's instead meet together on our real level: equally loved and accepted through God's boundless grace.

Jesus, whether my self-confidence is strong or shaky,
I will trust Your grace as my foundation.

EVENING
KNOW AND GROW

Jesus took Peter, James and John with him and led them up a high mountain, where they were all alone. There he was transfigured before them. . . . Then a cloud appeared and covered them, and a voice came from the cloud: "This is my Son, whom I love. Listen to him!"

MARK 9:2, 7 NIV

God's statement from the cloud affirmed Jesus' identity as the Son of God, beloved and trustworthy, telling them to "listen to Him!" God's declaration revealed a new truth to these disciples: Jesus was so much more than even the earthly messiah they had been hoping for.

Do you, like the disciples, have deep questions about Jesus and His ways? Follow the Father's words: listen to Him through the Word and prayer, and your trust will grow as you get to know Him better. He is indeed more than you could ever hope for.

Jesus, deepen my trust by showing me more of You.

MORNING
ENTRUSTED

"I have taken the Levites from among the Israelites in place of the first male offspring of every Israelite woman. The Levites are mine, for all the firstborn are mine. . . . They are to be mine. I am the LORD."
NUMBERS 3:12–13 NIV

In Christ we have the privilege of being "a royal priesthood, a holy nation" set apart for God (1 Peter 2:9 NIV), and He has given each of us talents and abilities to help grow His kingdom.

Regardless of your occupation, God wants you to work with Him in mind, whether your job is creative, collaborative, mundane, enjoyable, frustrating, or rewarding. Entrust your work to Him. Just as God used the Levites' everyday work to lead Israel into worship, we can be confident that our trustworthy, sovereign, loving God can use our work to grow us and bless others.

Father, I am Yours. I entrust my talents and work to You.

EVENING
HOPE FOR THE DRY TIMES

For this God is our God for ever and ever: he will be our guide even unto death.
PSALM 48:14 KJV

Tonight's psalm is full of truth about God's character: our righteous Lord is full of loving-kindness, His name endlessly worthy of praise (see Psalm 48:9–10). He chooses to be our guide, walking close to us "even unto death." No matter how distant we feel, He will not abandon us; even when we are disobedient, He will restore us as a loving parent.

It can be so discouraging when your spiritual walk feels desert dry. But take courage, daughter of God. Press on, and even if you can only manage a whisper, declare, "He is my God forever and ever; He *will* guide me through this season and the rest, until I meet Him face to face."

Father, help me trust Your truth and encourage others to do the same.

MORNING
SHINE ON US

"The LORD bless you and keep you; the LORD make His face shine upon you, and be gracious to you; the LORD lift up His countenance upon you, and give you peace."
NUMBERS 6:24–26 NKJV

Humble and lowly, God the Son would lift up His *human* countenance upon the people, face to face, to be gracious to them and give them peace. Through laying down His perfect life, Jesus would usher in something more precious than kingdoms and land: a no-holds-barred relationship with the Father, a God who is strong to answer His children when we pray (Mark 11:24).

Daughter of God, Christ still blesses you and keeps you; He looks on you with radiant love and grants you daily grace after grace. When all looks dark, turn your face to the Savior's. Let Him illuminate your heart with lasting peace.

Jesus, Light of the World, I'm so thankful for Your saving grace.

EVENING
ON THE MOVE

Whether the cloud stayed over the tabernacle for two days or a month or a year, the Israelites would remain in camp and not set out; but when it lifted, they would set out.
NUMBERS 9:22 NIV

Tonight, we've no pillar of fire to lead the way but Someone even better: the Holy Spirit, who lives and guides us as we seek God's will through the Word and prayer.

God put the Holy Spirit in your heart to be your "Comforter (Counselor, Helper, Intercessor, Advocate, Strengthener, and Standby)" (John 14:16 AMPC). The Spirit works for your good, teaching you God's truth (see 1 Corinthians 2:10–12) and praying on your behalf (see Romans 8:26–27). You aren't on your own. No matter your situation, you can depend on the Spirit to guide you forward.

Holy Spirit, grow my trust and strengthen my heart to follow Your leading.

MORNING
A TERRIBLE SIN?

*Have mercy on me, O God, according to your unfailing love;
according to your great compassion blot out my transgressions.*
PSALM 51:1 NIV

What makes complaining so bad? It's mistrust in action: when the Israelites complained, they were telling lies about God's character—"He hasn't and *won't* provide what we need"—and they implied that Egyptian slavery was preferable to God's freedom! Complaining ignores everything God has done and says, "God, since this didn't go the way I wanted, You aren't actually trustworthy, are You?" Yikes.

The Israelites needed the repentant heart shown in Psalm 51 to confess their sin and reaffirm God's unfailing love toward them. We too should repent when we complain, and God is faithful and just to forgive us (see 1 John 1:9). Better yet, let's make a habit of giving thanks instead of complaints!

Father, help me see all the blessings You give every day.

EVENING
WELL ROOTED

*But I am like a green olive tree in the house of God; I trust in and confidently rely
on the loving-kindness and the mercy of God forever and ever. . . . I will wait on,
hope in and expect in Your name, for it is good, in the presence of Your saints.*
PSALM 52:8–9 AMPC

How do we hold fast to our faith when the news reports have everyone in a panic? In Psalm 52, David paints a beautiful picture of steadfast trust: he is a "green olive tree in the house of God"—rooted deep in a secure place, confidently waiting for and relying on the good nourishment of God's love along with his fellow believers.

Is your confidence rooted in God as David's was? Deep roots will not be swayed even as high winds howl. Show others the firm ground of your confidence, encouraging people around you with God's solid truth.

Father, like David, help me stay well rooted in Your loving-kindness.

MORNING
TRUE BLUE

"God is not a man, so he does not lie. He is not human, so he does not change his mind. Has he ever spoken and failed to act? Has he ever promised and not carried it through? . . . God has blessed, and I cannot reverse it!"
NUMBERS 23:19–20 NLT

The Moabite king found out the truth: God keeps His promises, and absolutely no one can undo His blessings.

Sing of that truth with David, relying in all things on your Savior's care: "My heart is confident in you, O God. . . . No wonder I can sing your praises!" (Psalm 57:7 NLT). Trust God's integrity when He calls you to join His work, so you can experience the blessing Elizabeth gave Mary: "You are blessed because you believed that the Lord would do what he said" (Luke 1:45 NLT).

Be confident in your God! His character is firm—He's true blue through and through.

Father God, as spring renews the earth, let my heart be renewed by Your blessing today.

EVENING
FRUITFUL

"Produce fruit in keeping with repentance. . . . Every tree that does not produce good fruit will be cut down and thrown into the fire."
LUKE 3:8–9 NIV

How can you cultivate love-focused, God-honoring actions in your day-to-day work? Maybe it's by consistently doing your best work to support your team or choosing graciousness over grumbling when talking with a coworker. Or it could be practicing patience and forgiveness toward family members when they're on your last nerve. No matter your job, one thing is certain: God will strengthen you and guide you in living His way when you ask Him.

Father, I want to produce good fruit in my life. I'm ready to learn, and I trust You to accomplish Your good work in me.

MORNING
QUIET DAWN

*"A new day will dawn on us from above because our God is loving
and merciful. He will give light to those who live in the dark and
in death's shadow. He will guide us into the way of peace."*
LUKE 1:78–79 GW

Perhaps your story of meeting Jesus was like a slow sunrise: His light spread over the landscape of your heart, the blazing warmth of His love overtaking where death and sin had formerly reigned. Because God's kingdom is both "here and not yet"—Jesus is victorious over sin and death, but all things have not yet been "made new"—there are still places in your heart where you need His restoring light, whether it's to drive out icy fears, stormy anger, or the fog of nagging sins. In your times of confession, invite Jesus into those places. He will not condemn or criticize but will heal you and illumine the path to His ways of peace.

Jesus, You know where I need Your light today.

EVENING
VICTORY IN HIM

With God we will gain the victory, and he will trample down our enemies.
PSALM 60:12 NIV

When Jesus was tempted, He used God's Word to repel the devil, His God-breathed truth trampling the deceiver's lies.

Where's your battle right now? Whether you struggle against your sin nature or the enemy's discouraging whispers, whether temptation strikes or the world's unkindness stacks against you, practice David's lesson: pray to see God's deliverance, His strength, His mastery over your circumstances. He's your victorious Savior! He'll hold you up.

*Jehovah-Nissi ("the Lord is my banner"), when the battle is raging,
I will rally to Your banner of truth, looking for Your victory.*

MORNING
NO GUILT, JUST GRACE

*Yet the news about him spread all the more, so that crowds of
people came to hear him and to be healed of their sicknesses.
But Jesus often withdrew to lonely places and prayed.*

LUKE 5:15–16 NIV

You're not alone. Jesus probably felt pressures in His work too. As His fame spread, actual *multitudes* of people came to Him to be healed. Showing compassion, Jesus healed their diseases and preached God's good news. But we also see He "withdrew to lonely places" to pray. Jesus, fully God, was also fully human—He got hungry, tired, and probably emotionally drained from witnessing the brokenness in His creation firsthand. He met with the Father for rest and strength *so* He could be prepared to help those who needed Him.

Get out from under the guilt, and lean into His grace. God invites you to come to Him to exchange your cares for His strength, peace, and joy. He will meet you where you are.

Jehovah Jireh, my Provider, remind me throughout today that I can always rest in You.

EVENING
FAITH-FILLED IMAGINATION

*Truly my soul silently waits for God; from Him comes my salvation. He only is
my rock and my salvation; He is my defense; I shall not be greatly moved.*

PSALM 62:1–2 NKJV

Whether it's nagging daytime fears or Technicolor nightmares, worry is something all of us know. We're made to be creative thinkers, but all of us have wished now and then that our imaginations would just *slow down*. God knows the power of imagination, which may be why He gave us so many concrete pictures about Himself in scripture for us to hold on to. The Psalms are full of this imagery: God is a "rock" (Psalm 62:2), a "strong tower" (Psalm 61:3). He even has "wings" to cover us as a mother hen does her chicks (Psalm 91:4). A vivid image of God's strength and safety can help in the moments our worries overwhelm.

*Father, when I feel worried, help me dwell on things
that remind me of Your goodness and care for me.*

MORNING
ALL YOUR LOVE

"Listen, O Israel! The LORD is our God, the LORD alone. And you must love the LORD your God with all your heart, all your soul, and all your strength."
DEUTERONOMY 6:4–5 NLT

Let's love the One whose power rescued a nation from four hundred years of oppression, through mighty wonders bringing her out safely to a good land (see Deuteronomy 6:20–25). Let's adore the Creator whose words wrought the earth, whose command silences the angry winds and seas. Let's bow in reverence before the God who drew near to His creation to restore it, who "gave himself for us to redeem us. . .to purify for himself a people that are his very own" (Titus 2:14 NIV). Let's sing of His daily provision, His food for the hungry, His comfort to the hurt and lonely, His mercies that are new every morning.

Father, I'll walk in obedience, secure in Your love for me, responding in trust.

EVENING
MIRACLE UPON MIRACLE

"Go back and report to John what you have seen and heard: The blind receive sight, the lame walk, those who have leprosy are cleansed, the deaf hear, the dead are raised, and the good news is proclaimed to the poor."
LUKE 7:22 NIV

There are miracles in a baby's smile, the wrinkled hand of an elderly neighbor, the playful yap of a rowdy pup. There are supernatural reminders of God's grace in our bodies as well—a heart that beats in steady rhythm, hands that bend and move, legs that take us where we need to go.

May we never forget God started all of creation with just a word. And as we witness miracles in our lives, may we respond with words of awe and wonder, praising our amazing Father for all He continues to do.

Lord, I witness miracles every day of my life. From the rising of the sun, to its setting in the evening, the miracles never cease.

MORNING
REFINED AS SILVER

For You, O God, have tested us; You have refined us as silver is refined.
PSALM 66:10 NKJV

When we go through the fire (difficult or painful seasons), we undergo a holy refining. We become who we were meant to be. The good is separated from the not-so-good. When we are purified, we become stronger. Brighter. Purer. We will stand the test of time. No longer a lump of lead, we are bright and shining witnesses of God's transforming power.

The refining process is never easy. No one wants to go through fiery trials. But, oh, to shine like silver! To know that the work God is doing in us will last for all eternity. It makes the hard times worthwhile when we realize the Lord's purification process can be trusted.

Lord, I'll be the first to admit, I'm not a huge fan of the "refining" process. But when I come out on the other end, Father, what joy!

EVENING
WITH US

"When you go out to battle against your enemies, and see horses and chariots and people more numerous than you, do not be afraid of them; for the LORD your God is with you, who brought you up from the land of Egypt."
DEUTERONOMY 20:1 NKJV

Tonight, be reminded that God (who resides inside of you) is greater than any enemy you might face. No matter how many chariots or horses look you in the eye, don't give in to fear. The Lord is with you and will fight your battles.

Stand firm. Don't back down. He brought you out of Egypt. He can cause you to triumph even now.

It's easy to get overwhelmed, Lord. Those who are against me often seem greater than those who are for me. Thank You for the reminder that having You on my side tips the scale in my favor. You've brought me through so many scary places in the past, Father. I trust You to do it again.

MORNING
BEARING OUR BURDENS

Praise be to the Lord, to God our Savior, who daily bears our burdens.
PSALM 68:19 NIV

God has promised in His Word that He will bear our burdens not just occasionally but daily. Every problem we face can be placed into His mighty hands. He's more than capable. When we shift our attention away from our trials and onto Him, our perspective changes completely. The weight is gone! And when the weight is gone, we're better able to lift our hands and hearts in praise, which further strengthens our faith.

No matter what you're going through today, praise God! He's ready and willing to carry the load on your behalf. What a trustworthy and faithful God we serve!

Lord, what a gracious and kind Father You are!
I'm so grateful to You, my Burden Bearer.

EVENING
WHERE VALUE IS FOUND

"What is the price of five sparrows—two copper coins? Yet God does not forget a single one of them. And the very hairs on your head are all numbered. So don't be afraid; you are more valuable to God than a whole flock of sparrows."
LUKE 12:6–7 NLT

Perhaps you know how it feels to be devalued. Maybe you think you're not worth much. People don't include you. They don't consider your feelings. They push you to the outer fringes. Look to Jesus as an example of how to respond. Even in the face of His worst accusers, He found His value in His Father.

God looks at you with eyes of love. You're His precious child, worth more than a flock of sparrows. He numbers every hair on your head and sees you as priceless—so much so that He gave His only Son to die in your place.

Lord, You haven't forgotten me! I am Your beloved, more valuable than I'll
ever be able to comprehend. Thank You for the reminder that I matter, Lord.

MORNING
HE LEADS THE WAY

"The Lord your God himself will cross over ahead of you. He will destroy these nations before you, and you will take possession of their land. Joshua also will cross over ahead of you, as the Lord said."
DEUTERONOMY 31:3 NIV

Isn't it wonderful to realize that God wants to assume the leadership role in our lives? We don't have to be the ones in charge, making all the decisions. He leads, guides, directs, and encourages. Our role? To listen and to follow. We can trust His leadership to be the very best.

Who (or what) are you following today? Your gut? Your friends? Your peers? Those on social media? There is One who leads the way, and He stands ready to guide you even now. Shift your gaze to Him, and take possession of the land!

You're an amazing Leader, Father! I have nothing to fear as long as I stick close as You guide me into the Promised Land.

EVENING
PREPARING FOR THE MIRACLE

Then Joshua told the people, "Purify yourselves, for tomorrow the Lord will do great wonders among you."
JOSHUA 3:5 NLT

If you knew that God was going to perform a miracle for you tomorrow. . .what would you do differently today? If you were convinced He was about to move on your behalf, would it change your actions, your heart, or your mind? If so, in what ways?

When you think of preparing your heart to receive a miracle, what comes to mind? How would you begin the purification process? Tonight, as you pray for God's miraculous power to be revealed, ask Him to show you how to prepare. Then set yourself apart, purified, ready to receive His abundant blessings.

Lord, I choose to trust You, even in the fire. I give myself over to the purification process, Lord, so that I become a clean vessel, ready to be used in miraculous ways!

MORNING
BE MAGNIFIED!

I will praise the name of God with a song, and will magnify him with thanksgiving.
PSALM 69:30 KJV

Our holy and magnificent God deserves to be magnified. He is worthy of our praise. And when we examine Him in detail, we find a loving, patient Father who cares about His children, no matter their sinful state. How wonderful He is!

Today, spend some time magnifying the King of kings and Lord of lords. Proclaim His majesty. Exalt in His goodness. Adore Him with a song. Give Him your highest praise for He alone is worthy.

*Father, may I never forget to magnify You! May I sing Your praises
at every turn. May I praise Your name with each passing day.*

EVENING
REMARKABLE GROWTH

*Then He said, "What is the kingdom of God like? And to what shall I compare
it? It is like a mustard seed, which a man took and put in his garden; and it
grew and became a large tree, and the birds of the air nested in its branches."*
LUKE 13:18–19 NKJV

A mustard seed is a tiny thing—so small that you might look right past it and not see it at all. Yet from that tiny seed grows a magnificent tree. The same is true with our faith.

What are you believing God for right now? Does your faith feel small? Trust Him, even in your weakest moments, to accomplish great things. He has the ability to take the smallest thing and grow it beyond your wildest imagination. Best of all, He always carries through on His promises. If He said it, He will most certainly do it.

*I have to admit it, Lord, I sometimes doubt the process. I see a tiny
mustard seed and have a hard time imagining it blossoming into
a magnificent tree. Tonight, Father, I place every "small" thing into
Your hands and trust You will bring all things to fruition in my life.*

MORNING
NEVER FORSAKEN

O God, You have taught me from my youth; and to this day I declare Your wondrous works. Now also when I am old and grayheaded, O God, do not forsake me, until I declare Your strength to this generation, Your power to everyone who is to come.
PSALM 71:17–18 NKJV

No matter how badly broken your heart has been in the past, you can experience healing and wholeness again. Give that broken heart to the Lord and watch Him miraculously ease your pain. Best of all, He will stick close to you. In fact, He promises to never leave you. No rejection. No betrayal. No abandonment. When you enter a relationship with the Lord, it's for eternity. Now, that's a friendship worth having!

You've always stuck with me, Lord, even when I didn't deserve it. From the day I drew my first breath on planet Earth until this very moment, You've been right there, gently guiding me and giving me strength to overcome every obstacle.

EVENING
PROMISES FULFILLED

Not one of all the LORD's good promises to Israel failed; every one was fulfilled.
JOSHUA 21:45 NIV

God isn't like us. He doesn't make promises and then break them. If He said it, He will follow through. You won't have to wonder if He will make good on His promises to you. He is who He says He is, and He'll do what He says He'll do.

Tonight, look at several of the promises in God's Word. Put your name in each sentence, personalizing each promise. Then claim it as your own and watch in wonder as God brings every one of them to pass in your life.

Lord, You carry through on every promise. If You speak something in Your Word, You'll fulfill it. Knowing You're a Promise Keeper strengthens my faith and increases my trust in each new situation.

MORNING
FAITHFUL IN THE LITTLE THINGS

*"If you are faithful in little things, you will be faithful in large ones.
But if you are dishonest in little things, you won't be honest with greater
responsibilities. And if you are untrustworthy about worldly wealth, who will
trust you with the true riches of heaven? And if you are not faithful with other
people's things, why should you be trusted with things of your own?"*
LUKE 16:10–12 NLT

God is watching as you take care of the details. He's watching your heart, double-checking your attitude. He's smiling as you handle each small task with a smile. You are proving your trustworthiness with every step you take.

Don't fret over whether or not you'll be placed in charge of big things. For now, thank God for the small ones. . .and keep going.

*Lord, You're teaching me to be faithful, as You are faithful. You've given me
opportunity after opportunity with the small things so that You can make sure
I'm ready to handle the bigger things. Lord, may I be found trustworthy.*

EVENING
A WOMAN OF WISDOM

*Deborah, the wife of Lappidoth, was a prophet who was judging Israel at that
time. She would sit under the Palm of Deborah, between Ramah and Bethel in
the hill country of Ephraim, and the Israelites would go to her for judgment.*
JUDGES 4:4–5 NLT

Are you the sort of person who others come to for wisdom? Or do you often seek out a friend or loved one who happens to have a double dose? It's always a good idea to surround yourself with people who are wise.

The best way to obtain wisdom is to seek God's opinion on a matter. Don't make rash decisions. Listen carefully and follow as He leads. The very best sort of guidance is the kind that comes straight from the heart of God.

*Lord, I want to be a woman of great wisdom, so tuned in to Your
Word, heart, and voice that I make a difference in the lives of
others. I want to be a Deborah for my generation, Father.*

MORNING
TENACITY

Then Jesus told his disciples a parable to show them
that they should always pray and not give up.
LUKE 18:1 NIV

Aren't you glad that God never gave up on You? He never once looked at you and thought you were too much work. Instead, He saw you as a possibility, not an impossibility. Even when the musical notes on the page of your life were in chaos, He turned them into a beautiful symphony.

That's how you need to look at the situations in front of you even now. They're not impossible. Keep on keeping on. Don't give up. God has big plans, and you don't want to quit when you're so close to victory! So bend the knee. Pray. Then never ever give up.

Lord, in those moments when I feel like giving up, please strengthen
my resolve. Deepen my trust in You and in Your Word.

EVENING
TRUSTING TO THE END

"Every detail of your body and soul—even the hairs of your head!—
is in my care; nothing of you will be lost. Staying with it—that's what is
required. Stay with it to the end. You won't be sorry; you'll be saved."
LUKE 21:18–19 MSG

In the verses that follow this passage from Luke, Jesus tells His disciples that no matter what's happening in the world—famine, war, earthquake, betrayals, persecution—they aren't to worry. *For this world can take nothing from them*—as long as they trust in God, His promises, and His love. He will never leave them.

From first to last, it all comes down to a matter of giving God your all and trusting in God *for everything*, "every detail," to the very end. For that is how you will "win the true life of your souls" (Luke 21:19 AMPC).

Jesus, I give You my all and leave everything, every detail, in Your hands. I trust You.

MORNING
A FRESH START

And the children of Israel said to the Lord, "We have sinned! Do to us whatever seems best to You; only deliver us this day, we pray." So they put away the foreign gods from among them and served the Lord. And His soul could no longer endure the misery of Israel.
JUDGES 10:15–16 NKJV

Though we've been offered grace in abundance, we often do our own thing. We wander away, then crawl back, begging for forgiveness and mercy. God is good enough to show us where we got off-track but He never slam dunks us. Instead, He brushes us off and puts us on the right path again. He gives us a fresh start.

What area of your life needs a fresh start today? Even if you've painted yourself into a corner, even if your troubles are self-inflicted, cry out to God. In His mercy, He will answer and deliver you once again.

You are a God of fresh starts. Oh, how grateful I am, Lord!

EVENING
JUST AS HE SAID

I will [earnestly] recall the deeds of the Lord; yes, I will [earnestly] remember the wonders [You performed for our fathers] of old.
PSALM 77:11 AMPC

In Jesus' last days, the disciples were unsure about where to go to prepare the Passover meal for Jesus. But He told them exactly what would happen, who they would meet, and what they should do and say. Taking Him at His word, "they went and found it [just] as He had said to them" (Luke 22:13 AMPC).

Instead of worrying, go to God. Remember what He has done, the wonders He has performed in the past. Know that He will give you the information you need. And that when you take Him at His word, you'll be sure to find things just as He said you would.

Lord, I remember the deeds You have done, the wonders You have worked in my life in the past. And I go forth assured You will show me the path to take and that things will happen just as You say.

MORNING
SPEAK, WAIT, HEAR

Eli said to Samuel, "Go, lie down; and it shall be, if He calls you, that you must say, 'Speak, Lord, for Your servant hears.'" So Samuel went and lay down in his place.
1 SAMUEL 3:9 NKJV

Gone are the days when we have to travel to a church, temple, or tabernacle to speak to the One who was, is, and always will be. For having accepted Christ, God now dwells within us, leading us, guiding us, hearing us. But are we listening?

You may know who God is, but have you ever heard Him speak into your life? If you have, you know how amazingly wonderful that can be. Ask God to speak through His Word. Let Him know you're listening. Trust that He is within you, around you, beside you. Speak, and then wait quietly and patiently until you get a response, until you see the light He is so longing to give.

Speak to me, Lord. I'm waiting to hear Your sweet voice.

EVENING
GO IN PEACE

The king's officer pleaded with Him, Sir, do come down at once before my little child is dead! Jesus answered him, Go in peace; your son will live! And the man put his trust in what Jesus said and started home.
JOHN 4:49–50 AMPC

At that very moment, the officer took Jesus at His word. He believed what He said was reality. *He trusted Him.* And so the king's man started back home. On his way there, his servants came to tell him the boy had indeed recovered—at the same moment that Jesus had told the man, "Go in peace; your son will live!"

Put no limits on what Jesus and His Word can do in your life. There's no amount of time or space He cannot reach across with His power.

Lord, with You there are no limits. You can reach across time and space. I believe and trust in what You say. I go in peace, knowing Your truths are my truths.

MORNING
A WOMAN AFTER GOD'S OWN HEART

David said, The Lord Who delivered me out of the paw of the lion and out of the paw of the bear, He will deliver me out of the hand of this Philistine. And Saul said to David, Go, and the Lord be with you!
1 SAMUEL 17:37 AMPC

David's memory of how God had worked in the past is what gave him the courage to face Goliath in the present. His understanding the battle was God's and God would rescue him once more is what gave him the ultimate victory (see 1 Samuel 17:47).

Armed with this same amount of trust in and knowledge of God, you too may call yourself a woman after God's own heart and face your challenges in His power.

Because I trust You, Lord, and want what You want for my life, I'm ready—just as I am—to take on all challengers in Your name and power.

EVENING
OPEN WIDE

You called in distress and I delivered you. . . . O Israel, if you would listen to Me! . . . I am the Lord your God, Who brought you up out of the land of Egypt. Open your mouth wide and I will fill it.
PSALM 81:7, 8, 10 AMPC

God is longing for His people to trust in Him. Over and over again, He's rescued the Israelites from peril. And over and over again, they turn away after His deliverance. Thus, He laments, *"If only they would listen to Me!"*

God can do anything, rescue us from any situation. He'll walk with us through our wilderness. He'll carry us like a mother does a nursing child. Like a hen, He'll cover us with His feathers until we're able to go on again. And most fantastic of all, if we open ourselves all the way up to Him, He'll overflow us, so boundless are His blessings.

I'm listening, Lord, my Bread of Life and Living Water. I'm open wide. Fill me to overflowing!

MORNING
THE GATEWAY

*Guard my life, for I am faithful to you; save your servant who trusts in you. You are
my God. . .I call to you all day long. Bring joy to your servant, Lord, for I put my trust
in you. You, Lord, are forgiving and good, abounding in love to all who call to you.*
PSALM 86:2–5 NIV

Jesus knows your voice. Come through the door and into His fold. Trust Him. Speak
to Him. Call on Him throughout your day. Remind yourself *He* is God, your Joy
Giver, the love of your life. He's your front and rear guard, your gateway to security
and an abundant life. Then listen for *His* voice. He'll call you out by name and lead
you to where you are to go. He's also going on ahead, checking out the lay of the land,
paving the path for your feet.

*Thank You, Lord, for being my Good Shepherd and the door through which I can
find guidance and protection. I'm calling for You now. Speak, Lord. I'm listening.*

EVENING
DEEPLY MOVED

*When Jesus saw [Mary] weeping. . .he was deeply moved in spirit and troubled. . . .
Jesus wept. . . . Jesus, once more deeply moved, came to the tomb. . . . Then Jesus
said, "Did I not tell you that if you believe, you will see the glory of God?"*
JOHN 11:33, 35, 38, 40 NIV

Jesus isn't immune to your suffering. He knows what you're going through. He has so
much compassion for you that He cannot help but be moved, to hurt when you hurt,
weep when you weep. But He also knows about the power of faith, the strength of God
the Father, and the joy of the Spirit.

Trust that Jesus is walking with you through every trial and triumph. Know that
no matter what happens, you, as a believer, *will see* the glory of God.

*Thank You, God, for Jesus, the One who knows all about the human
experience. With Him by my side, I'm never alone in sorrow or in joy.*

MORNING
KNOWING GOD

Jesus shouted to the crowds, "If you trust me, you are trusting not only me, but also God who sent me. For when you see me, you are seeing the one who sent me."
JOHN 12:44–45 NLT

Not sure what God is all about? Uncertain as to His true character? You need not look any further than Jesus Christ. When you know Him, you'll know God. When you trust Him, you're trusting God.

Study His compassion for the mourning, the lame, the weak, the blind, the lepers, the sinners. Read of His attitude toward the political and religious leaders of His day. Walk with His disciples as they follow Him, forever trying to understand and often falling a little bit short. Allow Him to open up your eyes to what He reveals in the scriptures. Make a list of all the statements He begins with the words *I am*. And then find proof of His identity in the Word and in your own life.

Jesus, show me God through You and Your life. Open my eyes and heart to knowing You better.

EVENING
LEAN BACK UPON JESUS

The disciples kept looking at one another, puzzled as to whom He could mean. One of His disciples, whom Jesus loved [whom He esteemed and delighted in], was reclining [next to Him] on Jesus' bosom. . . . Then leaning back against Jesus' breast, he asked Him, Lord, who is it?
JOHN 13:22–23, 25 AMPC

Jesus isn't some god so far removed from you that you cannot reach Him. He's all around you, waiting for you to lean upon Him, ask Him questions, abide in His love. So go to Him now, knowing He'll provide you with all the knowledge you need. Trust that you can rely on both Him and His Word.

Lord, I'm leaning back on You, ready to whisper in Your ear, bathing in the intimacy of our love.

DAY 223

MORNING
RELAX, RELY, REJOICE

David. . . said: The Lord is my Rock [of escape from Saul] and my Fortress [in the wilderness] and my Deliverer. . . . As for God, His way is perfect; the word of the Lord is tried. He is a Shield to all those who trust and take refuge in Him.
2 SAMUEL 22:1–2, 31 AMPC

David was a man after God's own heart. Although he made mistakes, he was quick to confess to and humble himself before God. Because he trusted God, God became his Shield and Refuge. Because David trusted the Word and promises of God, God continually delivered him in the wilderness.

When you trust and take shelter in God your Rock, He will become your impenetrable Shield. And in following His Word, you'll find your way perfect. Relax. Rely. Rejoice in the Rock that is your God.

Thank You, Lord, for being my Rock and Fortress, my Deliverer and Shield!

EVENING
A PRAYER FOR YOU

"I am praying not only for these disciples but also for all who will ever believe in me through their message. I pray that they will all be one, just as you and I are one. . . . I have given them the glory you gave me, so they may be one as we are one. I am in them and you are in me."
JOHN 17:20–23 NLT

Thousands of years ago, while He was in human form on earth, Jesus, the Son of God, prayed a prayer for you, a believer. He prayed that you and other believers would be one, just as He and Father God are one. And He didn't stop there!

Make this awareness part of your daily walk. Know that Jesus has prayed for, is praying for, and will continue to pray for you. Know that He has been to you an example and will help you reflect the character of Father God.

I am amazed at Your prayer for me, Jesus! Thank You for its power and purpose.

MORNING
PRECONCEPTIONS

Then Naaman and all his attendants went back to the man of God. He stood before him and said, "Now I know that there is no God in all the world except in Israel."
2 KINGS 5:15 NIV

Naaman, commander of the Syrian army, took the advice of his wife's God-fearing servant girl. He headed to Israel to be cured of leprosy by the prophet Elisha. But when that man of God told him to wash in the Jordan seven times, Naaman balked because of his preconceptions of what Elisha's healing process would be.

When you're looking to God for answers, trust Him to have the right remedy. Let go of any preconceived notions of what your "cure" should look like. Step out in faith, knowing no matter how out-of-your-realm His notions are, they are what will work for you.

Help me have more faith in You than in my own ideas, Lord.

EVENING
FROM GLOOM TO BLOOM

Let all that I am praise the LORD; may I never forget the good things he does for me. . . . He fills my life with good things. My youth is renewed like the eagle's!
PSALM 103:2, 5 NLT

What if you looked at the things that happen as neither good nor bad? What if you constantly remembered God is in your corner, on your side (see Psalm 118:6)? What if you understood and kept in mind the idea that God has everything rigged in your favor?

To be sure, there are times when you need to grieve the loss of someone or something. Times when you need to regroup and take stock of what's happening. But the majority of the time, looking at things as being rigged by God in your favor may just change your life from gloom to bloom!

With You on my side, Lord, I can't lose!

MORNING
ADVENTURES WITH GOD

Hezekiah put his whole trust in the GOD of Israel. There was no king quite like him, either before or after. He held fast to GOD—never loosened his grip—and obeyed to the letter everything GOD had commanded Moses. And GOD, for his part, held fast to him through all his adventures.

2 KINGS 18:5–6 MSG

Hezekiah held fast to God. Imagine him following right in step with God, going wherever He led. Not once did Hezekiah let go; he did exactly what God told him to do when He told him to do it.

In return, God held fast to him too—like two best friends always together—in all their adventures.

The Bible says God doesn't play favorites (see Romans 2:11). That means you have the same opportunity to share adventures with God if you follow Hezekiah's example.

God, I put all my trust in You. By faith I will hold tight to You and obey all Your commands.

EVENING
SIGNS OF HIS PRESENCE

Keep your eyes open for GOD, watch for his works; be alert for signs of his presence. Remember the world of wonders he has made, his miracles, and the verdicts he's rendered—O seed of Abraham, his servant, O child of Jacob, his chosen.

PSALM 105:5–6 MSG

Put down your busy schedule and take a deep breath! What's God doing in your life? Perhaps at first glance you saw His fingerprints on your life as coincidence. Look a little closer. Where has He blessed you lately? When has He poured out His favor on you and given you opportunities you otherwise might not have had?

What great work is God doing now, and how can you join Him? When you see Him at work and join Him there, your soul is awake to His presence and in tune with Him.

God, open my eyes to see Your works. Help me be watchful and recognize Your presence.

MORNING
FREE AT LAST

Along about midnight, Paul and Silas were at prayer and singing a robust hymn to God. The other prisoners couldn't believe their ears. Then, without warning, a huge earthquake! The jailhouse tottered, every door flew open, all the prisoners were loose.
ACTS 16:25–26 MSG

Paul and Silas were beaten and unjustly thrown into jail simply for sharing their faith. They found themselves imprisoned with bruises and pain, no doubt on the inside as well as the outside. While they praised God through their suffering and heartbreak, God delivered them from their chains. He set them free, literally.

God's deliverance can happen rapidly, or it can take some time. Either way, God will set you free from the pain. While you're waiting, praise God. Doing so can comfort your heart and soothe the broken places in your life.

Lord, I'm in one of those difficult places now. I open my heart and my mouth in praise to You today. I trust You to set me free from the pain.

EVENING
ASKING RIGHTLY

God answered Solomon, "This is what has come out of your heart: You didn't grasp for money, wealth, fame, and the doom of your enemies; you didn't even ask for a long life. You asked for wisdom and knowledge so you could govern well my people over whom I've made you king. Because of this, you get what you asked for—wisdom and knowledge. And I'm presenting you the rest as a bonus—money, wealth, and fame beyond anything the kings before or after you had or will have."
2 CHRONICLES 1:11–12 MSG

Solomon's unselfish and thoughtful request for wisdom and knowledge pleased God. Not only did God grant Solomon's request, making him the wisest man to ever live, but He also gave Solomon the things he *didn't* ask for—wealth, honor, and a long life.

When you ask God for something rightly—know that you'll not only receive something better—but beyond what you imagine.

Heavenly Father, I'm determined to ask rightly, knowing when I do, You'll give me beyond what I imagine—for Your glory.

MORNING
GOD COMES DOWN

*When Solomon finished praying, a bolt of lightning out of heaven struck
the Whole-Burnt-Offering and sacrifices and the Glory of GOD filled
The Temple. The Glory was so dense that the priests couldn't get in—
GOD so filled The Temple that there was no room for the priests!*

2 CHRONICLES 7:1 MSG

It is often in those silent moments, when you're taking in God's creation, that you feel close to Him. It often feels that God comes down and you can experience His presence in a tangible way. Life's busyness fades away, and all of who He is envelops you like a waterfall, washing away the stress.

Take time today to step back from the traffic, the turmoil, the loud shouts of life, and into the calm of His creation. Embrace the silence, and step into the peace right now.

*Savior, You are welcome in this place. My body is Your temple. Come
and visit me today. Wash over me, and fill me with Your peace.*

EVENING
COUNT ON HOLY STRENGTH

*Then Asa cried out to the LORD his God, "O LORD, no one but you can help
the powerless against the mighty! Help us, O LORD our God, for we trust
in you alone. It is in your name that we have come against this vast horde.
O LORD, you are our God; do not let mere men prevail against you!"*

2 CHRONICLES 14:11 NLT

Complete dependence on God doesn't mean you're weak, passive, or unproductive. It means you're allowing His power to make you more effective for Him, enabling you to do so much more, often with eternal value.

If you're facing battles you feel you can't possibly win, don't give up. Study Asa, who, when standing against immense throngs of enemy soldiers, realized how incapable he was without God's holy power. When He prayed for God's intervention, God came through supernaturally and stupendously. In all things, trust in God alone.

God, I recognize my limitations and ask for Your help in all things.

MORNING
GOD OF YOUR UPS AND DOWNS

*Hallelujah! You who serve God, praise God! Just to speak his name is praise!
Just to remember God is a blessing—now and tomorrow and always. From
east to west, from dawn to dusk, keep lifting all your praises to God!*
PSALM 113:1–3 MSG

Through prayer, the writer of these psalms finds comfort in God for his brokenness and pain. He reminds himself of God's faithfulness and unfailing love and how it refreshes his spirit. Then he pulls himself up, encourages himself in the Lord, and becomes determined to experience the joy that only God can give. He rises again through faith in God, climbing ever higher with praise and thanksgiving.

Like the psalmist, you too can trust God with your ups and downs. Allow Him to go with you to the mountaintops and back down into the valleys.

*God, You are always with me. You faithfully walk with me no matter what situation
I face. I will rejoice in You at all times because I know I can count on You.*

EVENING
LEARNING TO REST IN HIM

*He shall not be afraid of evil tidings; his heart is firmly fixed,
trusting (leaning on and being confident) in the Lord.*
PSALM 112:7 AMPC

Pause for a moment and look back on your life. What things could you have done better or perhaps just a little differently? What would it have looked like if you would have trusted the Lord more? What if you'd let go and given Him control, especially knowing Him better now than you knew Him then?

How had God faithfully put things back together for you in the past? What are some examples of His faithfulness to you and to your family? What changes could you make in your thinking that would help you to lean on and rest in Him even more when difficulties arise?

*Lord, help me walk by faith and rely on You even when I can't see all
the details ahead, knowing You're working things out for my good.*

MORNING
HELP FROM THE HOLY SPIRIT

O Israel, trust the LORD! He is your helper and your shield. O priests,
descendants of Aaron, trust the LORD! He is your helper and your shield.
PSALM 115:9–10 NLT

The Lord remembers us. He sees us, thinks about us, and perfects those things that concern us. In His extraordinary love, He cares about everything—even the little things that we've lost track of. And He sent the Helper (see John 14:26 NKJV), the Holy Spirit, to assist us in everything, even in finding things we perceive to be lost.

Heavenly Father, thank You for sending the Holy Spirit to help me with all things.
Remind me that You care about even the littlest things that concern me.

EVENING
DEPEND ON GOD FOR EVERYTHING

You who [reverently] fear the Lord, trust in and lean on
the Lord! He is their Help and their Shield.
PSALM 115:11 AMPC

Throughout David's life, he often called on God to protect him from those who desired to end his life, including Saul, the king of Israel. Once King Saul stood just outside the cave where David hid. David could have easily taken Saul's life, but he refused to touch the king God had anointed. Instead, he relied on God to keep him safe.

You may not spend your days battling enemies with a sword or a sling and stones, but you have an enemy. Yet you also have a God who stands ready to shield you, protect you, and keep you in all of His ways.

My Help and Shield, my safety and security are found in You.

MORNING
WHAT GOD SAYS, HE WILL DO

*Abraham never wavered in believing God's promise. In fact, his
faith grew stronger, and in this he brought glory to God. He was
fully convinced that God is able to do whatever he promises.*

ROMANS 4:20–21 NLT

Abraham didn't waver during the long years separating the call to leave his home and travel to a new land (see Genesis 12), God's first promise of a son (see Genesis 15:4), and Isaac's birth (see Genesis 21:3). Instead of growing weaker, Abraham's faith grew stronger. He gave glory to God before the fact, *"fully convinced"* God had the power to do what He'd promised. Unfortunately, most of Abraham's descendants lacked his faith and ended up in exile.

Christians today have the same two choices: to believe God and trust Him, not depending on sight or immediate answers; or to give up and miss out on God's best. What choice will you make?

*Unchanging God, Your purposes never change. Ground my steps on the
foundation of Your Word, not on my feelings and shortsighted perceptions.*

EVENING
LIFE NOT DEATH

*Likewise reckon ye also yourselves to be dead indeed unto sin,
but alive unto God through Jesus Christ our Lord.*

ROMANS 6:11 KJV

Paul discusses that tension in Romans 5:20 (NIV). He says, "Where sin increased, grace increased all the more." He anticipates his audience's reaction: "Shall we go on sinning so that sin may increase?" (Romans 6:1 NIV). Paul slams the door shut. Absolutely not. You died to sin. Period. No questions. You're now alive in Christ. Live like it! Paul doesn't ignore the practical problems—he addresses them throughout the remainder of Romans and his other epistles—but the bottom line is this: Christians are alive in Christ.

God doesn't want you to worry over how to die to self. He wants you to revel in your new, spirit-filled life.

God, thank You for the new life You've given me in Christ.

MORNING
PASSING IT ON

*The gracious hand of his God was on him. For Ezra had
devoted himself to the study and observance of the Law of
the LORD, and to teaching its decrees and laws in Israel.*

EZRA 7:9–10 NIV

God had devoted Himself to His people, and Ezra devoted himself back to God by diving into His Word. God responded to Ezra's faithfulness by placing His hand on Ezra's life. When people met the scribe, they knew they'd seen God at work.

The world today needs more people like Ezra. The more time you spend with God, the more His work will be evident in your life, showing itself in your obedience, the words you speak, and your recognition of His faithfulness.

*Lawgiver and Living Word, thank You for Ezra's example. Broaden my
understanding as I study Your Word. Then help me pass this passion on. Amen.*

EVENING
GRINDING DOWN OR LIFTING UP?

*Then I pressed further, "What you are doing is not right! Should you not walk
in the fear of our God in order to avoid being mocked by enemy nations?"*

NEHEMIAH 5:9 NLT

The writer of Psalm 119:74 (NLT) hoped his own behavior would bring joy to others and not mockery: "May all who fear you find in me a cause for joy, for I have put my hope in your word." Like Nehemiah, the psalmist received a mixed reaction. Some accused him without cause (see Psalm 119:78).

Instead of giving up and backing away, the Jews fought back against the unfair practices and criticism. God made them overcomers.

If godly people and great presidents have their detractors, how much more so ordinary people? Whenever someone strikes to tear down what you're building up, you can choose to give up or to stand up with joy and confidence in God.

O Father, strengthen me with joy and hope according to Your Word.

MORNING
WHEN NOTHING MAKES SENSE—GOD DOES

Oh, the depth of the riches of the wisdom and knowledge of God! How unsearchable His judgments, and his paths beyond tracing out!

ROMANS 11:33 NIV

Although God's judgments are unsearchable, He's the most Supreme Court Justice. Bottom line: His decisions can be trusted.

People throughout history have discovered this rock-solid truth. God spared generations of Israelites from destruction because of His compassion, mercy, and goodness (see Nehemiah 9:28, 31, 36). In the nineteenth century, the great preacher Charles Spurgeon said, "We cannot always trace God's hand, but we can always trust God's heart."

God may not reveal the end, but He will always direct your next step.

God, may You shine brighter on my life so I may better see my path to Your goodness. Amen.

EVENING
BROAD PLACES

"But those who suffer he delivers in their suffering; he speaks to them in their affliction. He is wooing you from the jaws of distress to a spacious place free from restriction, to the comfort of your table laden with choice food."

JOB 36:15–16 NIV

God has ways and means that we cannot understand. He is better to us than we can imagine. He is more merciful and more powerful than we can comprehend. God may use the pain of our circumstances to get our attention. Then, coaxing us like reluctant sheep, He leads us away from the gaping jaws of an all-consuming anxiety and into a wide-open space, "to a place free from distress" (Job 36:16 NLT).

Ask God to open your heart to any truths He would like to teach you. Be transformed by the painful circumstance you find yourself in. Trust that God will rescue you and lavish you with things for your heart to enjoy. What would you like to ask God for tonight?

God, please lead me into a broad and peaceful place. I trust You with the journey.

MORNING
NOTHING BETTER

*I know that there is nothing better for people than to be happy and
to do good while they live. That each of them may eat and drink,
and find satisfaction in all their toil—this is the gift of God.*
ECCLESIASTES 3:12–13 NIV

Put a new spin on your work and its meaning by considering it as God's gift to you. What do you enjoy about what you do? Thank God for what's been placed in your hands, and your joyful mood will flourish.

To find even more satisfaction and joy, look for opportunities to bring more good into your day. "Good" can be as simple as connecting with a friend, sharing a smile with a child, or thanking God for a simple meal. Be intentional about enjoying today!

*God, help me be open to new ways of thinking about today's work. Help
me develop a joyful heart and attitude every moment of my life.*

EVENING
HIS MAJESTY

*God's voice thunders in marvelous ways; he does
great things beyond our understanding.*
JOB 37:5 NIV

God is both great and good at the same time.

He is the awesome Creator of everything we see. He is in control of the rain, snow, and sun. He holds the earth together with His thoughts. He is God of unlimited might.

At the same time, He is marvelously and unsurpassably good. There is no darkness or evil in Him.

Together, His greatness and His goodness mean that we can trust Him to work in our lives in an amazing way. We can trust that even when we struggle with hardships, He is working things out for our best. We can trust that when we experience success, it has been a good gift from His hand.

*God, I am grateful for Your mighty strength and
goodness. Please do great things in my life.*

MORNING
YOU ARE LOVED

*Love is patient, love is kind. It does not envy, it does not boast, it is not proud.
It does not dishonor others, it is not self-seeking, it is not easily angered, it keeps
no record of wrongs. Love does not delight in evil but rejoices with the truth.*
1 CORINTHIANS 13:4–6 NIV

Understanding how God sees us is critical to our trusting Him. Sometimes our brain tells us we're trusting when our emotions are still fearful. That's because head knowledge is different from heart knowledge. It's when our hearts are satisfied that His affection doesn't waver that we can trust God completely.

Take a deep breath and relax in the truth that God is good and you can trust Him with every part of your life: your family, work, relationships, health, and more. Look back over your life and remember the ways God has proven His great love for you. Rest in His affection today.

God, thank You for Your perfect love.

EVENING
ONE JUDGE

*Search me [thoroughly], O God, and know my heart! Try me and know my thoughts!
And see if there is any wicked or hurtful way in me, and lead me in the way everlasting.*
PSALM 139:23–24 AMPC

God's desire is for you to be free from the tight, constraining grasp of sin's chokehold. He wants you to be free to experience all the confidence, peace, and joy you were created for in life. Take His hand, and let Him lead you through the process of redeeming your heart and mind as only He can.

*God, please search my heart and mind, and show me what
You want to change in me. I trust You to break me free of old
thought patterns and feelings. Lead me in Your new way.*

MORNING
CONSIDER GOD

*They have harps and lyres at their banquets, pipes and timbrels and wine, but they
have no regard for the deeds of the Lord, no respect for the work of his hands.
Therefore my people will go into exile for lack of understanding; those of high
rank will die of hunger and the common people will be parched with thirst.*

ISAIAH 5:12–13 NIV

Acknowledge God in your day today. Recognize the unique beauty around you, and
praise the Creator. Did He bless you with sunlight, food, breath for your lungs? Reflect
on how He has worked in your life. Has He provided health, safety, work, family, or
friends? As you read the scriptures, ask God to reveal Himself to you in truth. Get to
know Him as a Savior, a Provider, a Pursuer, a Healer, and as a Friend. Peace and joy
will be your reward.

*God, let me know You in spirit and in truth. Remind me
to look for Your works today and to praise You.*

EVENING
FAITH IS THE VICTORY

For we live by faith, not by sight.

2 CORINTHIANS 5:7 NIV

In uncertain situations, we are to remember that faith, not the outcome, is the victory.
God is responsible for the results. Our job is the faith.

Trusting that God will take care of the outcome is a muscle that gets stronger each
time you practice it. Instead of worrying over the test results, the job interview, or the
bill payment, tell God you trust Him to take care of you. Tell Him that over and over
until both your mind and heart believe it. Know that no matter how the details play out
at the end, God is most assuredly in control and working for your best.

*God, thank You that You are responsible for all outcomes.
Help me to trust You now, to walk by faith, not by sight.*

MORNING
LIVE FREE

Now the Lord is the Spirit, and where the Spirit of the Lord is, there is freedom.
2 CORINTHIANS 3:17 NIV

God loves you and has given you the freedom to live each day loving Him, yourself, and others. He's given you the freedom to make the best choices. You are not restricted to living in a small and painful world but have been set free to celebrate being alive.

Christ fulfilled the law so that you don't have to. You can eat the foods you prefer, sing the songs you chose, dress in your own style, read what interests you, and attend church where you like.

Ask yourself what Christ wants you to enjoy today. Listen for His Spirit's promptings. Be free to enjoy the day He created.

God, help me to truly enjoy my freedom and this day with You.

EVENING
PERFECTLY PEACEFUL

You will keep in perfect peace those whose minds are steadfast, because they trust in you. Trust in the LORD forever, for the LORD, the LORD himself, is the Rock eternal.
ISAIAH 26:3–4 NIV

God gives you a clear picture of where to place your troubled thoughts. The Lord is the Rock eternal. He's powerful and able to hold whatever worries you. He can stop the storm but sometimes chooses to hold you through it. He's also everlasting and constant. God doesn't falter and disappear when you need Him most. He's always present.

What concerns do you wrestle with tonight? Take them to God. Tell Him you trust Him. Proclaim aloud, "There is no Rock like our God" (1 Samuel 2:2 NIV). Peace will fill you as your mind is stayed on Him.

God, there's no rock like You. Remind me of Your
faithfulness and power. I choose to put my trust in You.

MORNING
A SURE FOUNDATION

*Therefore, this is what the Sovereign Lord says: "Look! I am placing a
foundation stone in Jerusalem, a firm and tested stone. It is a precious
cornerstone that is safe to build on. Whoever believes need never be shaken."*

ISAIAH 28:16 NLT

You can trust Jesus to be your home base, the starting point of all your hopes, an unfailing infrastructure. He meets your needs when others fail you. He holds you close
when you're afraid. He heals your wounds. He successfully plans your future. He brings
peace to chaos.

No matter how tumultuous your circumstances, the promise is that you will not
be shaken. What threatens to throw you off balance today? What potential calamity
is stealing your confidence? Jesus is bigger than any problem you face. Put your trust
in Him alone.

God, I praise You for providing me with the precious cornerstone of Jesus Christ.

EVENING
NOT ONE MISSING

*Lift up your eyes and look to the heavens: Who created all these? He who
brings out the starry host one by one and calls forth each of them by name.
Because of his great power and mighty strength, not one of them is missing.*

ISAIAH 40:26 NIV

You are God's daughter made in His own image. He is aware of your every detail and
calls you by name. He hasn't lost a single star in all the vast galaxies despite the black
holes and endless space. *Not one is missing!* You will certainly not be lost either. Because
of God's "great power and mighty strength," you can trust Him with everything. You
need not be afraid.

Is there something that terrifies you? Some fear for yourself or a loved one that
haunts you? Trust God to use His *might* (outward strength) and His *power* (inner
strength) to keep you close and safe.

*God, I praise You for Your loving care toward me.
Help me entrust myself, my life, my all to You.*

MORNING
JOY OVERFLOWING

Then will the lame leap like a deer, and the mute tongue shout for joy.
Water will gush forth in the wilderness and streams in the desert.
ISAIAH 35:6 NIV

God's love is a constant and steady stream. This is a difficult truth to cling to when grief is the sun that parches you each morning. Trust God to break forth with water in your wilderness. Watch for it with hope. God will show you Himself in all His glory. He'll "strengthen the feeble hands, steady the knees that give way; say to those with fearful hearts, 'Be strong, do not fear; your God will come. . .he will come to save you'" (Isaiah 35:3–4 NIV). When you determine to look to God with hope amid great trials and have learned to trust Him in the process, you'll find you have a greater capacity for joy.

God, please send those waters of restoration and joy into my
day. Give me strength to watch for Your glory.

EVENING
NEW THINGS

"See, I am doing a new thing! Now it springs up; do you not perceive it?
I am making a way in the wilderness and streams in the wasteland."
ISAIAH 43:19 NIV

Do you struggle with change? Do transitions leave you anxious? Trust that God's plans for you are good and that His heart is loving. God will not give you more than you can handle.

Do not focus on previous years or past hurts. Be available for what God has for you right now. Look attentively for what may seem like a small trickle. Be ready for that trickle to turn into a spring and then a river. Prepare to get wet as you wade into your future personally designed by God with you in mind. He knows you better than you know yourself. Celebrate new life in abundance without looking back to the solid shore of your past. Go have your adventure with God at your side.

God, let my heart trust You as You prepare a "new thing" for my future.

MORNING
A BRUISED REED

"A bruised reed he will not break, and a smoldering wick he will not snuff out. In faithfulness he will bring forth justice."

ISAIAH 42:3 NIV

Jesus is called "a man of suffering" (Isaiah 53:3 NIV). He understands grief and rejection. Who better to turn to when you're sad and hurting? Your Savior seeks out the broken for healing and relationship. He knows exactly where your wounds are and how to heal them. You may carry the scar, but His touch works miracles.

You need not keep score of hurts, grievances, or harm done to you. Justice is Jesus' job. Let go of struggles to make things right for yourself. Let Jesus carry that burden for you. You get busy finding beauty in your day. Let gratitude and praise be your new song.

God, I trust in and praise Your healing touch in my life.

EVENING
REDEEMED

"I have swept away your offenses like a cloud, your sins like the morning mist. Return to me, for I have redeemed you."

ISAIAH 44:22 NIV

Although your heart may want to hide when you feel ashamed of your wrongdoing, God says, *"Come closer. I have redeemed you."* Is there something you have let come between you and God? Have you tormented yourself thinking He could never forgive that specific sin again? Know that God has blotted out all your missteps! Like a thick cloud that can't be seen through, He has covered your sin. Take a moment to confess any wrong attitudes, thoughts, or actions then praise God for His faithful and full forgiveness.

God, I confess I daily miss Your standard. I'm so grateful You are full of love and forgiveness. Help me run into Your open arms instead of hiding in shame.

MORNING
GOD'S SPIRIT IN YOU

And because we are his children, God has sent the Spirit of his Son into our hearts, prompting us to call out, "Abba, Father." Now you are no longer a slave but God's own child. And since you are his child, God has made you his heir.

GALATIANS 4:6–7 NLT

Your Father has put part of Himself, His Spirit, in you so that you'll never be alone. No matter how far you travel or what circumstances you're in, you have part of Him closer than your heartbeat.

This is your true reality. You have been adopted by the most generous of all Fathers, and nothing can separate you from His love. Not only that, but also everything He owns is yours!

Do you have needs? Bring them to your Abba Father. Do you have problems or concerns? Abba Father longs to help you. Spend time each day in the presence of your true Father.

Abba Father, thank You for making me Your own beloved child.

EVENING
BEAUTIFUL NEWS

How beautiful on the mountains are the feet of the messenger who brings good news, the good news of peace and salvation, the news that the God of Israel reigns!

ISAIAH 52:7 NLT

God's love is written on hugging arms that embrace reunited friends. His forgiveness is written in the tears of prisoners who confess their wrongs and accept His righteousness. His grace is written in the hands of mothers holding long-prayed-for newborns. His hope is written on the faces of those who wait for the doctor's prognosis, knowing that whatever happens, peace will come.

When you follow Jesus, it is not just your words that tell of His reign in your life but every step you take can bring good news to those around you.

Lord, may my life and the way that I live it tell the story of my love for You.

MORNING
KEEP RUNNING

You were running the race so well. Who has held you back from following the truth?
GALATIANS 5:7 NLT

In his letter to the believers in Galatia, Paul urges them to not get caught up in arguments about traditions and processes but to remember that the "only thing that counts is faith expressing itself through love" (Galatians 5:6 NIV).

Over and over, God reminds us that we are free in Him. We are free from any membership dues or tests of loyalty or conformity to human expectations. He loves us as we are, and He asks us to love like He does. That's it. And it's that love that will keep us running.

Lord of all, help me not be distracted by things
that are not designed to bring me closer to You.

EVENING
EVERLASTING LIGHT

"Your sun will never set again, and your moon will wane no more;
the Lord will be your everlasting light, and your days of sorrow will end."
ISAIAH 60:20 NIV

The apostle Paul writes to the believers at Ephesus and prays that the "eyes of your heart may be enlightened in order that you may know the hope to which he has called you, the riches of his glorious inheritance in his holy people, and his incomparably great power for us who believe" (Ephesians 1:18–19 NIV).

How often do we allow the darkness of this world's sorrows to blind us from the hope we have in Jesus? How many times do we let our greed or need for material goods cloud our knowledge of the treasures He has for us? How often do we run out of energy because we don't rely on His power?

Lord, help my eyes to be opened to the light of Your hope, glory,
and power that is readily available to me in this very moment.

MORNING
ECHOES OF ADVICE

When you walk, their counsel will lead you. When you sleep,
they will protect you. When you wake up, they will advise you.
PROVERBS 6:22 NLT

If you had the blessing of growing up with capable parents who were constantly telling you what to do and how to do it, you too have probably heard their voices speaking in your head. And sometimes you might wish you could find the "off" switch. But wisdom is wisdom, no matter how it comes to us or how often.

Next time you hear those familiar voices, thank God for the wisdom He's spoken through those who raised you. Thank Him for guidance that never leaves you. Trust that when you hear truth, God is the foundation of that truth.

Lord God, thank You for Your wisdom and truth that speak to me every day.

EVENING
WRESTLING MATCH

For we do not wrestle against flesh and blood, but against principalities,
against powers, against the rulers of the darkness of this age, against
spiritual hosts of wickedness in the heavenly places.
EPHESIANS 6:12 NKJV

Some days, every minute of the day, from before sunrise until that moment you drag yourself to bed, feels like one big wrestling match—and that's even when no other person is around! You fight against fatigue. You argue with your wants. You shout down the negative voices in your mind. You battle against irritation, impatience, and selfishness. It's a battle of the wills—and goodwill is losing.

It's vital to remember, on days like these, that God is not against us. We have the armor of God, and backed by the One who defeated even death; we can win this match any day!

Almighty Warrior and Lord, help me remember
who I'm fighting against and who I'm fighting for!

MORNING
BETTER

"For Wisdom is better than all the trappings of wealth;
nothing you could wish for holds a candle to her."
PROVERBS 8:11 MSG

Take some minutes to really consider carefully what your weeks look like. What things are pushing you along or holding you back? Do your goals match up with the way you are spending your time?

Whatever you are currently spending your time on, God's Word assures us of this: wisdom is better. It's better than running after wealth, or material possessions, or a good image, or a level of popularity. It's better than knowing about the latest funny TV shows or dramatic movies. It's better than keeping up with politics or listening to motivational speakers.

Wisdom is better. So go get that!

Lord, help me to want wisdom more than wealth or fleeting happiness.

EVENING
THE SECRET

I have learned the secret of living in every situation, whether it
is with a full stomach or empty, with plenty or little. For I can
do everything through Christ, who gives me strength.
PHILIPPIANS 4:12–13 NLT

The apostle Paul lived long before Columbus sailed the ocean blue, but he had as much faith as one of the first explorers. Time after time, he put his life in the hands of God. He gave up everything he knew to follow God's will and to teach others about Jesus. There were many times when he was beaten or imprisoned or run out of towns. But no matter what happened to him, he kept trusting in God's provision.

When you have been through hard times and survived, you have confidence that you can do it again. You know that you're not alone—that God never leaves you.

God, my Provider, I know I can trust You to get me through anything.

MORNING
WORKING FOR PEACE WHEREVER YOU ARE

"Work for the peace and prosperity of the city where I sent you into exile.
Pray to the LORD for it, for its welfare will determine your welfare."
JEREMIAH 29:7 NLT

Next time you find yourself feeling stuck someplace you don't want to be, don't get caught up in planning your exit. Instead, think about how you can make the best of the situation. Ask God to help you reach out to strangers. Think about ways you can help those around you succeed—no matter who they are or how welcome (or not) they've made you feel. Dig in. Participate. Join the team. Make solid connections. And trust that God will bless your efforts.

Lord, help me when I feel lost and far away.

EVENING
THE FEAR OF GOD

"And I will make an everlasting covenant with them, that I will
not turn away from doing them good; but I will put My fear in
their hearts so that they will not depart from Me."
JEREMIAH 32:40 NKJV

The fear that God wants to put in our hearts is the healthy, life-giving, transformational reverence and awe of Him. It is the feeling of wonder that comes when we know the Creator of the universe knows our names. It is the position of humility we take before the throne of the King of kings. It is the dazzling of our senses that occurs when we try to imagine His eternal glory. It is the absolute astonishment at being loved so fully, so fiercely, and so faithfully by our perfect Father in heaven.

This fear may well take our breath away. It may freeze us in our tracks or shock us into silence. But it will also fill us up, encourage our spirits, and speak to our hearts. It will cause us to stay instead of run away. It will make the impossible possible.

Lord, may I never stop fearing You.

MORNING
KEEP BUSY

We hear that some among you are idle and disruptive.
They are not busy; they are busybodies.
2 THESSALONIANS 3:11 NIV

It's actually quite hard to be a busy person and be a busybody at the same time. People who are diligent and productive don't have time to worry about what other people are doing. And they have no desire to cause trouble, as trouble might just slow them down.

We should strive to be busy—doing God's work, serving others, and taking care of those in need. There's always something to do in the kingdom of God!

Lord, I trust You to assign me to work You need me to do. Please keep me busy. Amen.

EVENING
TRUE FAITH

Those who won't care for their relatives, especially those in their own household,
have denied the true faith. Such people are worse than unbelievers.
1 TIMOTHY 5:8 NLT

True faith is believing that caring for others is more important than, well, anything else. True faith means sometimes putting ourselves in uncomfortable situations so that someone else may receive comfort. True faith is realizing that a momentary trial is worth the eternal reward of having our Father look at us and say, *"Well done."* True faith can mean putting up with complaints and crazy schedules and extra household work to make the last years of someone's life just a little bit easier. True faith means believing God can stretch our hearts to accept bigger families than we thought we could ever be able to love.

Lord, help me to look out for my relatives in the most honorable and loving way.

MORNING
IN GOD WE TRUST

Teach those who are rich in this world not to be proud and not to trust in their money, which is so unreliable. Their trust should be in God, who richly gives us all we need for our enjoyment.

1 TIMOTHY 6:17 NLT

God does not shift in value depending on the stock market, or the price of oil, or what battles are raging in faraway lands. No amount of human insecurity can touch God's everlasting consistency. And God is not just our Creator, not just our Sustainer, not just our Redeemer—He is our Provider. And He is our Friend. He knows everything that we need long before we need it. He knows everything that will please and delight us, even before we realize our need to be delighted. He is our loving, generous, gracious Father, ever ready to supply us with good gifts—even though we never did a thing to deserve them.

Why wouldn't we trust Him?

Father God, help me not to put my trust in earthly riches that will fade. Help me remember that all I ever need is You.

EVENING
A TRUSTWORTHY ANCHOR

So God has given both his promise and his oath. These two things are unchangeable because it is impossible for God to lie. Therefore, we who have fled to him for refuge can have great confidence as we hold to the hope that lies before us. This hope is a strong and trustworthy anchor for our souls. It leads us through the curtain into God's inner sanctuary.

HEBREWS 6:18–19 NLT

Thousands of years ago, God promised Abraham he would have a son. Although it took years for Abraham to see that promise be fulfilled, it did come to pass. Imagine the faith, patience, and trust Abraham needed to wait on God. But he had confidence that God would make good on His Word. And in God's grace and mercy, He did.

You too can count on the promises of God. As you do so, remember the patience of Abraham while riding out the storms with Jesus, your trustworthy Anchor.

Abba Father, I praise You for the many times You have been true to Your promises. Help me, amid my present storms, to remain anchored in Jesus.

MORNING
POWERFUL WORDS AND INSTRUCTIONS

In the past God spoke to our ancestors at many different times and in many different ways through the prophets. In these last days he has spoken to us through his Son. God made his Son responsible for everything. His Son is the one through whom God made the universe. His Son is the reflection of God's glory and the exact likeness of God's being. He holds everything together through his powerful words.

HEBREWS 1:1–3 GW

Today, consider meditating on God's Word. Reflect upon the instructions found in Proverbs 16:20 (NIV): "Whoever gives heed to instruction prospers, and blessed is the one who trusts in the LORD."

God will reward and prosper you as you study His Word and trust in Him—because through His Word, He's holding everything together, even the intricate details of your life!

*Father, help me to remain in Your Word. As I do,
may this increase my trust and awareness of You.*

EVENING
PURPOSE PREVAILS

All these people were known for their faith, but none of them received what God had promised. God planned to give us something very special so that we would gain eternal life with them.

HEBREWS 11:39–40 GW

Proverbs 19:21 (NIV) says, "Many are the plans in a person's heart, but it is the Lord's purpose that prevails." It's easy to see it was the Lord's purpose that prevailed in each and every one of the lives of Hebrews 11's heroes of faith. Sure, they may have had plans in their own heart. For example, Abraham and Sarah tried to "help" God by giving birth to Ishmael through their servant Hagar. Thankfully, they also repented and turned back to walking by faith, trusting in and waiting on God to fulfill His promise according to His timeline. And they were rewarded for doing so!

Whatever is going on in your life right now, commit it to Jesus. If He's given you a promise, hold on to it.

*Lord, I'm grateful that throughout history and my story,
Your purposes have always prevailed.*

MORNING
CONTENTMENT

Don't be obsessed with getting more material things. Be relaxed with what you have. Since God assured us, "I'll never let you down, never walk off and leave you," we can boldly quote, God is there, ready to help; I'm fearless no matter what. Who or what can get to me?

HEBREWS 13:5–6 MSG

If we trust in God, that He is for us, loves us, and is in control of our life, then trying to analyze or understand everything won't be something that consumes us. Instead, contentment can consume us. All of this sounds easier said than done, right? It happens through a process called *sanctification*. Sanctification occurs over time as the Holy Spirit works in our lives to mold us into the likeness of Jesus.

So when you have those moments where you become obsessed with trying to figure things out, stop, take a few deep breaths, and say out loud, "God, I trust You! I choose to be content!"

Abba Father, more than anything in this life, I desire contentment in You.

EVENING
TRUSTING IN TRIALS

Blessed is the one who perseveres under trial because, having stood the test, that person will receive the crown of life that the Lord has promised to those who love him.

JAMES 1:12 NIV

Have you ever found it challenging to trust God during a trial? Can you recall how you got through the test? Chances are you have a testimony that was cultivated, that came bubbling over from those pressure-cooker situations. In fact, chances are that one of the key ingredients that got you through was trusting God.

If you're walking through a trial right now, trust God. Even if you don't feel it, speak it. Consider saying these words out loud: "Lord Jesus, even though I don't feel it, I'm choosing to trust You. Even though my heart is heavy, and my soul is weak, I surrender all." Lord, may the words of my mouth and the meditations of my heart be pleasing to You. By faith, I thank You for blessing me with trials, believing such tests will be used to help me trust You more.

MORNING
REAP RIGHTEOUSNESS

But the wisdom that comes from heaven is first of all pure; then peace-loving, considerate, submissive, full of mercy and good fruit, impartial and sincere. Peacemakers who sow in peace reap a harvest of righteousness.
JAMES 3:17–18 NIV

Are you listening to God? Take a little inventory: How is the noise level in your life? Are you constantly running from one thing to the next? Do you feel worn out? Are you constantly filling what could be quiet time with constant chatter or noise like the radio, TV, or other forms of media?

If you want to reap the wisdom and righteousness that come from trusting in God, take some quiet time to be still and listen.

Lord, in these moments I have right now, help me listen to Your promptings.

EVENING
SPIRIT OF GOD

"Then my people will know that I am the LORD their God. I sent them into captivity among the nations, and I brought them back again to their land. I left none of them behind. I will no longer hide my face from them, because I will pour out my Spirit on the nation of Israel, declares the Almighty LORD."
EZEKIEL 39:28–29 GW

Proverbs 21:21 (GW) says: "Whoever pursues righteousness and mercy will find life, righteousness, and honor." As you pursue God, He'll fill you with more of Himself. As you trust God, you'll want to live in right standing with Him. He doesn't demand a perfect life from you, just one that is in relationship with Him. Ask Him for a new, fresh filling of His presence in your life. Trust that He'll supply enough for you.

Abba Father, I want to turn away from my sins. I ask for Your forgiveness and trust. I will receive it. Now, help me to forgive myself, and renew me by filling me with more of Your Holy Spirit.

MORNING
LET PRAYER SUSTAIN YOU

Then the king was exceedingly glad and commanded that Daniel should be taken up out of the den. So Daniel was taken up out of the den, and no hurt of any kind was found on him because he believed in (relied on, adhered to, and trusted in) his God.

DANIEL 6:23 AMPC

Daniel was found out and thrown into a den of hungry lions. Supernaturally, God delivered Daniel by shutting the lions' mouths so they could not harm him.

Life for most moves at a frenzied pace. Last-minute interruptions and busy schedules can easily push your time with God completely out of your day. Are you disciplined in prayer? If God can shut the lions' mouths for Daniel, then He can give you the time you need to do what's important when you give your time to Him in prayer first.

God, You have brought me through some pretty tough situations. Each time my confidence in You grows.

EVENING
ROCK-SOLID SAVIOR

Because of the Truth which lives and stays on in our hearts and will be with us forever: Grace (spiritual blessing), mercy, and [soul] peace will be with us, from God the Father and from Jesus Christ (the Messiah), the Father's Son, in all sincerity (truth) and love.

2 JOHN 2–3 AMPC

Your relationship with Jesus is the only thing that really offers you safety and stability while you navigate the violent maelstroms life often brings. When you can't depend on others, and maybe don't even trust yourself, you have a trustworthy, rock-solid Savior. He's the One you can always depend on. He faithfully points you in the way you should go. When life spins out of control, He stops the merry-go-round and with His truth helps you to focus.

Are you experiencing challenges that make you feel unstable right now? Ask Jesus to bring balance and stability tonight.

*Jesus, You are my stability. You are my strength.
I depend on Your truth to keep me in balance.*

MORNING
GOD IS UP TO SOMETHING GOOD

*Look around [you, Habakkuk, replied the Lord] among the nations and
see! And be astonished! Astounded! For I am putting into effect a work in
your days [such] that you would not believe it if it were told you.*
HABAKKUK 1:5 AMPC

Sometimes the difficulties you face can cause you to focus on what's not going right.
But you have a saving God. When things aren't going the way you'd hoped, look up. Ask
Him to help you tune in to Him. Open your eyes to see things from His perspective.

Even though you may not see it yet, God's at work, orchestrating an outcome that's
so much more than you imagined. He can turn your upside-down world right side up
again. You have a hope like no other. God is up to something good.

*God, I know You're at work in my life. Help me see even the smallest of positive things
You're doing. I give You praise for the good things about to happen even today.*

EVENING
RETURN TO HIM

*"So give to the people this Message from GOD-of-the-Angel-
Armies: 'Come back to me and I'll come back to you.'"*
ZECHARIAH 1:3 MSG

God wants His people to return to Him—and we all have the power to do so. In fact,
He wants us to return to Him even when we feel we don't deserve His favor or
forgiveness.

Take a few moments to look at your relationship with God. Do you feel distant
from Him? Are there things you need to share with Him in a way of returning to Him
with a willingness to serve Him fully and completely surrendered?

Zechariah 1:3 is a promise. Return to God—and He'll return to you.

*Heavenly Father, thank You for Your constant pursuit of relationship with me.
Tonight, I return to You and fully surrender all of my life to Your lordship.*

MORNING
A BLESSED LIFE

Blessed is the one who does not walk in step with the wicked or stand in the way that sinners take or sit in the company of mockers, but whose delight is in the law of the LORD, and who meditates on his law day and night. That person is like a tree planted by streams of water, which yields its fruit in season and whose leaf does not wither—whatever they do prospers.

PSALM 1:1–3 NIV

If you've accepted Christ as Savior, your life is made new. Gone are your old ways of thinking. . .you're on the path to righteous living! What's more, each and every one of the hundreds of promises in scripture are *yours* to claim.

Today, make a conscious decision to delight in the Lord. . .to meditate on His law. Don't live so you miss out on the blessings that God's Word promises. Let the theme of your life be one of beautiful transformation. You won't regret it!

Father God, I claim Your promise of blessing.

EVENING
A FAITHFUL FOCUS

After Jesus was born in Bethlehem village, Judah territory—this was during Herod's kingship—a band of scholars arrived in Jerusalem from the East. They asked around, "Where can we find and pay homage to the newborn King of the Jews? We observed a star in the eastern sky that signaled his birth. We're on pilgrimage to worship him."

MATTHEW 2:1–2 MSG

The lengthy journey of the wise men was likely arduous and not without uncertainty along the way. But still they persevered in faith and with focus. They traveled on, knowing they would eventually have the honor of being in the very presence of the long-awaited Messiah.

Like the wise men, our faith journey will not come without trials and tribulation. But we continue on, knowing that if we remain faithful and focused, actively seeking Jesus, He will see to it that we safely reach our final, heavenly destination—where we will spend eternity in praise and adoration of Him!

Father God, I trust You will help me to maintain a faithful focus.

MORNING
FROM DESPAIR TO HOPE

Many are saying of me, There is no help for him in God. Selah [pause, and calmly think of that]! But You, O Lord, are a shield for me, my glory, and the lifter of my head. With my voice I cry to the Lord, and He hears and answers me.
PSALM 3:2–4 AMPC

David could have easily allowed himself to be swayed by the world's words. But instead of allowing himself to wallow in despair, David recalled God's power, His faithfulness, His protection, and His love. David trusted in God and chose to cling to and focus on his heavenly Father, who "hears" and would no doubt restore David's joy.

As Christ followers, we can trust in our prayer-hearing God just as David did. . . and know without a doubt that God will lift our heads, offering us His protection and salvation from a world that wishes for our downfall. With our trust in God Almighty, we will overcome!

Father God, I praise You for the hope and joy I can find only in You!

EVENING
UNFAILING LOVE

Lord, do not rebuke me in your anger or discipline me in your wrath. Have mercy on me, Lord, for I am faint; heal me, Lord, for my bones are in agony. My soul is in deep anguish. How long, Lord, how long? Turn, Lord, and deliver me; save me because of your unfailing love.
PSALM 6:1–4 NIV

Like David, do thoughts of your sinful past interfere with a good night's sleep? Do your troubles weigh heavily on your spirit? Tonight is the night to approach the heavenly Father in bold confidence. Let Him know that you trust Him with the outcome. . .you trust Him to see you through to better days ahead. He will hear you, and He will act. Praise Him!

Heavenly Father, I trust You for my comfort. . .for deliverance from my troubles. Thank You for saving me!

MORNING
A STRONG FOUNDATION

Everyone who hears these words of Mine and acts upon them [obeying them] will be like a sensible. . .man who built his house upon the rock. And the rain fell and the floods came and the winds blew and beat against that house; yet it did not fall, because it had been founded on the rock.
MATTHEW 7:24–25 AMPC

These words of Jesus in Matthew 7 confirm that obedience to God *always* leads to a better life, creating a strong, faith-filled foundation to help you stand firm when the storms of life blow and batter against your weary soul. Allow your faithful obedience to transform your life—willingly give up your *imperfect* will for His *perfect* plan. Your house will stand strong!

Father God, help me build my house upon the Rock!

EVENING
A SURE FAITH

A centurion came to [Jesus]. . . . "Lord," he said, "my servant lies at home paralyzed, suffering terribly." Jesus said to him, "Shall I come and heal him?" The centurion replied, "Lord, I do not deserve to have you come under my roof. But just say the word, and my servant will be healed. . . ." When Jesus heard this, he was amazed and said to those following him, "Truly I tell you, I have not found anyone in Israel with such great faith."
MATTHEW 8:5–10 NIV

"*Just say the word*, and my servant will be healed," the centurion said to Jesus (emphasis added). Can you imagine a greater, surer faith than that? Just a *word* was all he asked for. . .nothing more, nothing less.

As a Christ follower, do you have a sure faith? The heavenly Father will assure your uncertain heart tonight! Just ask!

Father, I thank You for Your Word that gives me blessed assurance!

MORNING
YOUR RESCUER

*Break the arms of these wicked, evil people! Go after them until the last
one is destroyed. The LORD is king forever and ever! The godless nations
will vanish from the land. LORD, you know the hopes of the helpless. Surely
you will hear their cries and comfort them. You will bring justice to the
orphans and the oppressed, so mere people can no longer terrify them.*

PSALM 10:15–18 NLT

Maybe you've been bullied. . .cheated on. . .beat down. . . And maybe no one was there
to pick you up, dust you off, and breathe new life into your weary soul. If this is part of
your story, there is hope! As Psalm 10 states: "LORD, you know the hopes of the helpless. Surely you will hear their cries and comfort them."

And this same Lord Jesus promises to deliver you today. For He is your Rescuer. . .
the Justice Bringer. When you know Him as Your Lord and Savior, you never need to
feel helpless or hopeless again.

Lord Jesus, I look forward to the promise of heaven!

EVENING
PURE AND UNCHANGING

*Into the hovels of the poor, into the dark streets where the homeless groan,
God speaks: "I've had enough; I'm on my way to heal the ache in the heart
of the wretched." God's words are pure words, pure silver words refined seven
times in the fires of his word-kiln, pure on earth as well as in heaven.*

PSALM 12:5–7 MSG

When we've accepted Christ as our Lord and Savior, we can say with confidence, "He
will never let us down." He's in the business of promise keeping; His promises are a
sure thing. His words are pure.

The truth is:

Humans aren't trustworthy. . . God is.

Humans aren't faithful. . . God is.

Humans are promise breakers. . . God is a promise keeper.

Humans will fail us. . . God won't!

Where men and women fall short, God *always* comes through.

Promise-Keeper, my Savior, I trust in You alone.

MORNING
A LOVELY CAUSE FOR CELEBRATION

Take a good look at me, GOD, my God; I want to look life in the eye,
so no enemy can get the best of me or laugh when I fall on my face. I've
thrown myself headlong into your arms—I'm celebrating your rescue.
I'm singing at the top of my lungs, I'm so full of answered prayers.
PSALM 13:3–6 MSG

The old you may have been fearful, insecure, doubtful, depressed, and dismayed. But when you accepted the gift of salvation, you surely felt a significant shift within your spirit. With the power of Jesus Christ in you, you're rescued from the burdens that weigh down the soul. And a growing relationship with the heavenly Father brings about feelings of courage, confidence, belief, joy, and contentment. . .just the things you need to fulfill the wonderful purpose God has for you!

Father God, thank You for the lovely transformation You've
begun in my life. Because of You, I am a new creation!

EVENING
MORE JESUS

"Are you tired? Worn out? Burned out on religion? Come to me. Get
away with me and you'll recover your life. I'll show you how to take a
real rest. Walk with me and work with me—watch how I do it. Learn the
unforced rhythms of grace. I won't lay anything heavy or ill-fitting on you.
Keep company with me and you'll learn to live freely and lightly."
MATTHEW 11:28–30 MSG

When was the last time you had a real, honest-to-goodness rest? The kind that refreshes you both mentally and physically, that makes you feel completely revitalized and alive?

Instead of more *busy* in your life, get more of *Jesus*. He is just what your weary soul needs. He will pull you from the depths of your day-to-day burnout and give you rest like you've never experienced it before—a rest that leads to free and light living! Praise Him!

Father God, Rest-Giver, comfort my world-weary soul tonight. I am
exhausted! I trust You to show me the way to refreshing rest. Thank You!

MORNING
KNOWING HE WILL ANSWER

I am praying to you because I know you will answer,
O God. Bend down and listen as I pray.
PSALM 17:6 NLT

Imagine God bending down from heaven, intently looking you in the eye—you have His full attention. He's focused and waiting to hear what you have to share with Him. Now get this: that's what praying to God is really like. He is *that* focused on you! Talking with Him is like having a conversation with a friend who's the best listener on earth.

So if you've ever questioned whether the Father hears everything that's on your heart, ask Him to assure your spirit, to help you move from uncertain to knowing. Then thank Him for His love, one that is bigger than anything you could ever imagine.

Heavenly Father, thank You for being the best listener a girl could ever hope
for. . .thank You for helping to grow my trust in Your unfailing love!

EVENING
FINDING SHELTER IN THE STORMS

I love you, LORD; you are my strength. The LORD is my rock, my fortress,
and my savior; my God is my rock, in whom I find protection. He is my
shield, the power that saves me, and my place of safety. I called on the
LORD, who is worthy of praise, and he saved me from my enemies.
PSALM 18:1–3 NLT

When you have accepted Jesus as Lord and Leader of your life, you have a Protector on standby. He's waiting and ready to step in and provide shelter, a safe place where you will find strength and security just when you need it most. Call out to Him, and He will see you through the storm. Hold tightly to Him tonight!

Father, You are worthy of all my praise. In You I
find the peace and protection my soul craves.

MORNING
BEAUTIFUL BEGINNINGS

God made my life complete when I placed all the pieces before him. . . . God
rewrote the text of my life when I opened the book of my heart to his eyes.
PSALM 18:20, 24 MSG

While life with Jesus certainly isn't all sunshine and rainbows, this new way of living does have its perks. With God in the lead, you always have a guide to help you navigate the messiness of life. You have someone by your side to help you make sense of the madness, to turn your chaos into peace.

Truth is, God's story for you is so much better than anything you could ever write on your own. So don't attempt to write it all by yourself. Make sure you hand over the pen to the heavenly Author Himself. He'll see to it that your story of transformation has a beautiful, eternal theme of hope and security.

Father, thank You for rewriting my life story!

EVENING
LIFESAVING 101

Examine yourselves as to whether you are in the faith. Test yourselves.
Do you not know yourselves, that Jesus Christ is in you?
2 CORINTHIANS 13:5 NKJV

How many times do we almost drown in the floodwaters of fear? How often are we overcome by waves of discontent or pulled by currents of doubt? How often do we forget that Jesus Christ, the Master of the Universe, is within us?

Jesus, the One with the power to rebuke the winds and calm the waters, is our lifesaver. The knowledge that He is within us boosts us up above the waves of fear and into the peace of His presence. When caught up in the riptides of life, we are to examine ourselves to make sure we are acknowledging the fact that Christ resides within us. Buoyed by His presence, we can withstand the storm and rise up in the power of His strength.

Jesus, You are the one who has saved my life, the one who resides within me.
Give me the wisdom to keep this in my mind throughout my day, and give me
the power to do Your will in this world, knowing You have overcome it. Amen.

MORNING
PERFECT PEACE

You will keep in perfect peace all who trust in you, all whose thoughts are fixed on you! Trust in the LORD always, for the LORD GOD is the eternal Rock.
ISAIAH 26:3–4 NLT

Our lives are a series of moments. And that's what our minds get caught up in, the day-to-day minutiae, the little niggling worries, the what-ifs, the how-comes, and the why-fors. But God wants us to have a different perspective, not an in-the-moment viewpoint but an eternal one.

So fix your mind on the One who sees and knows so much more than you ever will. Put your confidence in the One who has your name written on the palm of His hand. Practice being in His presence during quiet hours. And then, the moment stress and chaos begin creeping in, call God to mind, and He will surround you with that big-picture, perfect peace.

I need Your perfect peace, God. Take me out of the present and into Your presence where peace will reign and blessings abound.

EVENING
FLAWLESS!

As for God, his way is perfect: The LORD's word is flawless; he shields all who take refuge in him. For who is God besides the LORD? And who is the Rock except our God? It is God who arms me with strength and keeps my way secure.
PSALM 18:30–32 NIV

While there are many things in life that bring us sheer delight because of their wonderful qualities, the truth is none of those things is truly perfect or flawless. But you *do* know someone who is the very definition of flawless Himself: the Lord and Savior, Jesus Christ. And He alone offers just what you need—security, strength, protection, comfort, and more! He is your Shield and your Rock. He sets you on the right path with His flawless Word and ways.

Praise Him for drawing your heart near to His, for being the perfection you need today and all your days to come.

My Redeemer, I thank You for Your flawless ways, for Your perfect Word that guides my life!

MORNING
GOD'S PERFECT LAWS

The law of the LORD is perfect, refreshing the soul. The statutes of the LORD are trustworthy, making wise the simple. The precepts of the LORD are right, giving joy to the heart. The commands of the LORD are radiant, giving light to the eyes.

PSALM 19:7–8 NIV

No matter how good man-made laws are, they all fall short—which is why many laws are often amended over time. In contrast, the laws of our heavenly Father are "perfect," "trustworthy," and stand firm forever. His commands are righteous—because they stem from His goodness and love.

The bottom line? God is good. And obeying His laws and commands will *always* lead to good things as well. If you're in need of a soul refreshing today, ask Him to give you His wisdom and to lead you all your days. Commit to obeying His laws—and your heart will be filled with joy!

Heavenly Father, thank You for Your perfect, enduring laws. You are so, so good, and I love You!

EVENING
NOTHING BUT GOOD PLANS

In times of trouble, may the LORD answer your cry. . . . May he grant your heart's desires and make all your plans succeed. May we shout for joy when we hear of your victory and raise a victory banner in the name of our God. May the LORD answer all your prayers.

PSALM 20:1, 4–5 NLT

Whether you're asking God for hope, healing, help, or safety from harm, you can know with certainty that He will do what's best for you—He has nothing but good plans for you, sister! His promise in Jeremiah 29:11 (NIV) says, "For I know the plans I have for you. . .plans to prosper you and not to harm you, plans to give you hope and a future."

So pray with complete confidence to the One who offers protection, strength, hope, and success and know that an answer is coming your way!

Heavenly Father, You love me and want only the best for me. Thank You for Your answers to my prayers!

MORNING
THE GOD OF POSSIBLE!

Jesus. . .took the five loaves and two fish, lifted his face to heaven in prayer, blessed, broke, and gave the bread to the disciples. The disciples then gave the food to the congregation. They all ate their fill. They gathered twelve baskets of leftovers.
MATTHEW 14:18–21 MSG

The famished crowd was impossibly large. Feeding a group of five thousand men, women, and children would have been no small task, even if the supplies had been readily available. But Jesus didn't hesitate to ask for what little food there was. He seemed quite sure of Himself—and He remedied the situation! Jesus multiplied the amount of food—enough that each person was able to eat—*and there were leftovers!*

When life throws seemingly impossible situations your way, remember the story of the fives loaves and two fish, and know that the same God who fed the five thousand can handle whatever hardship you're facing today.

Father God, I believe! I know You can help with any situation—even the impossible ones!

EVENING
ERASING YOUR FEARS

The LORD is my shepherd; I shall not want. . . . Even though I walk through the valley of the shadow of death, I will fear no evil, for you are with me; your rod and your staff, they comfort me.
PSALM 23:1, 4 ESV

No matter *what* you fear and no matter *how big* your fear, it can be erased—because of Jesus! He will calm your deepest, darkest fears. And because of His loving sacrifice on the cross, even the fear of death can be overcome! What a beautiful promise His Word gives you: "For God so loved the world that he gave his one and only Son, that whoever believes in him shall not perish but have eternal life" (John 3:16 NIV).

Jesus died so that you might live and spend eternity in heaven! If you haven't already, say yes to His gift of fearless living!

Lord Jesus, thank You for saving me! Help me to overcome my fears!

MORNING
PERFECTLY IN STEP

Clear my name, GOD; I've kept an honest shop. I've thrown in my lot with
you, GOD, and I'm not budging. Examine me, GOD, from head to foot,
order your battery of tests. Make sure I'm fit inside and out so I never lose
sight of your love, but keep in step with you, never missing a beat.
PSALM 26:1–3 MSG

If you've accepted Jesus Christ as Lord and Leader of Your life, you share a bond with Him that can never be broken. Simply trust Him to keep your spiritual "fitness" in check, and you'll never lose sight of His amazing, unconditional love. You can be confident that, no matter what life brings, the Lord will keep you on the right path—staying in step with Him—so you won't waver in your Christian journey.

Father, examine me; know my heart. I long to keep in
step with You today and all my days to come.

EVENING
FOLLOWING YOUR HEART

Jesus. . .said to them, "Why do you trouble the woman? For she has done a
beautiful thing to me. . . . Truly, I say to you, wherever this gospel is proclaimed
in the whole world, what she has done will also be told in memory of her."
MATTHEW 26:10, 13 ESV

Some days you may feel nameless. That what you do in this world seems to have little effect. Yet when you allow God and His Spirit to work in your heart and hold sway over your actions, you too will find yourself doing beautiful things for Jesus, in His name. And your deeds on His behalf will never be forgotten.

Show me what I can do tonight to worship You, Jesus. To honor You as Your and
God's Spirit work in me. Direct my heart and move my hands to do beautiful things.

MORNING
AS THE SON RISES

Now in the morning, having risen a long while before daylight,
He went out and departed to a solitary place; and there He prayed.
MARK 1:35 NKJV

How is your daily prayer life? Are you making going to God your first priority? And what happens after you pray? Do you expect anything in your day to change? Are you placing all your hope and expectations in God (Psalm 39:7) and His power or in yourself and your own strength?

Perhaps it's time to reenergize your prayer life. Consider setting your alarm five, ten, fifteen, or twenty minutes earlier than usual, giving you time to seek God's face before anyone else in the house stirs.

Today, make it a priority to go to God in prayer, expecting Him to meet all your needs—and more!

Father, help me make meeting alone with You my first and most blessed priority.

EVENING
A WILLING JESUS

Now a leper came to Him, imploring Him, kneeling down to Him and saying to Him,
"If You are willing, You can make me clean." Then Jesus, moved with compassion,
stretched out His hand and touched him, and said to him, "I am willing; be cleansed."
MARK 1:40–41 NKJV

Jesus' heart was deeply stirred at seeing this man's plight. And He not only stated His willingness to make the leper clean but prefaced it by actually stretching out His hand and touching him! Then, "as soon as He had spoken, immediately the leprosy left him, and he was cleansed" (Mark 1:42 NKJV).

No matter where you are, what you've done, how much of an outcast you are, Jesus doesn't just *see* you. He reaches *out* for you. But first you must come to Him, humbly, believing He's willing to help you, that He will effect in you a change—for the better.

Jesus, if You are willing, I humbly ask You to. . .

MORNING
HEART—AND MIND—GUARD

For as he thinks in his heart, so is he.
PROVERBS 23:7 NKJV

Why not take a leap of faith today? Ask God to help you change any thoughts that are contrary to His will and way, to give you the verses you need to hear and focus on, ones that will change your life (and mind) around. Choose the blessings He has brought before you (Deuteronomy 30:19). Allow Him to transform you into a new person by changing the way you think (Romans 12:2). Pray God would help you dismiss thoughts and opinions that are not in line with His, "and take every thought captive to obey Christ" (2 Corinthians 10:5 ESV).

Change up your mind to God's way of thinking, and He'll change your life.

Lord, help me monitor my thoughts and guard my heart.
Change my mind to Your way of thinking.

EVENING
CONSTANT PRAYER

Be unceasing in prayer.
1 THESSALONIANS 5:17 AMPC

Nonstop prayer? How can we ever achieve that in our hectic world? By our awareness of God. Through it, we become conscious of Him and discern His active involvement in our lives. God wants to have a relationship with us, and prayer demonstrates our faith in Him. His Word tells us to stay in constant contact.

Prayer strengthens us for any battle. It's our armor and our mightiest weapon against fear, doubt, discouragement, and worry. Prayer changes our perspective and allows us to face the cares of each day. When our whole world is falling apart, prayer can keep us together.

Dear Father, I want to be in the center of Your will.
Please help me to "be unceasing in prayer."

MORNING
WHAT'S THAT UP AHEAD?

The bride, a princess, looks glorious in her golden gown. In her beautiful
robes, she is led to the king, accompanied by her bridesmaids. What a
joyful and enthusiastic procession as they enter the king's palace!
PSALM 45:13–15 NLT

Psalm 45 celebrates the joys and anticipations of weddings and the changes that come along with marriage, but it also invites you to think about the other ways in which you are transformed over time, whether it be owing to professions, relocations, or simply aging. You can reflect on the joys of these changes and the positive anticipations that can come with them. You can look for the beauty in them. How often are you made over new through life changes?

Lord, let me look for Your glory in each season of life.

EVENING
STRENGTH IN LOVING FORGIVENESS

"Now may the Lord's strength be displayed, just as you have declared: 'The
LORD *is slow to anger, abounding in love and forgiving sin and rebellion. . . .'*
In accordance with your great love, forgive the sin of these people, just as
you have pardoned them from the time they left Egypt until now."
NUMBERS 14:17–19 NIV

Here we find Moses interceding before God for the rebellious Israelites. Having received bad reports about the Promised Land, the Israelites begin to complain bitterly to Moses and Aaron. The Lord is so exasperated by the people that He's ready to destroy them and create anew. Moses implores God not to destroy but to forgive the Israelites.

When things are going poorly in our lives and a bright future seems doubtful, how often do we blame God for what has gone awry? How often do we fail to ask God for the strength and fortitude we need to envision a brighter future both in the world and within ourselves?

Lord, transform my heart when it weakens in the face of life's troubles.

MORNING
MY BANNER AND MY SHIELD

For those who fear you, you have raised a banner to be unfurled against the bow.
Save us and help us with your right hand, that those you love may be delivered.
PSALM 60:4–5 NIV

In the world, there will be shows of power, demonstrations and strikes, petitions and drives of all sorts. But those are all nothing in comparison to the strength that comes from an alliance with God. For God loves you with a love far greater and far beyond the love of any human being. And God knows your needs. So the psalmist sings to Him to "save us and help us with your right hand."

Dear God, help us place our trust in You in times of trouble and desperation. Amen.

EVENING
PRAISE GOD

Because your love is better than life, my lips will glorify you. I will praise you as long as I live, and in your name I will lift up my hands. I will be fully satisfied as with the richest of foods; with singing lips my mouth will praise you.
PSALM 63:3–5 NIV

Life is good. But the love of the Lord is better than life. For it is the love of the Lord that gives meaning to life.

With the love of the Lord, the soul is filled and satisfied as with the finest food. It is filled with the kind of joy that brings a song to the lips spontaneously, a song of praise that never ceases.

How often are you drawn to look around and see the love of God in its various forms? How often are you moved like the psalmist to sing the praises of God, whose love is better than life?

Dear God, please draw me closer to You. Help me to feel
Your love as better than life, prompting me to praise.

MORNING
LOVE ON DISPLAY

When we were overwhelmed by sins, you forgave our transgressions.
PSALM 65:3 NIV

As you realize the depth of your sin and that God's forgiveness is deeper still, you can willingly pour out all that is precious to you for Him. You can make your lives a bold display of your love for the One who forgives and makes you new. You can hear Jesus' words every day: "Your faith has saved you; go in peace" (Luke 7:50 NIV).

Lord, I kneel today seeking forgiveness. I've sinned, and right now the sin weighs heavily on me. But You are able to remove that sin and replace it with Your forgiveness, Your peace. Thank You!

EVENING
WAIT FOR IT. . . .

"A sower went out to sow his seed. . . . And some fell into good soil and grew and yielded a hundredfold."
LUKE 8:5, 8 ESV

When we hear God's Word and believe, it grows down deep into our hearts, and through Him we begin to yield a crop. Yet don't miss Jesus' words on how we bear fruit—*with patience.* The New International Version translates the end of verse 15: "and by persevering produce a crop." The Message says: "sticking with it until there's a harvest." But let's face it, in a fast-paced, instant-download culture, aren't we more likely to become *impatient* waiting for that bounty of fruit? While some fruit we do see immediately, often the working of God in our lives takes time. As we continue to obey, though—as we persevere and stick with it—we *will* see a harvest!

God, I want to be fruitful. Help me hold Your Word fast in my heart and not give up before I yield an abundance of good works for You.

MORNING
WHAT ARE YOU WAITING FOR?

"Woe to you, Chorazin! Woe to you, Bethsaida! For if the mighty works done in you had been done in Tyre and Sidon, they would have repented long ago."
LUKE 10:13 ESV

Dealing with sin in our lives isn't easy, but as God forms us from the inside to be more like Christ, repenting of bad behavior and living in obedience is vital. We shouldn't close our ears to the things God calls us to do and be like the unrepentant cities that Jesus spoke about. Think on what Moses told Israel: "All these blessings shall come upon you and overtake you, if you obey the voice of the LORD your God. Blessed shall you be in the city, and blessed shall you be in the field. . . . Blessed shall you be when you come in, and blessed shall you be when you go out" (Deuteronomy 28:2–3, 6 ESV).

Is God whispering to your heart? Don't wait.

Father, please forgive me and help me start fresh.

EVENING
WORRILESS

Fear not, little flock; for it is your Father's good pleasure to give you the kingdom.
LUKE 12:32 KJV

Since worry achieves nothing but more worry, what should you do instead? "Seek the Kingdom of God above all else, and he will give you everything you need" (Luke 12:31 NLT). Your God—the One who fills the bellies of the birds and clothes the lilies like royalty—knows your needs, and He is capable and faithful to satisfy them. More than that, it is His *pleasure* to care for you. So turn every anxious thought into a chance to focus on your Father. With eyes fixed on Him, the kingdom itself is yours.

Father, use this anxiety to draw me toward You. I can be calm because You care.

MORNING
PASS THE SALT, PLEASE

"Salt is good, but if it loses its saltiness, how can it be made salty
again? It is fit neither for the soil nor for the manure pile; it is
thrown out. Whoever has ears to hear, let them hear."
LUKE 14:34–35 NIV

In a rotting world, we as believers need to be salt—*and* to maintain our saltiness! To do this, we're to have salt in ourselves (Mark 9:50). But the source of that pure salt isn't us; it's God. His Word and the Spirit rubbed into our hearts not only stop the decay but also reverse the damage, making us new and seasoning our interactions with Him and others.

So no skimping on the purest of salt. Add whole cupfuls of scripture and prayer to your day, and let the world see what salt can do.

I can't be salt without You, Lord. Keep me salty so others will notice and seek You.

EVENING
TRUST HIM

Not one of all their enemies had withstood them. . . .
Not one word of all the good promises that the LORD had
made to the house of Israel had failed; all came to pass.
JOSHUA 21:44–45 ESV

Can I trust God? Has that thought ever crossed your mind? When looking for an answer, don't overlook the Word. It's a sixty-six-book chronicle of God's faithfulness—from the beginning of time to the end times—that you can hold in one hand.

You have the record of how God kept His promise in the book of Joshua. True, your eyes might glaze over as you read the lists of allotments and inheritances, but the detail goes to show the intimacy of the Lord in His children's lives, the meticulous attention He gives to the ones He loves.

God hasn't changed since then and never will (Hebrews 13:8).

God, You are faithful from generation to generation, age to age, time without end.
Whatever You've done in my life and whatever You're going to do, I can trust You.

MORNING
A NEW RÉSUMÉ

Jesus said to him, "Today salvation has come to this house, because this man, too, is a son of Abraham. For the Son of Man came to seek and to save the lost."
LUKE 19:9–10 NIV

Zacchaeus: chief tax collector, wealthy, disloyal to the Jews. He would receive Jesus joyfully, repent of his old ways, and make restitution. Zacchaeus's new résumé read "son of Abraham; saved by the Lord."

Jesus came to seek and save sinners—people like Zacchaeus, like us. While the crowds grumbled and thought of Zacchaeus as beyond redemption, Jesus knew better. *No one* is barred from salvation because *nothing* is impossible for God. He can radically change even the worst sinners (1 Timothy 1:15).

Yes, Jesus came to seek and save sinners, to change lives. How will He revise your résumé?

Lord, give me eyes to see as You see. You look through the sin to the soul, to the difference You can make there. Rewrite my life as I seek You.

EVENING
KNOW YOUR PURPOSE

"You will become pregnant and give birth to a son, and his hair must never be cut. For he will be dedicated to God as a Nazirite from birth. He will begin to rescue Israel from the Philistines."
JUDGES 13:5 NLT

Although you may sometimes feel small and insignificant and unable to do anything really worthwhile in this messed-up world, know this: when God designed your life, He didn't roll the dice and arbitrarily place you. No, He crafted your unique position—the years you live, the family you belong to, the career you pursue, the friends you choose, your passions and abilities—to give you the opportunity to make an everlasting impact on the world. Big, earth-changing revivals or small, personal kindnesses alike—you can make a difference.

God, please show me how to make an everlasting impact. Use me, Father.

MORNING
SERVANT LEADERS

*"Those who are the greatest among you should take the lowest
rank, and the leader should be like a servant."*
LUKE 22:26 NLT

By being a servant—choosing to honor others above Himself—Jesus demonstrated just one aspect of the upside-down nature of God's kingdom. The first will be last and the last will be first (Matthew 19:30). To have new life in Christ, one must give up one's life (Matthew 16:24–25). Return hate with love (Romans 12:19–21). True wealth results from giving generously (Luke 6:38).

Not one aspect of Jesus' teaching is easy; each rubs against the grain of our selfish desires. But they are surprisingly simple. And the rewards of doing as Jesus said (and as He does) are immeasurable—both as a peaceful present and as a joyful future.

*Jesus, fix my vision to see and fully understand Your right-side-
up kingdom. I will serve. I will love. I will give. Amen.*

EVENING
KEEP YOUR GUARD UP

About an hour later, someone else spoke up, really adamant: "He's got to have been with him! He's got 'Galilean' written all over him." Peter said, "Man, I don't know what you're talking about." At that very moment, the last word hardly off his lips, a rooster crowed.
LUKE 22:59–60 MSG

We, like Peter, are vulnerable to temptation—especially during times of great stress. Hard lines we've set for ourselves get blurry as we struggle through difficulties. But, when in the Garden of Gethsemane, Jesus gave us an example of what to do to resist:
1. Pray (Mark 14:35).
2. Seek support of others (Mark 14:33, 37, 40, 41).
3. Focus on God's purpose for you (Mark 14:36).

Peter's story doesn't end at the rooster crow. He found redemption and forgiveness through Jesus and went on to do mighty works in forming the early church. Don't let your failures define you either. God can and will use a willing and humble heart for great things.

Jesus, create in me a pure heart that resists temptation. I'm living for You and You only!

MORNING
NOT A GHOST

*"Why are you troubled, and why do doubts rise in your minds?
Look at my hands and my feet. It is I myself! Touch me and see; a
ghost does not have flesh and bones, as you see I have."*
LUKE 24:38–40 NIV

Following Christ sometimes means you don't have all the *why* and *how* answers to your questions. Scripture tells you that living a life of faith requires setting aside your human desire to understand the whole picture (see 2 Corinthians 5:7; Hebrews 11). But while Jesus, in His newly risen body, isn't here with you today, He *will* give you clarity and insight through His Word if you continually seek Him there.

*Jesus, give me a hunger for Your Word and clarity
from its living, powerful message. Amen.*

EVENING
ALWAYS A BEST MAN

"He must become greater and greater, and I must become less and less."
JOHN 3:30 NLT

What was John's secret to humility? God had given him a heart for the Messiah—an uncanny understanding of the hope Christ's salvation would bring to the world. John was tapped into the power of God, and nothing would distract his focus.

What about you? What singular calling has God placed on your life? Ask Him to make that calling clear and to show you how amid your ministry—and life—Jesus will become greater and you less.

*Father, may the love of Jesus overtake my thoughts, actions, and speech in
everything so that my circle no longer sees me—but a beautiful reflection of You.*

MORNING
THE HEART'S JUDGE

*"The LORD doesn't see things the way you see them. People judge
by outward appearance, but the LORD looks at the heart."*
1 SAMUEL 16:7 NLT

When God sent Samuel to Bethlehem to find King Saul's replacement among Jesse's sons, Samuel thought he had a pretty good idea who was God's "type." But before Samuel could crack open the anointing oil, God warned him against judging on appearance alone.

God knows it's human nature to judge by how someone looks. But appearance doesn't reveal the true self or a person's actual value. God judges on heart and character. And because only He can see what's on the inside, only He can judge fairly.

If you're like most women, your daily outer-beauty routine is almost second nature. But how about your *inner*-beauty routine? Are you putting in enough time to cultivate the true beauty God looks for?

God, fill me with Your pure and holy love. Amen.

EVENING
OUR GREATER PURPOSE

*"For I have come down from heaven, not to do
my own will but the will of him who sent me."*
JOHN 6:38 ESV

Jesus understood God's plan in a personal way that gave Him a mission unlike any other human in the past or in the future. Doing God's will meant that Jesus' actions and decisions had a greater purpose than His own human desires and temptations. For us, that means that we don't have to make an educated guess about what God's will is. God's written instruction for our lives comes down to four simple letters: L-O-V-E.

Take comfort in the fact that you're working for All of Creation's Greatest Boss. Follow His instruction, carry out His will, and live a life of greater purpose.

God, give me a Christlike desire to lay aside my own will and do only Yours.

MORNING
MICHAL'S MISSTEP

As the ark of the LORD was entering the City of David, Michal daughter of Saul watched from a window. And when she saw King David leaping and dancing before the LORD, she despised him in her heart.

2 SAMUEL 6:16 NIV

Bitterness and resentment are insidious emotions that may simmer on the back burner of a relationship for some time before coming to a boil. But bitterness has no power to change circumstances, and resentment only makes a bad situation worse. Left unchecked, they can destroy a relationship. Although you may not have control over what happens to you, you *do* control how you respond. When you feel those simmering emotions, reset, ask God for clarity, and deal with your feelings.

God, I cannot live with this bitterness in my heart. Cleanse me and give me a new heart full of love and patience.

EVENING
PROVE TO THE WORLD

"So now I am giving you a new commandment: Love each other. Just as I have loved you, you should love each other. Your love for one another will prove to the world that you are my disciples."

JOHN 13:34–35 NLT

It's easy to fall out with people, especially in today's volatile political climate. But God longs for His kids to enjoy fellowship. Don't rob yourself of that by letting animosity get in the way. Tear down walls. Learn to love so that a watching world will catch a glimpse of Jesus from your example. As God transforms your heart, offer it to others as a gift.

Father, I want to prove to the world that I'm a lover, not a hater. It's not easy, I confess. But You've shown me in Your Word, Lord, that there's a better way to be a light to others.

MORNING
GUIDED INTO TRUTH

*"But when he, the Spirit of truth, comes, he will guide you into
all the truth. He will not speak on his own; he will speak only
what he hears, and he will tell you what is yet to come."*
JOHN 16:13 NIV

So many people are aiming themselves at happiness instead of following the Spirit's lead toward truth. What good would it do you if you found one but missed the other?

Today, yield to the Holy Spirit. Follow His course. Relinquish yourself to the sovereign hand of God. He wants the very best for you and is the only One capable of bringing you into the fullness of His truth.

*Father, thank You for the reminder that this Christian walk isn't just about my
happiness, though I know You want me to experience fullness of joy. It's about finding
truth in You. Guide me, Holy Spirit; nudge me in the direction I need to go.*

EVENING
TAKE HEART

*"I have told you all this so that you may have peace in me. Here on earth you will
have many trials and sorrows. But take heart, because I have overcome the world."*
JOHN 16:33 NLT

When Jesus says to "*take* heart" (emphais added), He's implying that somewhere along the way you may have *lost* heart. But not to worry. As God transforms your life, He will gift you with His courage and peace, hope and confidence, joy and patience. For He works to replace your fearful, discouraged, worry-filled, and broken heart with His. When you yield yourself to the Master's ministrations, you'll experience His supernatural ability to overcome any circumstance that might come your way. What an amazing heart swap that would be!

*Father, how grateful I am that You have overcome the world!
I would despair, otherwise. Thank You for the reminder that
You're my Courage Giver, my Peace, my Overcomer.*

MORNING
HIS GLORIOUS PRESENCE

When the priests came out of the Holy Place, a thick cloud filled the Temple
of the LORD. The priests could not continue their service because of the cloud,
for the glorious presence of the LORD filled the Temple of the LORD.

1 KINGS 8:10–11 NLT

What do you picture as you read those words from 1 Kings—a magnificent cloud, weighty with the glory of God? The hum of an angelic chorus with an unfamiliar but heavenly melody pouring forth? Goosebumps on your arms and shivers running down your back?

If you've ever been in a service where God's presence was undeniable, then you've had a small foretaste of what's to come once you make the transition to heaven. Until then, keep pressing in. Draw close. Experience God's glory on a new level. Make room for the Spirit of God, and He will overwhelm You with His presence.

Father, I want to know You more! I want to experience Your
glorious presence, as men and women did in days of old.

EVENING
RESTING IN HIS SHADOW

Whoever dwells in the shelter of the Most High will rest in the shadow of the Almighty.
I will say of the LORD, "He is my refuge and my fortress, my God, in whom I trust."

PSALM 91:1–2 NIV

Finding the time to bask in God's presence, resting heart, mind, and spirit, is critical to survival! The Lord longs for you to draw close, to experience His goodness, His heart, His words of wisdom for whatever situation you happen to be walking through.

Where are you now? Are you resting in God's shadow or striving in the shadows of life? Run to Him right now and experience true rest.

Father, I'm so tired of striving! I'm constantly going, 'round the clock, trying to
figure things out on my own. I give up! Help me learn how to rest in You.

MORNING
IT'S YOU, OH LORD

When I said, "My foot is slipping," your unfailing love, LORD, supported me.
When anxiety was great within me, your consolation brought me joy.
PSALM 94:18–19 NIV

If you've ever walked through a particularly difficult period, you know what it's like to feel deflated.

When you hit your jumping-off point, God is right there, catching you midleap. When your feet are stuck in clay, He reaches down and plucks you up again. When the stresses are weighing you down, bringing nothing but tears and despair, He consoles and brings joy.

God cares deeply about your situation, and He longs to be your all in all. Don't give up on Him. He will never give up on you.

I needed that reminder, Lord, that You will never give up on me. So many times, my feet have slipped out from under me, but I can count on You not to let me go, Father. I'm so very grateful for that.

EVENING
A JUST KING

The King's strength also loves justice; you have established equity;
you have executed justice and righteousness in Jacob.
PSALM 99:4 NKJV

Aren't you glad God is a just King? He doesn't discriminate. He doesn't just randomly issue orders for one person to rule over another. He longs for equity and righteousness. Tonight, if you've been treated unjustly—at the hands of someone you thought you could trust or someone in your school or workplace—give your situation to God. He longs to heal the pain caused by the unjust treatment. At the same time, He wants to show *you* how to treat others fairly.

What seems "just" to some might be unjust to You, Lord. I'm so glad You're a just Father, one who makes all things right in the end. Thank You, Father.

MORNING
ABOVE REPROACH

I will search for faithful people to be my companions. Only those who are above reproach will be allowed to serve me. I will not allow deceivers to serve in my house, and liars will not stay in my presence.

PSALM 101:6–7 NLT

God is searching the earth for people who want to live godly lives, people who've turned their backs on sin and are willing to follow wholeheartedly after Him. And He's not just looking at famous/well-known people either. He's checking out the supermarket clerk, the mail carrier, the single mom, the CEO, the high school coach, the secretary, and so on. And He's finding willing candidates, those who say, "I will do my best to live for You and not bring shame to Your name, Lord."

Have you made a faith-filled commitment to your heavenly Father? If not, today is the perfect day to do so.

Father, today I recommit myself to You. I want to be who I say I am, a woman above reproach. May my name always bring joy to Your heart.

EVENING
FACE-TO-FACE

But he, being full of the Holy Spirit, gazed into heaven and saw the glory of God, and Jesus standing at the right hand of God, and said, "Look! I see the heavens opened and the Son of Man standing at the right hand of God!"

ACTS 7:55–56 NKJV

Heaven will be wonderful, but our focus won't be on all of the shimmer and shine. It will be on the One at the right hand of the Father—Jesus, our Savior. All that we've waited for, all that we've longed for, will be complete in that moment, as we gaze at Him face-to-face.

As you think about eternity, don't let fear take root. You won't be losing your life here—or there! You'll be gaining an amazing life that will continue forever in the presence of God.

Father, I can hardly wait to see heaven for myself. How glorious it will be!

MORNING
REGAIN SIGHT

So Ananias went and found Saul. He laid his hands on him and said, "Brother Saul, the Lord Jesus, who appeared to you on the road, has sent me so that you might regain your sight and be filled with the Holy Spirit." Instantly something like scales fell from Saul's eyes, and he regained his sight. Then he got up and was baptized. Afterward he ate some food and regained his strength. Saul stayed with the believers in Damascus for a few days.

ACTS 9:17–19 NLT

The same God who helped Saul regain his sight is the same God who wants to help you regain eyes of faith. If you don't know where to start, look up and praise God for the good things He has already done. Praise Him for how He wants to increase your faith. Then when He works in Your life, let all that you are praise the Lord (Psalm 103:22).

Jesus, I'm in need of Your touch. Help me regain strength in You and have the faith to believe You are transforming me.

EVENING
LISTENING AND MOVING

And Hezekiah prayed before the LORD and said: "O LORD, the God of Israel, enthroned above the cherubim, you are the God, you alone, of all the kingdoms of the earth; you have made heaven and earth."

2 KINGS 19:15 ESV

When you pray, know this: God hears you! You might not see anything happen immediately, right before your eyes. But you can trust that the God of the universe is listening and moving behind the scenes for your good. And even though you might not even feel any different after you pray, you can be sure you've done something courageous. You humbled yourself enough to seek God.

Lord, as I read Psalm 104:10–23, I reflect on how You are constantly at work in creation. Help me to trust that You are working on me, sanctifying me, molding me to be more of who You desire me to be.

MORNING
CHOSEN CHILD

While they were worshiping the Lord and fasting, the Holy Spirit said, "Set apart for me Barnabas and Saul for the work to which I have called them." So after they had fasted and prayed, they placed their hands on them and sent them off.
ACTS 13:2–3 NIV

As a daughter of Christ, you have a transformation story. One that's beautiful and amazing! One that has the power to change a life and remind others they are also God's chosen.

If you haven't done so already, take some time to write down your testimony. "Remember the wonders he has performed, his miracles" (Psalm 105:5 NLT). Then pray and ask God to show you who to share your story with. He'll be sure to give you the strength to do it (Psalm 105:4).

Lord, thank You for showing me that I'm Your dearly loved, chosen child. I love You!

EVENING
STANDING IN FAITH

In Lystra a certain man without strength in his feet was sitting, a cripple from his mother's womb, who had never walked. This man heard Paul speaking. Paul, observing him intently and seeing that he had faith to be healed, said with a loud voice, "Stand up straight on your feet!" And he leaped and walked.
ACTS 14:8–10 NKJV

When you have faith in God, others will notice it, including Him. Because of that faith, God will help you not just to stand—but to leap and walk!

If you want God to perform a miracle in your life, shore up your faith by spending time in His presence. Open yourself up to His Word. And pray, asking God to work in your life.

Lord, help me shore up my faith. Show me how to pray for the areas in my life where I desire to see You work out for my good and for Your glory.

MORNING
SPRING IN YOUR STEP

Praise ye the LORD. O give thanks unto the LORD; for he is good: for his mercy endureth for ever. Who can utter the mighty acts of the LORD? who can shew forth all his praise?
PSALM 106:1–2 KJV

In the early days of the church, a message was delivered to the Antioch believers, bringing the new Christians great joy as it was read aloud. Then the prophets Judas and Silas spoke to "the believers, encouraging and strengthening their faith" (Acts 15:32 NLT).

If you need an extra dose of support and encouragement, consider tapping into old messages that have increased your faith in the past—or seek out new ones. As you do so, God's joy will bubble up within you, giving you that extra spring in your step and prompting praise to roll off your lips.

Father God, if joyful words are not flowing from my mouth, help me get there by reading or hearing the encouraging messages of others.

EVENING
KEEP PRESSING ON

All Israel gathered before David at Hebron and told him, . . . "In the past, even when Saul was king, you were the one who really led the forces of Israel. And the LORD your God told you, 'You will be the shepherd of my people Israel. You will be the leader of my people Israel.'"
1 CHRONICLES 11:1–2 NLT

When you are walking through times of questioning and doubt, feeling like your prayers are hitting a roadblock, it can be tempting to take matters into your own hands. Instead of turning away from the faith, keep pressing on. Be like the mighty fighters who stood for God and supported David. But do so without their armor and swords. For you, woman warrior, will be able to stand your ground with God at your side, armed with the weapons of His Word of truth, the power of your prayers, and the strength of your praise.

Lord, when I'm tempted to go in another direction, help me find scripture to hold on to.

MORNING
TRANSFORMATION PROCLAMATION

Sing to the Lord, all the earth! Tell of his salvation from day to day. Declare his glory among the nations, his marvelous works among all the peoples! For great is the Lord, and greatly to be praised, and he is to be feared above all gods.

1 CHRONICLES 16:23–25 ESV

When going through tests or trials, you may be tempted to entertain negative thoughts or adopt a bad attitude. If that happens, if your old ways begin to rise up in your heart and mind, then rest assured that God sees you and understands! He has compassion for you. And because of that compassion, He has a word for you, a scripture verse or a prayer, a transformation proclamation that you can write down, one that reminds you that you're a new creation. That the old way of thinking and reacting is gone. That you have been transformed by the renewing of your mind.

Lord, lead me out of all darkness and into Your light.

EVENING
A GOD INCIDENCE

When Solomon finished praying, a bolt of lightning out of heaven struck the Whole-Burnt-Offering and sacrifices and the Glory of God filled The Temple. The Glory was so dense that the priests couldn't get in—God so filled The Temple that there was no room for the priests! When all Israel saw the fire fall from heaven and the Glory of God fill The Temple, they fell on their knees, bowed their heads, and worshiped, thanking God: Yes! God is good! His love never quits!

2 CHRONICLES 7:1–3 MSG

Chances are you too have experienced God incidences. It's when your faith aligns with reality and crosses over into your everyday life. It's those moments you look back on in awe and wonder. You tell others about the experience, and all you can do is praise God!

As you think about God at work in your life and in the lives of others you know, consider those God-incidence moments. Ask God to give you more of them, because when He does, it will increase your faith and others'.

Father God, I want to experience more of You in my everyday moments.

MORNING
GOD REIGNS

"To this day I have had the help that comes from God, and so I stand here testifying both to small and great, saying nothing but what the prophets and Moses said would come to pass: that the Christ must suffer and that, by being the first to rise from the dead, he would proclaim light both to our people and to the Gentiles."
ACTS 26:22–23 ESV

In today's passage in Acts, Paul is brought before King Agrippa. What might seem like a very intimidating situation for Paul becomes an opportunity for him to share about his conversion to Christianity. Once again, God reigns!

Whatever you face today or in the days ahead, remember: God reigns!

Father, You are on the throne of this world and the throne of my life. You rule over all the nations. Thank You for being in control over everything.

EVENING
HELPER AND SHIELD

O Israel, trust and take refuge in the Lord! [Lean on, rely on, and be confident in Him!] He is their Help and their Shield. O house of Aaron [the priesthood], trust in and lean on the Lord! He is their Help and their Shield.
PSALM 115:9–10 AMPC

Consider all the instances you've witnessed God being your Helper. Although not physically seen right there beside you, He provided people to come alongside you, to support and encourage you. Likewise, consider the times God has been your Shield. Although you may not have seen Him there, you may recall situations that turned out better than they could have.

Every day, continue to invite God to be your Helper and Shield, confident that He's always with you as He continues to mold and shape you.

Lord, You mean so much to me! There are so many ways about You that I have yet to fully understand. I invite You into all that I am so that I can experience more of Your presence.

MORNING
NEW COURAGE

*And the [Christian] brethren there, having had news of us, came as
far as the Forum of Appius and the Three Taverns to meet us. When
Paul saw them, he thanked God and received new courage.*
ACTS 28:15 AMPC

When you need a break, when you're disheartened and dispirited, when nothing seems to be going your way, take heart. God will send just what you need at just the right time to give you new courage. To lighten your heart, spirit, and mind. To renew you.

Today, thank God for seeing you through some dire situations. And when He sends others to come alongside you, lift up your heart and voice in praise. His help and their encouragement will make a new woman out of you.

*Thank You, Lord, for seeing me through so many things and for
sending brothers and sisters in Christ to renew my courage.*

EVENING
AN AGENT OF CHANGE

*GOD is gracious—it is he who makes things right, our most compassionate God.
GOD takes the side of the helpless; when I was at the end of my rope, he saved
me. I said to myself, "Relax and rest. GOD has showered you with blessings."*
PSALM 116:5–7 MSG

Looking for reasons to love the Lord? Check out Psalm 116, and you'll find a myriad of them!

All that God does to turn your life around gives you a new purpose and perspective, making you want to "give back to GOD. . .the blessings he's poured out on" you (v. 12 MSG). That, in turn, prompts you to reach out to others, to help transform their circumstances and perspectives as He works through you to make their lives a little more "right."

Lord, thank You for all the blessings that make me an agent of change for You!

MORNING
FINDING YOUR WAY BACK

*Manasseh sought the Lord his God and sincerely humbled himself
before the God of his ancestors. And when he prayed, the
Lord listened to him and was moved by his request.*

2 Chronicles 33:12–13 NLT

No matter what you've done, if you sincerely repent (turn around), if you change and come back to God, then you can move the One who moves the world.

Consider where God may be speaking into *your* life, where He may be wanting you to change. Then pray, knowing God is listening and, if you're sincere, will be moved by your plea—and will bring you back home to Him, where you belong.

God, open my ears to Your voice. Help me find my way back home to You.

EVENING
OPENING THE GATES

*Open for me the gates where the righteous enter, and I will go in and
thank the Lord. These gates lead to the presence of the Lord, and
the godly enter there. . . . This is the day the Lord has made. We will
rejoice and be glad in it. . . . The Lord is God, shining upon us.*

Psalm 118:19–20, 24, 27 NLT

Tonight, consider areas in your life in which you may not be giving God full sway. Where are you feeling resistance to His message, hints, and commands? What things or people have you not turned over to Him, surrendered to His gentle care and touch? Which worries are leading you to places of doubt and fear?

Ask God to open your eyes to concerns that are best left in His care. Then surrender them to Him as you walk through the gates that lead to His presence. And rejoice, for God has made this day for you.

*Lord, reveal then tear down any barrier that exists between us.
I desire to enter Your gates with praise upon my lips.*

DAY 286

MORNING
KEEP HOPING

*Abraham believed in the God. . .who creates new things out of nothing.
Even when there was no reason for hope, Abraham kept hoping. . .
fully convinced that God is able to do whatever he promises.*
ROMANS 4:17–18, 21 NLT

Abraham's original name, *Abram*, means "high, exalted father" (Genesis 17:5 AMPC). But God changed his name to Abraham, meaning "father of a multitude" (Genesis 17:5 AMPC). God did this when Abraham was already ninety-nine years old and Sarah was eighty-nine, well past childbearing years! In other words, God spoke of Abraham being the father of many before he even had his son Isaac with Sarah!

God is already changing things in your life, creating something new for you out of nothing. So be like Abraham. Hope even when you see no reason for hope, fully convinced God is doing and has the power to do whatever He's promised.

Lord, my hope lies in You!

EVENING
POWER TOOL

Then the king said to me, "What do you request?" So I prayed to the God of heaven.
NEHEMIAH 2:4 NKJV

Prayers come in all different shapes and sizes. That's because different situations require different prayers. Nehemiah's first and longer prayer was his way of unburdening himself. It also allowed him to remind God (and himself) of His promises—and to ask for help (see Nehemiah 1:3–11). But the next day, before the king, Nehemiah wisely used an arrow prayer, a quick opening up to God for help to speak wisely (see Nehemiah 2:4).

No matter what the length or content of your prayer, be assured of its power to transform you, your words, and the situation at hand.

Thank You, God, for gifting me with the tool and power of prayer.

MORNING
STAYING FIRM

I sent him back this: "There's nothing to what you're saying. You've made it all up." They were trying to intimidate us into quitting. They thought, "They'll give up; they'll never finish it." I prayed, "Give me strength."
NEHEMIAH 6:8–9 MSG

While overseeing the rebuilding of Jerusalem, Nehemiah met with continual opposition. Instead of giving in, changing his mind because of outside pressure, Nehemiah prayed for God to give him strength. In the end, the wall was finished in fifty-two days. And when all the Israelites' enemies heard about it, they "totally lost their nerve. They knew that God was behind this work" (Nehemiah 6:16 MSG).

Don't let the falsehoods of others intimidate you. Don't let lies and bullies keep you from doing what God has called you to do. Instead, go to God for strength to persevere in your endeavor. And in the end, all who witness the completion of your work will realize it was God's doing after all.

Give me strength, Lord, to stay on Your track and not be influenced by others.

EVENING
WADE RIGHT IN

Each one of us needs to look after the good of the people around us, asking ourselves, "How can I help?" That's exactly what Jesus did. He didn't make it easy for himself by avoiding people's troubles, but waded right in and helped out.
ROMANS 15:2–3 MSG

Jesus went against societal norms. Some thought He also went against all human reasoning. Yet nothing could deter Him from helping the helpless. And so He transformed this world and continues to do so through those who follow in His footsteps.

You too can transform the world, or at least your little part of it, by reaching out to others. By asking yourself, *How can I help that person?* And then actually helping. For you have been called to "follow in His footsteps" (1 Peter 2:21 AMPC).

Jesus, I want to transform this world, just like You transformed mine. Show me how I can help someone this week.

MORNING
PERFECT TIMING

I wait for the Lord, I expectantly wait, and in His word do I hope.
I am looking and waiting for the Lord more than watchmen for
the morning, I say, more than watchmen for the morning.
PSALM 130:5–6 AMPC

God wants us to learn how to wait. To expect He will answer when the time is absolutely right. For as we watch and wait, our faith and expectations grow, making us ever stronger and dependent on Him.

So instead of tapping your toes with arms folded, be still and open to the knowledge that God loves you, and He will act when the time is just right.

On You, Lord, I wait, leaving all things to Your perfect timing
and continuing to hope in Your good Word.

EVENING
A GOD-CENTERED LIFE

Except the Lord builds the house, they labor in vain who build it; except the Lord keeps
the city, the watchman wakes but in vain. It is vain for you to rise up early, to take rest
late, to eat the bread of [anxious] toil—for He gives [blessings] to His beloved in sleep.
PSALM 127:1–2 AMPC

The Lord knows that a life lived without Him at the center is a life not worth living. So be sure to put God in the center of your processes as you build your life with Him by your side. As you do so, you will find yourself blessed with peace and so much more, including a good night's rest.

Lord, too often I get so wrapped up in my work, family, and church that I
forget to include You in the process. Remind me each day to look to You for all
things, to do my best in all endeavors, and to leave all the results to You.

MORNING
LIFE LIVED LARGE

The moment I called out, you stepped in; you made my life large with strength.
PSALM 138:3 MSG

Since God—the almighty, all-seeing, all-good God—is on our side, how can we ever feel weak? All we have to do is call out and He answers—He will be our Strength. He will help us when we can't see a way out of our troubles. He will walk with us when we are in the middle of difficult situations. He will keep the ground where we are standing firm when everything and everyone else is crumbling away.

So how should we live? We should live large—not filled with our own pride but as humble servants emboldened by the holy, glorious, mighty power of God.

Lord God, thank You for being my Strength. Amen.

EVENING
FINDING MEANING

Yet when I surveyed all that my hands had done and what I had toiled to achieve, everything was meaningless, a chasing after the wind; nothing was gained under the sun.
ECCLESIASTES 2:11 NIV

The words of the writer of Ecclesiastes often sound to the modern reader like someone singing the blues. Nothing ever happens. Nothing ever changes.

But if we look more closely at this little book in the Bible, we see a different message. We see that God "has made everything beautiful in its time. He has also set eternity in the human heart; yet no one can fathom what God has done from beginning to end" (Ecclesiastes 3:11). We ask these questions about meaning because God put the questions inside us. Because He wanted us, through the questioning, to find Him. To know that our meaning is found in Him.

Lord, thank You for the longing for purpose that leads me to You.

MORNING
BY GRACE

But whatever I am now, it is all because God poured out his special favor on me—and not without results. For I have worked harder than any of the other apostles; yet it was not I but God who was working through me by his grace.
1 CORINTHIANS 15:10 NLT

Even Paul felt he was "not. . .worthy to be called an apostle" (1 Corinthians 15:9 NLT). But the difference between Paul and many others who feel unworthy is that Paul didn't let his feelings get in the way of God's faithfulness. Grace does that for us. Grace gives us a position we have no right to take and access to power we have no authority to use, in exchange for nothing we can do or deserve.

Grace is the beautiful, life-changing, heart-shaping gift of your loving God. Whatever you are or will be is because of His grace.

Lord, thank You for Your gift of grace. Help me to use it to work for You.

EVENING
NEW LIFE

Now we look inside, and what we see is that anyone united with the Messiah gets a fresh start, is created new. The old life is gone; a new life emerges!
2 CORINTHIANS 5:17 MSG

When we accept the salvation of Jesus Christ our Lord, we are given the gift of a new life with a new hope. We no longer have to be ashamed. We no longer have to perform acts to try to get rid of our sins—which no person can do. We can rest in the Spirit of God, united with Christ in the death of our old selves and joined with Him on a new path. Our heart is made clean, once and for all. Our minds look to Jesus, to understand better how to follow Him—not because we must do better but because His love compels us to become more like Him, to come close to Him.

Lord, thank You for a new life! Help me live it well.

MORNING
MORNING GUIDANCE

*Let me hear of your unfailing love each morning, for I am
trusting you. Show me where to walk, for I give myself to you.*
PSALM 143:8 NLT

The first light of the day, whether it comes from the lamp beside your bed or from the
sunrise, can serve as a reminder that today is a new beginning. The first page of a new
chapter. The first line of a new story. Whatever has gone before need not be forgotten—in
fact, it's good to remember the days that have passed and to recall the times God has
been with you, each step of the way showing His love for you. And on this new day, in
full confidence of His unfailing love, you can commit once again to put your life in His
hands. You can trust Him. He will not lead you down a wrong path. He will not leave
you to walk any path alone.

Lord of love, call me every morning to wake up in Your Word.

EVENING
AN AUTUMN HYMN

Let everything that breathes sing praises to the LORD!
PSALM 150:6 NLT

Let the colors of the trees reflect the variety of His blessings. Let the crisp, fresh air
remind you of the life He breathes into your lungs. Let the birds that greet the sun give
thanks for the new day. Let the fox that slips through the shadows of the night bow in
submission to the Lord of all creation. Let the wings of the geese that migrate beat out
the rhythm of His provision. Let the deer freeze in poses of graceful beauty, revealing
the thoughtful details of His design. Let the flowers that close their petals to the cold
and the fronds that curl in the dew show you the intricate miracles He works around
you every day.

Lord, You're so beautiful; I praise You and You only.

MORNING
SOW NOW

*Remember this—a farmer who plants only a few seeds will get a small
crop. But the one who plants generously will get a generous crop.*

2 Corinthians 9:6 nlt

There is one fact we can be sure of. God will do good with whatever we give Him. So if we know that to be true, wouldn't we want to give everything we have to God? Wouldn't we want to give Him every coin we could spare? Wouldn't we want to hand over to Him every gift, every thought, every moment?

What you give to God, He will multiply. He will maximize your investments beyond any earthly calculations. And He will supply you with more than you need and so much more than you deserve. Just try Him.

*Lord, I want to give everything to You. Help me to let go
of my worries and give generously today.*

EVENING
BLOOMING GLORY

*The desert and the parched land will be glad;
the wilderness will rejoice and blossom.*

Isaiah 35:1 niv

Your God is the One who can strengthen the feeble and steady the unstable. He's the One who can turn fear into courage and doubt into bravery. He's the One who can open blind eyes, unstop deaf ears, and cause mute tongues to shout for joy (Isaiah 35:3–6). And for all this and more, you follow Him.

Lord, thank You for glorious change.

MORNING
WEAK MADE STRONG

*Therefore I will boast all the more gladly about my
weaknesses, so that Christ's power may rest on me.*

2 CORINTHIANS 12:9 NIV

Paul is delighted by his own failures and losses—in the insults that are hurled at him and in the difficulties he faces and in the persecution he suffers. For he knows that through all these things, he is being made into a more perfect witness of the glory of God. And that witness doesn't just testify to others but also serves as a daily reminder to us of the God who loves us so much—and loves us exactly as we are.

Lord, when I am in the middle of hard times, help me to lean fully on You.

EVENING
NO LONGER A SLAVE

*So you are no longer a slave, but God's child; and since
you are his child, God has made you also an heir.*

GALATIANS 4:7 NIV

Before you know God, you are a slave to the impulse of your nature and a slave to the rules you create for yourself. But when you know God and accept His salvation, you don't just become a member of a group of believers. You become His child—His. He adopts you, making you His daughter—an heir to the inheritance of eternal life with Him. You are no longer an orphan. No longer a slave. You no longer have to live in fear or wonder about your worth. You are a child of the King.

Lord, I'm so glad I'm Yours!

MORNING
LEAVE IT ALL AT THE CROSS

*As for me, may I never boast about anything except the cross of our
Lord Jesus Christ. Because of that cross, my interest in this world
has been crucified, and the world's interest in me has also died.*

GALATIANS 6:14 NLT

When Jesus died on the cross, He accomplished all that needed to be accomplished. His death, burial, and resurrection didn't just ensure our place in heaven, but also gave us a way to live in victory and peace, unencumbered by the troubles each day might bring.

What's holding you back today? Have you left it at the cross? Release it to the Lord and watch Him free you up to live a full, abundant life.

*Father, today I come to the cross not just to lay my burdens at Your
feet but to thank You for being my Burden Bearer. How can I ever
repay You? From the bottom of my heart, I bring You praise.*

EVENING
BRINGING HIS PEOPLE HOME

*"And what do I see flying like clouds to Israel, like doves to their nests?
They are ships from the ends of the earth, from lands that trust in me, led
by the great ships of Tarshish. They are bringing the people of Israel home
from far away, carrying their silver and gold. They will honor the LORD
your God, the Holy One of Israel, for he has filled you with splendor."*

ISAIAH 60:8–9 NLT

Maybe you've felt like a child lost in the wilderness, wanting to go home. Tonight, God is calling you back to Himself. No matter where you are, no matter how far you've wandered, no matter how many times you've convinced yourself that going home isn't an option, He's right there, crying out for you to run into His arms.

Don't wait another minute. Like a dove, fly to your nest and find true rest in Him once and for all.

*Lord, I want to go home! No more wandering for me. Tonight, I choose
to run back into Your arms, as the Israelites sprinted toward Jerusalem.
There's no place sweeter than being at home with You, Father.*

MORNING
ABOVE ALL WE COULD ASK OR THINK

*Now to Him who is able to do exceedingly abundantly above all that we
ask or think, according to the power that works in us, to Him be glory in
the church by Christ Jesus to all generations, forever and ever. Amen.*
EPHESIANS 3:20–21 NKJV

The power of our God is so far beyond anything our finite minds can comprehend.
Why, then, do we doubt Him when we pray? The same God who created everything
we enjoy in this life cares about our requests, our needs. He won't leave us hanging.
He's got the power to save marriages, to transform lives, to turn wayward children
back toward home. And His plan for His children, including you, darling daughter, is
for good, not evil.

What are you facing today? Stop fretting over what you can't do, and start trusting
what God can do. It will be far above anything you could ask or think.

*Father, I know I can trust You with every facet
of my life, and today I choose to do just that.*

EVENING
BEFORE YOU WERE FORMED

*"Before I formed you in the womb I knew you; before you were born
I sanctified you; I ordained you a prophet to the nations."*
JEREMIAH 1:5 NKJV

How long has God known you? Most would answer, "Since I was born!" In truth, He's
known you longer than that.

It's remarkable to think about God's vast ability to "know" His kids, even before
He ushers them into the world as babies. But we can see from His words to Jeremiah
how much planning goes into the birth of each child: "Before you were born I sanctified you; I ordained you a prophet to the nations." God doesn't just "know" us. . .He
sanctifies and ordains us. Wow, what a God we serve!

You know me, Lord. . .better than anyone. More than anything, You know my heart.

MORNING
EVERYTHING SET RIGHT

I'm whistling, laughing, and jumping for joy; I'm singing your song, High God. The day my enemies turned tail and ran, they stumbled on you and fell on their faces. You took over and set everything right; when I needed you, you were there, taking charge.
PSALM 9:2–4 MSG

In this psalm, we find David singing praises to God, the Doer of great things—the One who sets everything to right. David isn't praising halfheartedly, oh no. He's putting his *whole* heart and soul into it. He's "whistling, laughing, and jumping for joy." His *entire being* is directed in praise to almighty God.

We can experience this same kind of bubbling-up joy that David did. When hard times come, when nothing is going our way, we can trust our heavenly Father with the outcome. He can—He *will*—transform our troubles.

Today, I ask You to take complete charge of my life, Lord. No matter what, You are always the One who can set things right. I praise You!

EVENING
THIS IS WHAT THE LORD SAYS

"This is what the LORD says: 'When people fall down, don't they get up again? When they discover they're on the wrong road, don't they turn back?'"
JEREMIAH 8:4 NLT

There will be seasons when you tumble, when you make mistakes. But God doesn't want you to stay down long. Sure, it's not easy to pick yourself up, admit you've made a mistake, and then get back to walking the straight and narrow. But it is possible. And don't spend too much time worrying about the recovery period. God will see you through all of that, no matter how long it takes.

Father, I've stumbled and fallen more times than I can count. Tonight, I'm ready to admit my flaws, my imperfections. Pick me up (again), I pray. I'm so grateful for Your staying power, Lord.

MORNING
SET YOUR MIND ON THINGS ABOVE

Since, then, you have been raised with Christ, set your hearts on things above, where Christ is, seated at the right hand of God. Set your minds on things above, not on earthly things.

COLOSSIANS 3:1–2 NIV

How do you set your mind on things above? Focus on what is good, what is right, what is true, what is lovely. Ask the Lord to give you His opinion on everything (even the little things). Don't focus on self. Instead, keep your eyes on Him. That's where you will find your answers, after all.

Today, I choose to set my mind on things above, Lord. I won't let the daily troubles get me down. I'll shift my eyes up, up, up to You, my Maker and Creator.

EVENING
NO NEED FOR ACCOLADES

We were not looking for praise from people, not from you or anyone else, even though as apostles of Christ we could have asserted our authority. Instead, we were like young children among you.

1 THESSALONIANS 2:6–7 NIV

Tonight, the LORD wants to remind you that the only praise that matters is His. He adores you and is your biggest cheerleader. So don't seek the praise of those around you. They can't give you what the Lord can. Applause is short lived, but the love of the Lord lasts forever. And best of all, He's not asking you to perform for Him. He simply wants your heart.

Father, I've been such a performer, such a people pleaser. I'll admit, the accolades felt good. But I see now that the only audience I need is an audience of One.

MORNING
JESUS IS MY BROTHER

Both the one who makes people holy and those who are made holy are of the
same family. So Jesus is not ashamed to call them brothers and sisters.
HEBREWS 2:11 NIV

Hebrews tell us that, despite our imperfection, Jesus makes us holy. That's why He's not ashamed to call us His sisters. And not second-class sisters in name only. No, Christ Jesus is proud to share His inheritance with each of His siblings: salvation that provides eternal life in the Father's presence.

Don't get so comfortable in your salvation that you lose perspective on the awe factor of just how amazing your salvation is. Your today, tomorrow, and forever is secure—and glorious, not to mention totally awesome!

Jesus, thank You for claiming me as Your sister and making me holy.
I don't deserve Your good gifts, but I am thankful for them. Amen.

EVENING
FORWARD THINKERS

All these people were still living by faith when they died. They did not
receive the things promised; they only saw them and welcomed them from
a distance, admitting that they were foreigners and strangers on earth.
HEBREWS 11:13 NIV

If you're going through a difficult time, God's promises may seem far away. Don't give up! Take courage from these heroes of faith who lived and died without seeing the reward of their belief on earth but who are now at home in God's presence. Ask God to show you what He has promised from afar—even a glimpse of what's to come can help you stand strong.

God, I know this place is not my home, and I'm trying to keep that in
perspective as I grow more and more homesick to be with You. Thank You
for the heritage of faith in Your family tree. I am blessed to be a part of it.

MORNING
EXTREME TRANSFORMATION: SPIRITUAL EDITION

"Speak a prophetic message and say, 'This is what the Sovereign
Lord says: Come, O breath, from the four winds! Breathe
into these dead bodies so they may live again.'"
EZEKIEL 37:9 NLT

If you've been a Christian for a while, you've probably experienced some seasons of being spiritually alive and others of being on spiritual life support. If God can take long-dead, dried-up, crusty bones and transform them into living, breathing people, take hope in the fact that He *can* and *will* bring your faith back from the dead. Ask Him to start that extreme transformation *now*!

God, I'm ready for a change. Breathe new life into me so I may live fully in You again!

EVENING
HANDPICKED

God the Father knew you and chose you long ago, and his
Spirit has made you holy. As a result, you have obeyed him
and have been cleansed by the blood of Jesus Christ.
1 PETER 1:2 NLT

Before Jesus came, only the nation of Israel could claim to be God's chosen people. But because of Christ, all believers—Jews and Gentiles—belong to God. Here's a beautiful truth in scripture, sister: When you were born, God had already chosen and accepted you. Your salvation and security rest in the free and merciful choice of your almighty God, and nothing can take away His love for those who believe in Him (Romans 8:38–39).

Father, You chose me first, but I choose You now and forever. Thank You for
wanting me even if others reject me. You hold my heart, God. I trust You with it.

MORNING
COMFORT FOOD

My son, eat honey, for it is good; yes, the honey from the comb is sweet
to your taste; know that wisdom is the same for your soul; if you find
it, then there will be a future, and your hope will not be cut off.
PROVERBS 24:13–14 NASB

The speaker here in Proverbs 24 instructs his son to nurture his heart as well as his body with sweetness—with the taste of *wisdom*. Wisdom nourishes and brightens the soul—it will guide a woman forward, giving her confidence and a hopeful outlook on her future. For the woman who savors wisdom in her heart is spending time with its Author, her Savior, who has promised to care for her.

Fill your heart with your Savior's sweetness—He will give you hope for the time to come.

Jesus, thank You for the comfort You've provided in Your Word. Help me to
taste its sweetness, to be nourished by it, no matter what part I am reading.

EVENING
LIKE HE IS

"And those who are wise shall shine like the brightness of the sky above;
and those who turn many to righteousness, like the stars forever and ever."
DANIEL 12:3 ESV

How can we be more like Christ now? Tonight's verse from Daniel offers an answer: by being wise and turning many to righteousness. After all, Jesus' main task in His work before the cross was loving others and sharing the good news of the kingdom—that God had restoration for all who knew their brokenness and came to Him.

Until our image bearing is restored to full brightness like dazzling stars, let's work as Jesus did, following God's good commands to love others and to share His good news, knowing Jesus will help us do both.

Jesus, thank You for Your promise and the hope I have of being like You.

MORNING
KNOWING HIM

We know also that the Son of God has come and has given us understanding,
so that we may know him who is true. And we are in him who is true by
being in his Son Jesus Christ. He is the true God and eternal life.
1 JOHN 5:20 NIV

Relationships can't thrive without intentional effort. Humanly speaking, it would be like having a friend who gives presents on birthdays or holidays, but whom you'd hardly hear from otherwise. How can a friendship grow without time spent together or shared memories? It would quickly fade, even with pleasantries exchanged from time to time.

Jesus gave us the gift of access to the Father, of communing in spirit and in truth. Even in this busy month, aim to go deeper in your friendship with God, for knowing Him "who is true" gives you new life.

Jesus, my heart feels its deep need of You and fellowship
with You. Please keep revealing Yourself to me.

EVENING
MERCY WILL BE THERE

But you, beloved, building yourselves up on your most holy faith,
praying in the Holy Spirit, keep yourselves in the love of God, looking
for the mercy of our Lord Jesus Christ unto eternal life.
JUDE 20–21 NKJV

No matter the danger you see ahead or the worst-case scenarios that leave you trembling, Christ's mercy will be there. The One who promised is faithful. Ask yourself: In your starkest imaginings, how could God's mercy show up? Then look for it—*expect* it—to show up in your life, doing so in the Spirit, submerging yourself in God's love, enriching your faith. And trust Him to be merciful to you as you strive toward the good.

Jesus, Your goodness and mercy will follow hard after me all the
days of my life, for You are good and perfectly faithful—when fear
hits, help me to be looking for how Your mercy will show up.

MORNING
SOVEREIGN IN EARTH AND HEAVEN

*The Lord GOD of hosts, he who touches the earth and it melts. . .and all
of it rises like the Nile, and sinks again. . .who builds his upper chambers
in the heavens and founds his vault upon the earth; who calls for the
waters of the sea and pours them out. . .the LORD is his name.*

AMOS 9:5–6 ESV

Heaven and earth testify to God's glory, and God is sovereign over them both. His gracious rule extends over you and *your* life as well. Where do you need to see God's awesome power, His grace, today? His hand is there, working where you cannot see; His love is already with you to hold you up. Praise God for His matchless grace!

*Jesus, Father, Holy Spirit, I long to grow in greater awe of Your
power and love. Your holiness and glory are incomparable! Thank
You for Your Word that paints pictures of them for me.*

EVENING
JESUS OUR SHEPHERD

*"The Lamb on the Throne will shepherd them, will lead them to spring
waters of Life. And God will wipe every last tear from their eyes."*

REVELATION 7:17 MSG

Using Jesus' names can direct your prayers in a new, powerful way. Consider how you can address Him as your Good Shepherd tonight, using Psalm 23's depiction to guide you:

Shepherd me, oh Jesus, for I am one of Your precious lambs. Lead me to good pasture, where I can feed on Your Word and grow strong in the faith. Show me anew Your springs of Living Water that I may be refreshed with You, for You are the Truth. Pull burrs from my coat and thorns from my flesh; nurture me by Your hand. Protect me from the wolves that would wound; show me Your strong staff is always near. And, Lord Jesus, help me to be a willing sheep who hears only Your voice calling amid the cacophony. Amen.

Jesus, my Good Shepherd, tonight I pray. . .

MORNING
KEEP ASKING

You shall have charge over my house, and all my people shall be governed
according to your word [with reverence, submission, and obedience].
Only in matters of the throne will I be greater than you are.
GENESIS 41:40 AMPC

Sometimes it's hard to continue praying for God's intervention over and over and over again. Our perseverance peters out. We worry He may grow tired of our request, or we give up altogether because we think His answer is a firm *no*. But the truth is that it's not yet time for the next right step.

It's hard to understand God's timing, so we have to choose to trust it because God is God and we are not. Yet we need not grow weary of asking, for we won't wear God out. And we'll have peace if we live our lives knowing that when it *is* the right time, God's answers *will* come.

Lord, please give me perseverance to keep asking and
patience to wait for Your perfectly timed answer!

EVENING
THE PRISON OF PARANOIA

But Benjamin, Joseph's [full] brother, Jacob did not send with his brothers;
for he said, Lest perhaps some harm or injury should befall him.
GENESIS 42:4 AMPC

Too often, we live our lives afraid that bad events will happen. That mindset keeps us from branching out and trying new things. It makes us second-guess our plans or cancel them altogether. It breeds distrust in relationships and robs us of joy and peace.

While it's wise to be aware, it's foolish to let worry take control, because it will always point to horrible outcomes and endings. And if you choose to live here, your life will be wasted on *what-ifs*.

Ask God to replace your fears with faith.

Lord, living in a place of fear is a dead-end street and one road I don't want to travel.
Will You give me courage and confidence to trust You instead? Help me be brave!

MORNING
SUFFICIENT GRACE

"Therefore you shall do my statutes and keep my rules and perform them, and then you will dwell in the land securely. The land will yield its fruit, and you will eat your fill and dwell in it securely. And if you say, 'What shall we eat in the seventh year, if we may not sow or gather in our crop?' I will command my blessing on you in the sixth year, so that it will produce a crop sufficient for three years."

LEVITICUS 25:18–21 ESV

These words from Leviticus are a reminder that God's grace is sufficient enough for all of your needs. You love, serve, and obey a God who cares about your deepest needs and desires. When you worry about the things of this earth, you sink into despair and rage. Yet when you look up at God and recount His goodness, you can rest assured that everything—including you and His plans for your life—is under His control.

Heavenly Daddy, please show me You are truly in control of my life.

EVENING
WORSHIP WITH ABANDON

When David returned home to bless his household, Michal daughter of Saul came out to meet him and said, "How the king of Israel has distinguished himself today, going around half-naked in full view of the slave girls of his servants as any vulgar fellow would!"

2 SAMUEL 6:20 NIV

Regardless of how you do it, you have the ability and right to worship with freedom like David. You can make a joyful noise however you see fit.

Don't worry about the judgers. It's okay if they don't understand. Don't concern yourself with naysayers. God is worthy of your praise, and He delights to receive it from you in authentic and intentional ways.

Lord, give me the confidence to worship You my way—our way.

MORNING
IN GOOD COMPANY

*Then Jesus told them, "A prophet is honored everywhere except
in his own hometown and among his relatives and his own family."*
MARK 6:4 NLT

If, because of your faith, you have ever experienced the cold shoulder from those closest to you, you're in good company. Jesus understands. Yet the fact that you stood up and decided to follow Him and then went to tell others is very important.

Keep looking up to Jesus for wisdom and guidance about how to share His good news. Don't worry if you get rejected every now and then. The Lord sees what you're doing and will reward you in due time.

*Lord, I've told those I care for about You. I pray that my
words planted seeds of love and faith in their hearts.*

EVENING
YOUR DAY TO CHOOSE

*And [Jesus] said to His disciples, Therefore I tell you, do not be anxious
and troubled [with cares] about your life, as to what you will [have
to] eat; or about your body, as to what you will [have to] wear. For
life is more than food, and the body [more] than clothes.*
LUKE 12:22–23 AMPC

Jesus says your worrying will get you nowhere. It only subtracts from your life. Yet not worrying can be difficult if you were raised with the conviction that you need to be able to take care of yourself. So it can take some time to let go so that you can let God take care of you. But it can be done. How? By choosing to seek the Lord and His kingdom above all things and before all people. That means looking to God and His Word in the beginning of the day before your feet even touch the ground.

Lord, above all other things and people in my life, I choose to trust and seek You.

MORNING
DON'T LOOK BACK

But Lot's wife looked back and turned into a pillar of salt.
GENESIS 19:26 MSG

When God asks you to let go of something—be it a bad relationship, a dangerous addiction, the hold of unforgiveness, a negative influence, or some other unhealthy person, posture, or place—what's your reaction? God loves you so much, and He wants you to experience freedom in Him—something that can't happen when you're continually glancing back.

Choose to keep your eyes on God, willing to follow wherever He leads.

Lord, I don't want to settle for the wrong things. I don't want to compromise what I know is Your will. Instead, help me find contentment in a relationship with You that meets my every need.

EVENING
NO MORE TEARS

"'He will wipe every tear from their eyes. There will be no more death' or mourning or crying or pain, for the old order of things has passed away."
REVELATION 21:4 NIV

In Revelation 21:4, God guarantees there will be no more sadness, mourning, pain, or death. You will no longer be separated from your loved ones. Worry and anguish will be things of the past. It will literally be a new world, a time of peace and joy!

If you are struggling with sadness, if your face is stained with tears, do not lose hope. Your current situation is temporary, and your God promises brighter days will come. The old order of things will pass away to be replaced with the blissful happiness found in dwelling in and with God.

Dear Lord, help me to remember better times will come, times when I'll feel no more pain, times when night will disappear and You will be my only Light.

MORNING
THE GOD WHO ANSWERS

Then let us arise and go up to Bethel, and I will make there an altar to God Who answered me in the day of my distress and was with me wherever I went.
GENESIS 35:3 AMPC

When you pray and ask God for answers, you must surrender your ideas and trust the provision He's made for your life. You have to let God be God. Hard to do? Yes! But the Word says His plans for you are filled with hope for a future that will help you become more like Christ. And at the end of the day, isn't that the goal of your life anyway?

Lord, thank You for being a God who answers me. Help me trust Your will and ways and Your timing. You've never let me down, and I know You won't start now!

EVENING
AN ANOINTED ASSESSMENT

But now, do not be distressed and disheartened or vexed and angry with yourselves because you sold me here, for God sent me ahead of you to preserve life.
GENESIS 45:5 AMPC

Where do you need divine perspective right now? Maybe it's in a relationship that's falling apart or finances that are failing. It could be a child who's making horrible choices or a career that feels like a dead end. Maybe you're just tired of trying to hold everyone and everything together, wrestling with discouragement as you wait for a response from God.

We all have seasons and moments that need an anointed assessment from time to time. Ask God for perspective, and then ask for an extra measure of faith to trust Him through it.

Lord, sometimes I just need a peek deeper into my situation to help settle my heart. If it's Your will, would You give me that? If not, would You help me trust Your plan?

MORNING
THE BEAUTY OF RESTORATION

Joseph had his chariot made ready and went to Goshen to meet his father Israel. As soon as Joseph appeared before him, he threw his arms around his father and wept for a long time.

GENESIS 46:29 NIV

When God brings restoration, it's magical. He softens hearts, shortens distances, heals hurts, and changes attitudes so we're able to embrace one another again.

Is there someone you're wanting to reconnect with? Are you hoping for a reunion with someone once dear to you? Pray for God to make it possible.

Lord, my heart aches for reconciliation. I want to work through the issues and have a relationship with that person. I know this is something only You can make happen. Would You do that for me?

EVENING
BLESSING FOR OBEDIENCE

And because the midwives honored God, God gave them families of their own.

EXODUS 1:21 MSG

It's not always easy to stand up for what's right, especially when a threat's involved. From losing your job to compromising a friendship to risking your reputation, taking a hard stand for true and right isn't often convenient or simple. It takes guts and grit to hold the line so many others cross without consideration. But when you do the hard thing and follow God's way, He will not only see it but also promises to bless your obedience.

What keeps you from doing the things you know will please God?

Ask God for courage. Ask Him to make you brave. Ask for wisdom. And rest knowing that if God is asking something from you, He'll give you everything you need to walk it out.

Lord, give me confidence to stand for what's true and pleasing to You.

MORNING
THE TANGLE OF INSECURITY

*Moses objected, "They won't trust me. They won't listen to a word
I say. They're going to say, 'GOD? Appear to him? Hardly!'"*
EXODUS 4:1 MSG

God didn't make a mistake when He made you. He knew exactly what He was doing. He created you with specific gifts and talents that would bless others and benefit your community. He put you together with intentionality from head to toe. He decided details like where you'd live, the jobs you'd have, the money you'd make, and the friends you'd have. And in God's eyes, you are complete and perfect.

There is nothing *less than* about you.

Lord, please untangle me from insecurity, and remind me of who I am because of You.

EVENING
AND THEN SOME

*The LORD had made the Egyptians favorably disposed toward the people,
and they gave them what they asked for; so they plundered the Egyptians.*
EXODUS 12:36 NIV

God's love is lavish! Can you think of a time when His favor shined brightly on you? Maybe money showed up when you needed it most or a new job offer came out of nowhere. Maybe someone offered to fix your car for free or your child's school tuition was covered anonymously. Maybe groceries were on your doorstep after a long day of work or you walked into a spotless house, courtesy of your teenagers.

You serve a generous Father who will make sure your needs are met. . .*and then some.*

*Lord, thank You for being a God of "and then some." I am so thankful for
Your kindness and generosity toward me! I'm so grateful for Your favor!*

MORNING
WHO OR WHAT IS YOUR GOD?

You shall have no other gods before or besides Me.
EXODUS 20:3 AMPC

God wants the number one place in your heart. He wants no one or nothing to be above Him. He wants you to include Him in your day, your struggles, your challenges, as well as your joys. God desires a robust relationship with *you*.

What are some things you can change today that will help you keep priorities in the right order? How can you reorder your to-do lists? What needs to shift on your calendar? God is eager to be your God above all else.

Lord, I am sorry that I've not always put You first.
You are my only God. Help me live that way.

EVENING
A STANDING INVITATION

The LORD said to Moses, "Come up to me on the mountain and
stay here, and I will give you the tablets of stone with the law
and commandments I have written for their instruction."
EXODUS 24:12 NIV

God's invitation is a standing one. Whether it be one o'clock in the afternoon or one o'clock in the wee hours of the morning, God is available. No matter how many times you've shared your thoughts and feelings with Him before, He'll listen again, for He welcomes you into His presence whenever you want and wherever you are.

What keeps you from reaching out to God? Is it a busy schedule? Do you feel like an annoyance? Is it pride? Do you think He has bigger fish to fry? Well, friend, just like He did for Moses, God is inviting you to come and spend time with Him. Will you?

Lord, thank You for the standing invitation to spend time with You. In a
world where many are too busy for me, I'm grateful You never are.

MORNING
A GLIMPSE OF GRACE

And the rest of the oil that is in the priest's hand he shall put upon the head of him that is to be cleansed, to make an atonement for him before the LORD. And he shall offer the one of the turtledoves, or of the young pigeons, such as he can get; even such as he is able to get, the one for a sin offering, and the other for a burnt offering, with the meat offering: and the priest shall make an atonement for him that is to be cleansed before the LORD.

LEVITICUS 14:29–31 KJV

In today's reading of Leviticus 14:29–31, you'll get a glimpse of grace. Look closely to read words that convey that a priest was willing to look upon lepers and help make them right with God.

No matter what physical or relational ailment may be plaguing you, causing discord and division in your life, remember God loves and accepts you just as you are! His grace is ready and waiting. Simply go to Him and ask for it.

Lord, keep my eyes and mind open to the reality that Your grace is all around me. Thank You for loving and accepting me just as I am.

EVENING
SABBATH REST

On that day offerings of purification will be made for you, and you will be purified in the LORD's presence from all your sins. It will be a Sabbath day of complete rest for you, and you must deny yourselves. This is a permanent law for you.

LEVITICUS 16:30–31 NLT

The most important thing you will ever do throughout your daily routine is spend time with your heavenly Father and Creator. Without staying in line with the One who knitted you together and knows your every thought and feeling, how can you keep a good attitude through it all? You can't. But with God's help, you can.

So, take five minutes to breathe deeply and talk to God. He wants to hear from you.

God, I come before You in need of some rest. From the top of my head to the bottom of my feet, please relax my body and renew me tonight.

MORNING
WHEN THE LORD SPEAKS

*"You and your brother Aaron are to speak to the rock while they watch,
and it will yield its water. You will bring out water for them from the
rock and provide drink for the community and their livestock."*
NUMBERS 20:8 HCSB

When the Lord speaks, He wants you to totally trust Him in every detail, no matter how strange His request. So, if and when you find yourself doubting, humble yourself and ask for forgiveness. Then walk forward, trusting your Creator, taking Him at His word.

Lord, please forgive me for not trusting You at times. Keep my ears open to what You have spoken to me through Your Word, through the prompting of Your Holy Spirit, and through the testimonies of others. Keep my ears open, Lord, to what You're saying.

EVENING
GREAT LENGTHS

*And God said to Balaam, You shall not go with them; you
shall not curse the people, for they are blessed.*
NUMBERS 22:12 AMPC

If the same God who went to great lengths for the Israelites is the same God you follow today, to what great lengths are you willing to go to express your love and devotion to Him?

Take some time to inventory your relationship with God. How have you seen Him come through for you? What miracles has He performed? What prayers has He answered? How can you praise Him for all that He has done and will yet do? Thank Him for being available right now, in this moment, to hear you, love you, and lavish you.

Father God, You are worthy of my praise and admiration. Thank You for continuing to pursue me even when I forget to look up and pursue You!

MORNING
FAITHFUL TO THE END

Then the Lord said to Moses, "On behalf of the people of Israel,
take revenge on the Midianites for leading them into idolatry.
After that, you will die and join your ancestors."

NUMBERS 31:1–2 NLT

Has God ever brought you through a challenging season? Chances are He has. As you went through it, it most likely felt hard, overwhelming. You might have questioned God or even thrown your hands up and railed at Him, asking, "How long, Lord? When will my situation *finally* change?"

Stay faithful until the end. Your time of rest is coming, both now here on earth and later when you get to spend eternity with God in heaven.

Lord, help me remain faithful. When I'm in seasons of blessing and harvest, help
me remember it was You who provided abundantly. When I'm in seasons that are
humbling, help me remember that life is fragile and shaky, but You are stable and solid!

EVENING
HE DELIGHTS IN YOU

The Lord your God will delight in you if you obey his voice and keep
the commands and decrees written in this Book of Instruction, and if
you turn to the Lord your God with all your heart and soul.

DEUTERONOMY 30:10 NLT

Did you know that God delights in you? It's true! You bring such joy to the heavenly Father's heart.

For some women, that might be hard to hear. . .or believe. Many are convinced that they are a disappointment to the Lord, that their mistakes have somehow separated them from Him. Nothing could be further from the truth. Tonight and every night, turn to God and see that He has a sparkle in His eye and hands extended. You're His daughter, and you bring Him such joy!

I'm so glad my presence brings You joy, Father!

MORNING
AND THE WALLS CAME TUMBLING DOWN

*When the people heard the sound of the rams' horns, they shouted
as loud as they could. Suddenly, the walls of Jericho collapsed, and
the Israelites charged straight into the town and captured it.*
JOSHUA 6:20 NLT

Joshua and the Israelites marched around the city for seven days, just as the Lord instructed. Then, when the moment was right, the ram's horn was blown, and the walls collapsed right in front of them.

Maybe you've faced some walls in your own life. There are areas you feel are impenetrable. Perhaps it's time to march around those "nevers" a few times and blow the ram's horn. If you have faith as the Israelites did, those walls might just come tumbling down!

*Thank You for knocking down the walls in my life, Father! Please increase
my faith as, with Your help, I march around the "nevers" in my life.*

EVENING
WHILE YOU'RE WAITING

*But the descendants of Manasseh were unable to occupy these towns
because the Canaanites were determined to stay in that region.*
JOSHUA 17:12 NLT

Maybe you're not in a position to take that big trip like the one your neighbors are taking. And maybe you're not able to cruise the Caribbean. But while you're waiting, God can still do amazing things.

The Israelites knew what it was like to wait. Even after they entered the Promised Land, the descendants of Manasseh ran into a hitch. Surely it dashed their hopes to realize they would have to wait to occupy their portion of land. Still, they didn't give up in the waiting, and God doesn't want you to give up, either. . .no matter how long it takes.

*I won't give up while I'm waiting, Lord. I'll keep
the faith no matter how things look in the moment.*

MORNING
THERE'S STILL WORK TO BE DONE

When Joshua was an old man, the LORD said to him, "You are growing old, and much land remains to be conquered."

JOSHUA 13:1 NLT

Maybe you are reaching the point in your journey where you feel your best days are behind you. You don't know what—if anything—is next. Your "glory days" were wonderful, but you're just tired. Depleted.

God still has plenty of adventure ahead for you. The work isn't done yet and neither is His plan for your goodness. Get the rest you need, but don't give up. Rise up from that bed and face new adventures, new joys.

Lord, thank You for the reminder that there are still adventures ahead. Amen.

EVENING
A RESCUER

But when the people of Israel cried out to the LORD for help, the LORD raised up a rescuer to save them. His name was Othniel, the son of Caleb's younger brother, Kenaz. The Spirit of the LORD came upon him, and he became Israel's judge. He went to war against King Cushan-rishathaim of Aram, and the LORD gave Othniel victory over him.

JUDGES 3:9–10 NLT

Over two thousand years ago, God heard the cries of His people and sent His Son, Jesus, as the Ultimate Rescuer. He did what none of the former "gods" could do—He offered eternal rescue to all who would place their trust in Him.

Tonight, when you cry out to God, trust that He will hear your prayer. Know that Jesus will rescue you from whatever's coming against you. For that's His business today, tomorrow, and forever.

*Thank You for hearing the words of my prayer, Lord.
Jesus, how can I ever thank You for coming to save me?*

MORNING
A WOMAN OF HONOR

Deborah, the wife of Lappidoth, was a prophet who was judging Israel at that
time. She would sit under the Palm of Deborah, between Ramah and Bethel in
the hill country of Ephraim, and the Israelites would go to her for judgment.
JUDGES 4:4–5 NLT

God still uses women today. They speak into the lives of their children, friends, loved ones, and the church body. They write and teach Bible studies, direct plays, lead ministries. They manage companies, travel the globe, and impact people world-round.

What a blessing to know that God values the giftings inside of His women. What gift is He stirring in you right now?

Thank You for using women, Lord. I'm so grateful
for the gifts You've placed inside of all of us.

EVENING
WHERE YOU GO, I'LL GO

But Ruth replied, "Don't ask me to leave you and turn back. Wherever you go,
I will go; wherever you live, I will live. Your people will be my people, and your
God will be my God. Wherever you die, I will die, and there I will be buried. May
the LORD punish me severely if I allow anything but death to separate us!"
RUTH 1:16–18 NLT

Wow. Naomi must've been shocked. Ruth was so bonded with her mother-in-law that Ruth couldn't bear the idea of separating from her.

God wants us to be as bonded to Him as Ruth was to Naomi. When He moves to the right, He wants us to move to the right. When He moves to the left. . .well, you get the point. Where He goes, we go. Where He stays, we stay.

Wherever You go, Lord, I'm going too.

MORNING
OUR UNSTOPPABLE GOD

*And Jonathan said to his young armor-bearer, Come, and let us go over to
the garrison of these uncircumcised; it may be that the Lord will work for us.
For there is nothing to prevent the Lord from saving by many or by few.*
1 SAMUEL 14:6 AMPC

We serve a mighty God who always wins. He has been, He is, and He will always be victorious because He is above all. God's plans are perfect, and His will is wonderful. There is nothing to prevent the Lord from doing what He sees fit to do.

Nothing.

Let God do the heavy lifting. Activate your faith in His abilities, because, unlike you, He is unstoppable.

*Lord, what a relief to know that Your will. . .will be
done. Thankfully, You're God, and I am not.*

EVENING
DECLARE IT OUT LOUD

*David answered, "You come at me with sword and spear and battle-ax. I come
at you in the name of GOD-of-the-Angel-Armies, the God of Israel's troops,
whom you curse and mock. This very day GOD is handing you over to me."*
1 SAMUEL 17:45 MSG

David had complete faith in the Lord. He knew the victory was his, and he was confident in that truth enough to declare it out loud for all to hear.

It's one thing to believe God will give you victory over the giants you face. It's another thing altogether to speak it.

Trust God enough to voice your faith in Him. Tell others you believe in Him. It's encouraging when you're bold enough to declare your faith in God.

Lord, I believe You. I trust You. My faith will always be in You.

MORNING
BACK TO PRAYER

So David went back to God in prayer. God said, "Get going.
Head for Keilah. I'm placing the Philistines in your hands."
1 Samuel 23:4 MSG

God puts no limits on your sharing. He doesn't roll His eyes when "that topic" comes up again and again. He never grows weary of your requests. God wants to hear all, all the time.

What are the lies you've been believing about prayer? What are the misconceptions you've been entertaining? Do you believe God is "all ears" for you?

Woman of the Way, you are God's daughter. Because you're the daughter of the King, you can always come back to prayer.

Lord, thank You for the open invitation to pray to You anytime, anywhere.

EVENING
GOD ALONE

So Saul ordered his officials, "Find me someone who can call
up spirits so I may go and seek counsel from those spirits."
His servants said, "There's a witch at Endor."
1 Samuel 28:7 MSG

Friend, God is Lord over everything. There is none above Him and none beside Him. God alone rules the heavens and the earth, and He determines your next steps. Don't allow anything to pull you away from Him. Have faith that He loves you fully and completely. And decide to trust God even when you don't understand His ways and will.

Lord, I believe You're 100 percent for me and will never leave nor forsake me.
Forgive me for the times I've doubted You. You alone I'll seek and trust.

MORNING
STRENGTHENING YOURSELF IN HIM

David was greatly distressed, for the men spoke of stoning him because the souls of them all were bitterly grieved, each man for his sons and daughters. But David encouraged and strengthened himself in the Lord his God.
1 SAMUEL 30:6 AMPC

Like David, it's vital we know how to strengthen ourselves in the Lord. It might consist of desperate conversations with Him. It might entail reading His Word or speaking out scriptures that remind us who He is. It might be listening to worship music or figuratively crawling into our Daddy's lap and crying those big tears.

Remember, you have everything you need to encourage and strengthen yourself in God as you walk out this hard season.

Lord, help me learn to strengthen myself when no one is around. I'm so thankful that You always make a way.

EVENING
THE TEMPTATION OF LOVELY

One evening David arose from his couch and was walking on the roof of the king's house, when from there he saw a woman bathing; and she was very lovely to behold.
2 SAMUEL 11:2 AMPC

What are the lovely things that tempt you? What do you find so irresistible that you compromise what you know is good and right?

The truth is that we won't escape this life without being enticed by something or someone. It's common to every one of us. Let's just settle that right now. But when the pressure to compromise feels too much, God will help you hold steady and not give in.

Remember that you're not alone. And you don't have to rely on your own strength to stay strong.

Lord, there are lovely things that weaken my resolve. On my own, I can't always withstand their pull, so thank You for Your promise to help me.

MORNING
IS IT GUILT OR SHAME?

*But when it was all done, David was overwhelmed with guilt because he had counted
the people, replacing trust with statistics. And David prayed to God, "I have sinned
badly in what I have just done. But now God forgive my guilt—I've been really stupid."*
2 Samuel 24:10 MSG

Guilt says you've *done* something bad. Shame says you *are* bad.

It's important to know the difference because shame is often a hidden belief that
operates within without you even knowing it. Unless it's uncovered, it will be the lens
you look at life through. It will decide what you think about yourself.

Just as David took his guilt to God, you can too. Even more importantly, you can
take the shame you're feeling to Him as well. Confess them both, and then ask for the
Lord to remove them and remind you of your value.

*Lord, I realize I'm living with both of these joy-draining feelings.
Please either remove them or break their hold over me. Then,
Lord, restore my value as I live and breathe in You.*

EVENING
PRAYING FOR OTHERS

*Then the king said to the man of God, "Intercede with the Lord your God and
pray for me that my hand may be restored." So the man of God interceded with
the Lord, and the king's hand was restored and became as it was before.*
1 Kings 13:6 NIV

Have you been asked to pray for someone and it frustrated you? Or have you thought
you were too busy and already praying for enough people?

Ask God to help you embrace the opportunity, because the Bible tells us prayer
matters. The Lord hears every word, every request, every plea. Not only does He listen,
but we're also told in the pages of His Word that we will be answered. Sometimes He
says, "Yes," other times He says, "No," or "Wait for it," but God will answer.

*Lord, I want to be open to praying for others when they need it,
without their request feeling too heavy. Change my heart when needed.*

MORNING
LIMITLESS GOD

"Thus says the LORD, 'Because the Syrians have said, "The LORD is a god of the hills but he is not a god of the valleys," therefore I will give all this great multitude into your hand, and you shall know that I am the LORD.'"
1 KINGS 20:28 ESV

God wants you to know that He can do anything, be anywhere, and reigns over all things, creatures, and places—in heaven and on earth. Your God is bigger, greater, mightier, and more wonderful than anything or anyone you could ever meet or imagine.

If you have a problem, don't fear. Just look to God. Know that He's bigger than any obstacle that stands before You. And He will give you the victory, the ways, the means to overcome it.

Lord, I rejoice that You are so mighty, so much bigger than any obstacle looming before me! Because of You, I fear nothing and no one!

EVENING
BEFORE YOU DO ANYTHING. . .

He turned to Jehoshaphat and said, "Will you join me in fighting for Ramoth Gilead?" Jehoshaphat said, "You bet. I'm with you all the way—my troops are your troops, my horses are your horses. . . . But before you do anything, ask GOD for guidance."
1 KINGS 22:4–5 MSG

James 1:5–6 (MSG) says, "If you don't know what you're doing, pray to the Father. He loves to help. You'll get his help, and won't be condescended to when you ask for it. Ask boldly, believingly, without a second thought."

Tonight, before you do anything, ask God for guidance. He'll be sure to head you in the right direction, from here to eternity.

Lord, I'm in need of Your guidance. What would You have me do?

MORNING
ARMS AND HEART OPEN WIDE

But the Lord was gracious to them and had compassion on them and
turned toward them because of His covenant with Abraham, Isaac, and
Jacob, and would not destroy them or cast them from His presence yet.
2 KINGS 13:23 AMPC

Just as God was gracious to His people and had compassion on them thousands of years ago, your God-who-never-changes has grace and compassion for you today. As a Christ follower, rest assured your God is waiting to hold you in His arms, to love and comfort you just as a mother comforts her child (Isaiah 66:13 NIV).

Today, seek out your God. When you do, He'll turn to you, arms and heart open wide.

Lord, hold me. Love me. Be to me as a loving parent. Amen.

EVENING
PRESENCE AND PROSPERITY

Hezekiah trusted in, leaned on, and was confident in the Lord. . . .
For he clung and held fast to the Lord and ceased not to follow Him,
but kept His commandments, as the Lord commanded Moses. And
the Lord was with Hezekiah; he prospered wherever he went.
2 KINGS 18:5–7 AMPC

What's your relationship with God like? What do you trust Him with? How close do you cling to Him—in good times and bad? How well do you keep His Son's commandments?

There is a connection between God's presence in your life and your prosperity. Tonight, contemplate your answers to the foregoing questions. Then pray for God to increase your faith, trust, and confidence in Him.

Lord, I want to grow my trust and faith in You alone. Please help me
follow You no matter what, for I desire Your presence in my life here and
beyond! So please be with me, Lord, prospering me wherever I go.

MORNING
THE POWER OF HEARTFELT PRAYER

Hezekiah turned his face to the wall and prayed to the LORD, "Please LORD, remember how I have walked before You faithfully and wholeheartedly and have done what pleases You" . . . " 'The LORD God. . .says: I have heard your prayer; I have seen your tears. Look, I will heal you.'"

2 KINGS 20:2–3, 5 HCSB

God, hearing Hezekiah's heartfelt prayer, sent Isaiah back to tell Hezekiah that He had heard his prayer, seen his tears, and would heal him. To prove it, Hezekiah asked God to reverse the course of a shadow, making it go back ten steps. And He did!

When you find yourself in dire straits, follow the wisdom of good King Hezekiah. Go directly to God. Put your case before Him. Allow the tears to flow and the heart to speak. Then know that God has heard you. He has seen your tears. And He will heal you—if not in this life, then the next.

Lord, You have my heart. Now hear my prayer.

EVENING
READ AND PRAY

"Go and pray to GOD for me and for this people—for all Judah! Find out what we must do in response to what is written in this book that has just been found! GOD's anger must be burning furiously against us—our ancestors haven't obeyed a thing written in this book."

2 KINGS 22:13 MSG

Can you imagine trying to live life without the Bible, God's voice, His words to train you, inform you, advise you, and call you ever closer to Him? Can you imagine losing His precious Word?

Tonight, grab your Bible. Pray that God will open your eyes, ears, mind, and heart to the message meant for you. Then read God's words. Allow His direction and wisdom to flow into you.

Open Your Word to me, Lord. Show me what You would have me know, see, hear, and do.

MORNING
RAISE A PRAISE

And then there were the musicians, all heads of Levite families. They had permanent living quarters in The Temple; because they were on twenty-four-hour duty, they were exempt from all other duties.
1 CHRONICLES 9:33 MSG

When was the last time you praised God, making a joyful noise to Him with songs of praise (Psalm 95:1–11)? James tells you to pray if you're suffering and sing praise if you're cheerful (James 5:13). Yet can you imagine how wonderful it would be if you'd praise God even on your down days? If you do, if you burst into song when you're unhappy, your sorrow will soon fade away because you'll be focusing on the Lord instead of yourself or your troubles.

Lord, I lift my voice in praise to You each day and, in so doing, lift myself in You!

EVENING
ALL THE COURAGE YOU NEED

"If the Arameans are too much for me, you help me; and if the Ammonites prove too much for you, I'll come and help you. Courage! We'll fight might and main for our people and for the cities of our God. And GOD will do whatever he sees needs doing!"
1 CHRONICLES 19:12–13 MSG

When you find yourself between a rock and a hard place, don't allow yourself to feel defeated. Instead, look for or give help where needed. Then remind yourself that you can find all the courage you need in the God you trust. At the same time, be sure to acknowledge that your victory lies in knowing God Himself will do whatever else He sees needs doing.

I'm stuck in a tough situation, Lord. Yet in You I find the courage I need and the knowledge that You'll do whatever I cannot.

MORNING
ENOUGH TIME

Be strong and courageous, and do it. Fear not, be not dismayed, for the
Lord God, my God, is with you. He will not fail or forsake you until you
have finished all the work for the service of the house of the Lord.
1 CHRONICLES 28:20 AMPC

Have you ever considered you would never have enough time to do all you wanted to do in your day or lifetime? If so, take heart. God has a certain purpose for you, a role He would have only you fill, work that you alone can accomplish. And He will not leave or fail you until you've done what He created you to do. So let go of that "I'll never have enough time to do what needs to be done" feeling. Stop rushing to accomplish what God has put in your hands. Instead, be calm, quiet, and confident that your Lord is with you, helping you, and allowing you all the time you need.

Lord, help me to slow down, to seek to live for and serve
You, knowing You'll stick with me till the end.

EVENING
ALL THAT YOU ARE

King Solomon surpassed all the kings of the earth in riches and
wisdom. And all the kings of the earth sought the presence of Solomon
to hear his wisdom which God had put into his mind.
2 CHRONICLES 9:22–23 AMPC

All that you have, all that you are, all that you do, in fact your very life itself, are gifts from God. He is the One who created you, then breathed life into you. He is the One who sustains, protects, and provides for you. And He is the One who will, at some point, bring you back to Himself. So when others laud you for your talents, possessions, insights, knowledge, etc., remind yourself (and perhaps them) that what others admire about you is from God, giving credit where credit is due.

You are the One who has made me what I am, Lord. So when
others praise me, remind me to give all of the credit to You alone!

MORNING
TAKE COURAGE

"Take courage! Do not let your hands be weak, for your work
shall be rewarded." As soon as Asa heard these words, the
prophecy of Azariah the son of Oded, he took courage.
2 CHRONICLES 15:7–8 ESV

When Asa heard these encouraging words, he "rolled up his sleeves, and went to work" (2 Chronicles 15:8 MSG) removing idols and renovating altars. As a result of his endeavors, the Judeans sought God with all their hearts and minds and found Him. And "the LORD gave them rest all around" (2 Chronicles 15:15 ESV).

You have the truth and wisdom of God at your fingertips, so when you need some extra courage, seek out His good Word. Look for Him with all your heart and mind. And you too will find God, as well as His strength, courage, peace, and rest.

Lord, please give me the courage and strength to do what You've called me to do.

EVENING
EYES ON GOD

For we have no might to stand against this great company that is coming against us.
We do not know what to do, but our eyes are upon You. . . . The Lord says this to you:
Be not afraid or dismayed at this great multitude; for the battle is not yours, but God's.
2 CHRONICLES 20:12, 15 AMPC

Hearing these words from Jehoshaphat, God tells him not to be worried or afraid of this great mass of warriors at Judah's gate for this battle is His. All His people need to do is "take your positions, stand still, and see the deliverance of the Lord [Who is] with you" (2 Chronicles 20:17 AMPC).

When you find yourself about to panic, stop. Let God know your situation. Then, with your eyes on Him and your faith in Him, stand still and witness the victory.

I don't know what to do, Lord. But my eyes are on You, and my faith is in You.

MORNING
THE BEST LIFE THERE IS

While they were bringing out the money that had been taken into the temple of the LORD, Hilkiah the priest found the Book of the Law of the LORD that had been given through Moses. Hilkiah said to Shaphan the secretary, "I have found the Book of the Law in the temple of the LORD." He gave it to Shaphan.

2 CHRONICLES 34:14–15 NIV

Today, we have done a great job of snubbing the Word of God and even removing parts of the Bible that make us squirm. We've extracted the Good Book from our schools, businesses, and even our hotel rooms. And now, the Word of God is fading from the hearts of people, leaving each of them in spiritual peril.

The great news is that what was lost can be found. Look for that family Bible or buy a new one. Open its pages and discover real life in Christ—the best life there is—both now and forevermore.

Lord, at times we're guilty of ignoring You and the Bible.
Please awaken us to the truth of Your Word.

EVENING
A COMING HOME OF THE SOUL

But many of the older priests and Levites and family heads, who had seen the former temple, wept aloud when they saw the foundation of this temple being laid, while many others shouted for joy. No one could distinguish the sound of the shouts of joy from the sound of weeping, because the people made so much noise. And the sound was heard far away.

EZRA 3:12–13 NIV

Making things right with God, well, there's nothing else like that divine reconnection. One might come to think of remorseful or joyous weeping or jubilant shouts before God as a sacred song or a "coming home of the soul."

Have you connected to God lately? Have you come to know that "coming home of the soul"? It is only a prayer away.

God, please forgive me for all that I've done to harm our relationship. I want to be close to You both now and forevermore. In Jesus' holy name I pray.

MORNING
FROM DISCOURAGEMENT TO JOY

*Then the peoples around them set out to discourage the people of Judah
and make them afraid to go on building. They bribed officials to work
against them and frustrate their plans during the entire reign of Cyrus
king of Persia and down to the reign of Darius king of Persia.*

EZRA 4:4–5 NIV

In our modern world, there will be people who will pretend to help us in our endeavors,
but in the end, we may discover their hidden motives might not be so pure or helpful.
Yet just as God allowed the Jewish exiles to succeed in the end, may we always pray for
His will to be done in our lives no matter the worldly hostilities and the ploys of the
enemy. May God give us wisdom and perseverance as we follow His lead in helping to
build His kingdom!

*Lord, please allow me to know Your will and follow through with it no
matter the oppositions. Please turn my discouragements into joy!*

EVENING
CHOOSING TO HONOR GOD

*Praise be to the LORD, the God of our ancestors, who has put it into the king's
heart to bring honor to the house of the LORD in Jerusalem in this way and
who has extended his good favor to me before the king and his advisers and
all the king's powerful officials. Because the hand of the LORD my God was
on me, I took courage and gathered leaders from Israel to go up with me.*

EZRA 7:27–28 NIV

Today, we can choose who will be our lawmakers from the voting booth. Are we prayerfully considering who we select to lead us? Does he or she follow scripture, including
honoring the biblical view of marriage, the sanctity of life, and watching out for the
needy and elderly? Or do the people running for office call good evil and evil good?
With God's help, may we be diligent in finding godly leaders.

*Lord, I want to honor You in all that I do, including
choosing the right people to lead our nation.*

MORNING
CHOICES

King Xerxes imposed tribute throughout the empire, to its distant shores. And all his acts of power and might, together with a full account of the greatness of Mordecai, whom the king had promoted, are they not written in the book of the annals of the kings of Media and Persia? Mordecai the Jew was second in rank to King Xerxes, preeminent among the Jews, and held in high esteem by his many fellow Jews, because he worked for the good of his people and spoke up for the welfare of all the Jews.
ESTHER 10:1–3 NIV

Today, every choice you make is not only remembered by God but has the potential to change the flow of history—for good or for evil.

What will your choices be today?

Dearest Lord Jesus, please help my choices to be good and lovely ones. Help them to shine Your light in a world that is in great need of Your radiant presence.

EVENING
TRIALS

Then the LORD said to Satan, "Have you considered my servant Job? There is no one on earth like him; he is blameless and upright, a man who fears God and shuns evil." "Does Job fear God for nothing?" Satan replied. "Have you not put a hedge around him and his household and everything he has? You have blessed the work of his hands, so that his flocks and herds are spread throughout the land. But now stretch out your hand and strike everything he has, and he will surely curse you to your face."
JOB 1:8–11 NIV

If we endured a few Job-like catastrophes, how would we fare? Would we curse God? Would we doubt His power, sovereignty, or love for us? Or in the end would we, like Job, still find ourselves in love with God, no matter our circumstances?

Lord, help me to stay true to You even during the rough patches. Amen.

MORNING
RIVER OF DELIGHTS

Your love, LORD, reaches to the heavens, your faithfulness to the skies. Your righteousness is like the highest mountains, your justice like the great deep. You, LORD, preserve both people and animals. How priceless is your unfailing love, O God! People take refuge in the shadow of your wings. They feast on the abundance of your house; you give them drink from your river of delights. For with you is the fountain of life; in your light we see light.
PSALM 36:5–9 NIV

Read and reread this passage in Psalms, and embrace the delights of God Almighty.

Remember, of course, that the greatest delight comes from Jesus Christ Himself, whose sacrifice and redemption make for the most radiant light and most irresistible goodness and most powerful love this world will ever know.

Father God, be ever near me. I want to know You. I want to drink from Your river of delights.

EVENING
PRAISE HIM!

Praise the LORD!
PSALM 150:6 ESV

"Let everything that has breath" (Psalm 150:6 ESV). . . When you're feeling up or down—praise the Lord! In good times and bad—praise the Lord! At the beginning of each new morning, at the end of your longest days—praise the Lord! Maybe praising God doesn't come naturally to you, or maybe your praise muscles are a little out of shape—praise the Lord anyway! It's amazing what praise can do. And God deserves nothing less. As the psalmist declared, "Hallelujah! It's a good thing to sing praise to our God; praise is beautiful, praise is fitting" (Psalm 147:1 MSG).

Lord, there's so much to praise You for. Oh, that praise would fill my life and rise straight to You!

MORNING
IN THE END

When the tempest passes, the wicked is no more,
but the righteous is established forever.
PROVERBS 10:25 ESV

When all the storms of this life pass, the righteous will end in good and the wicked will end period. It's a promise:

"*Count on this: The wicked won't get off scot-free, and God's loyal people will triumph*" (Proverbs 11:21 MSG).

"*The godly can look forward to a reward, while the wicked can expect only judgment*" (Proverbs 11:23 NLT).

"*The light of the righteous rejoices, but the lamp of the wicked will be put out*" (Proverbs 13:9 ESV).

God of justice, all that goes on—well, it makes me mad,
and it makes me sad. But I trust You for the future.

EVENING
POLAR OPPOSITES

To every thing there is a season, and a time to every purpose under the heaven.
ECCLESIASTES 3:1 KJV

Perhaps you tend to zoom in on the negative. You read Solomon's words, "What do people really get for all their hard work? I have seen the burden God has placed on us all" (Ecclesiastes 3:9–10 NLT), and your heart adds, *Ain't it the truth!*

Yes, it's the truth, but don't call it quits there. We may not be able to escape the bad, yet we *can* cling to the good. We can hold on to the assurance that "God has made everything beautiful for its own time," *and* we can hold on to the God-given promise of a perfect time to come: "He has planted eternity in the human heart" (Ecclesiastes 3:11 NLT).

God, help me hold tightly to the good.

MORNING
L.O.V.E.

Love flashes like fire, the brightest kind of flame. Many
waters cannot quench love, nor can rivers drown it.
Song of Solomon 8:6–7 nlt

Truth is, even the deepest, most joyous human love will let us down if we don't let Love Himself love us first. Our souls won't be satisfied nor our desires met until we find satisfaction in Him and He becomes our highest desire. No true love can complete us—only the One with the truest love of all. But praise God! He's reaching out with that love. Will you reach out too?

Lord, Your love is greater than any other, and You've given it to me! Earthly
love may disappoint me, but I can rejoice and rest in Your love forever.

EVENING
JESUS

For unto us a child is born, unto us a son is given: and the government shall
be upon his shoulder: and his name shall be called Wonderful, Counsellor,
The mighty God, The everlasting Father, The Prince of Peace.
Isaiah 9:6 kjv

These days, we might fear that troubled times lie ahead. Our world is aching, and there's already abundant gloom. But Isaiah's words promise dawn on the horizon. The Messiah is coming back! He's coming back to put things right for good and for certain: "His government and its peace will never end. He will rule with fairness and justice . . .for all eternity. The passionate commitment of the Lord of Heaven's Armies will make this happen!" (Isaiah 9:7 nlt). Look beyond any hardship to the returning King.

Jesus, You are the Light of the World—and of my life!

MORNING
ABSOLUTE POWER

Who has purposed this. . . ? The LORD of hosts has purposed it. . . .
He has stretched out his hand over the sea; he has shaken the kingdoms.
ISAIAH 23:8–9, 11 ESV

Out with the bad! And in with the good. God replaced Shebna with Eliakim, whom He called "my servant" (Isaiah 22:20) and described him in terms reminiscent of Christ: "I will give him the key to the house of David. . . . When he opens doors, no one will be able to close them; when he closes doors, no one will be able to open them" (Isaiah 22:22 NLT; see Revelation 3:7).

However troubling leadership may be, you can be sure that our Sovereign Lord is still holding the reins. He's in control! Of leaders. Of nations. And nothing can thwart His purposes.

I rest easy in Your will, Lord. How great You are!

EVENING
KEY TO HAPPINESS

He will be the sure foundation for your times, a rich store of salvation and
wisdom and knowledge; the fear of the LORD is the key to this treasure.
ISAIAH 33:6 NIV

What is "this treasure" of which Isaiah speaks? Unlike a chest overflowing with gold and jewels, Isaiah refers to a treasure far more valuable. This treasure offers safety, peace of mind, knowledge, and wisdom. As Proverbs 8:11 (NIV) tells us, "Wisdom is more precious than rubies, and nothing you desire can compare with her."

Remember to let God be your foundation, and you will certainly reap the bounty of His treasure.

Dear Lord, help me to trust in You, to respect You, and to be secure in
the knowledge that my confidence lies in You. Help me seek the treasure
You offer, the true treasure of salvation, wisdom, and knowledge.

Day 334

MORNING
GREEN THUMB

For as the soil makes the sprout come up and a garden causes seeds to grow, so the Sovereign LORD will make righteousness and praise spring up before all nations.
ISAIAH 61:11 NIV

Just as plants are a part of your garden, you are a part of God's garden. So create in yourself the perfect environment to cultivate God's blessings. Prepare yourself to be as good a vessel as you possibly can. God has planted the seed in you. Now it's up to you to help it along.

God is the Master Gardener. Allow yourself to blossom under His hand and with His help.

Dear God, You are the Grower of all good things. Help me to prepare a proper environment within myself to receive Your blessings. Let my heart be a vessel worthy of Your promises of love and eternal life.

EVENING
BRAGGING RIGHTS

"But let the one who boasts boast about this: that they have the understanding to know me, that I am the LORD, who exercises kindness, justice and righteousness on earth, for in these I delight," declares the LORD.
JEREMIAH 9:24 NIV

It is comforting to read the God-inspired words of Jeremiah, wherein God reminds you and all His children that He is loving, is caring, and delights in justice and righteousness. So if you feel the tendency to boast rising up within you, consider that your greatest claim to fame should be that you know the Lord your God, that you understand and fear Him. When you do, giving Him all the credit, He, in turn, will delight in you and your adherence to His Word.

Dear Lord, let my lips brag of no one but You. Help me sing Your praises day and night. In You I can boast confidently, knowing that You delight in me.

MORNING
WINNING THE RACE

*"If you have raced with men on foot and they have worn you out,
how can you compete with horses? If you stumble in safe country,
how will you manage in the thickets by the Jordan?"*

JEREMIAH 12:5 NIV

God tells His people that if they don't have the stamina to race men, how will they compete with horses? If they stumble on a safe road, how will they ever make it through thickets? God would have you learn to pace yourself in any race. To take things slow and steady. Remember, this is how the tortoise won the proverbial race against the hare. By pacing yourself, you save energy for the larger problems in life. In other words, don't sweat the small stuff.

*Dear Lord, help me pace myself in this relay of life. Help me recognize
the difference between small inconveniences and severe situations. Help
me to remember that You are with me through the small stuff as well as
the large because You are my salvation in all ways and for all days.*

EVENING
HEART TO HEART

*"I will give them a heart to know me, that I am the LORD. They will be my
people, and I will be their God, for they will return to me with all their heart."*

JEREMIAH 24:7 NIV

In Proverbs 4:23 (NIV), you are warned, "Above all else, guard your heart, for everything you do flows from it." There is nothing more important than your heart and your love, so guard that heart. And love your God. Know Him with your whole heart, returning to Him tonight and every night.

*Dear Lord, I thank You every day for the gift of my life, for the heart You
have given me, and for the ability to love You and know You with that whole
heart. Thank You for being my God, the One who loves and cares for me.*

MORNING
SHOUTING FROM THE ROOFTOPS

"This is what the Lord says: Stand in the courtyard of the Lord's house and
speak to all the people of the towns of Judah who come to worship in the house
of the Lord. Tell them everything I command you; do not omit a word."
JEREMIAH 26:2 NIV

The subject of Jeremiah's message is timeless, for God tells His people (including us) to stand in the courtyard, the very center, the hub of the area, and speak to all who come to worship. Speak up, share the good news! Shout it from the rooftops; repeat it to all who will listen.

And what is that good news? Well, it's all about Jesus and the fact that He is the Way, the Truth, and the Life. That no one comes to the Father except through Him (John 14:6). It can't get any clearer than that! Take joy in knowing that through God's Son, you have the promise of eternal life.

Dear Lord, help me share Your message of hope and salvation to all I can.

EVENING
GODLY PLANETARIUM

This is what the Lord says, he who appoints the sun to shine by day,
who decrees the moon and stars to shine by night, who stirs up the
sea so that its waves roar—the Lord Almighty is his name.
JEREMIAH 31:35 NIV

Did you ever sit on the beach and marvel at the massive oceanic expanse before you? Probably one of the most beautiful earthly sights is a sunrise over a sea. The roar of the waves as they crash on the beach; the sound of the sea gulls as they fly low overhead, searching for a morning bite of crab; the colors of the sun peeking over the horizon; all are a part of God's morning masterpiece. He appoints the sun to rise each day and later to set, bringing with it darkness and slowly but surely beautiful twinkling stars to dot the sky.

Dear Lord, my God Almighty, thank You for Your grace,
for the beauty that You have created here on earth.

MORNING
UNCONDITIONAL OBEDIENCE

"Whether it is favorable or unfavorable, we will obey the LORD our God, to whom we are sending you, so that it will go well with us, for we will obey the LORD our God."
JEREMIAH 42:6 NIV

Sometimes the right course in your life may seem counterintuitive. That's when you need to let go and let God. Once you renounce what you feel you should do, and do what you realize God wants you to do, your situation will improve and peace will be restored to your soul. Within God's plan lies your correct course. Although His course may appear difficult, in the end your pledge of obedience will be the best choice you can make to lay the foundation for the best course you can take.

Dear Lord, I ask that You help me to be Your obedient servant, to trust in Your supreme plan for me, and to rest assured that Your will is the best course for me.

EVENING
CHIN UP

"Do not be afraid, Jacob my servant; do not be dismayed, Israel. I will surely save you out of a distant place, your descendants from the land of their exile. Jacob will again have peace and security, and no one will make him afraid."
JEREMIAH 46:27 NIV

In tonight's scripture, God reassures the surviving Israelites that they will be safe. These exiles, now living in a strange place away from their homeland, having lost everything, were certainly alone and afraid. But God was there to reassure them that He would restore peace and security once again.

God holds out that same promise to you. He wants you to know that you are safe and sound in His hands. All you need to do to tap into that peace is to "let be and be still, and know (recognize and understand) that I am God" (Psalm 46:10 AMPC).

Dear Lord, grant me Your peace, the peace You promised Your people many years ago and that You continue to promise to me today. Help me to trust in You always.

MORNING
GUILT-FREE

*"In those days, at that time," declares the LORD, "search will be made
for Israel's guilt, but there will be none, and for the sins of Judah,
but none will be found, for I will forgive the remnant I spare."*

JEREMIAH 50:20 NIV

To the survivors of Israel and Judah, God declares there will be no guilt and no regret. The people are to look forward, not back. Yesterday is done, and if you strayed from God's path, ask His divine forgiveness and move on. He will gladly grant it. Once forgiven, forget it. Don't let guilt be a weight that drags you down into the depths of regret.

Each day, God gives you a new page to write the next chapter of your life. So learn from your mistakes, but don't get lost in them. Just as God gifted Israel and Judah with a guilt-free life, He will do the same for you.

*Dear Lord, I am grateful for Your forgiveness when I stray.
Grant me wisdom to ask for Your forgiveness when I fail.*

EVENING
RUMOR HAS IT

*"Do not lose heart or be afraid when rumors are heard in the land; one rumor comes
this year, another the next, rumors of violence in the land and of ruler against ruler."*

JEREMIAH 51:46 NIV

Most people have been a victim of the rumor mill. Unsubstantiated information tends to spread like wildfire. What's worse, as it spreads, it tends to get more colorful and less factual. This is not a new phenomenon—throughout the history of humankind, rumors have been born and spread.

It's good to remember God's preemptive words, counseling His people not to lose heart or be afraid. You, as one of His chosen people, can rise above the rumors that run rampant each day via social media, radio, television, and newspapers.

Although some would like you to panic, remember God has given and continues to give you the inside scoop.

*Dear Lord, help me steer clear of unsubstantiated sources of
information and heed only information that contains Your truth.*

MORNING
OVERWHELMED

*What can I say for you? With what can I compare you, Daughter
Jerusalem? To what can I liken you, that I may comfort you, Virgin
Daughter Zion? Your wound is as deep as the sea. Who can heal you?*
LAMENTATIONS 2:13 NIV

The accounts related in the book of Lamentations make it clear the people of Jerusalem were going through tough times. However, their struggle would not last forever. God alone was the solution to their problems. God alone was able to heal their afflictions.

God alone can help you too. Allow Him to uplift you right now with these words: "I will restore you to health and heal your wounds" (Jeremiah 30:17 NIV).

*Dear Lord, sometimes I feel overwhelmed by hardship and can see
no way out. Please open my eyes to see You and my ears to hear You.
I trust that You will heal me and restore peace in my life.*

EVENING
DEEP WITHIN THE PIT

*But I called on your name, LORD, from deep within the pit. You heard
me when I cried, "Listen to my pleading! Hear my cry for help!"
Yes, you came when I called; you told me, "Do not fear."*
LAMENTATIONS 3:55–57 NLT

Perhaps you can relate to the people of God who'd hit rock bottom, as revealed in tonight's verses. Yet hope remains, for these verses also show that God hears our cries, no matter how low we've fallen. His response to us, even while we're sinking deep in our sin? *"Do not fear!"*

Isn't that the most gracious thing you could say to a person who's buried in a pit, terrified she will stay there forever? God, the Rescuer, comes to save even the ones most hopeless. What a wonderful Father!

*Father, You've rescued me more times than I could count.
How I praise You for snatching me out of the pit!*

MORNING
THE SPIRIT SPEAKS

"Stand up, son of man," said the voice. "I want to speak with you." The Spirit came
into me as he spoke, and he set me on my feet. I listened carefully to his words.
EZEKIEL 2:1–2 NLT

A strange voice spoke to Ezekiel, and it didn't take long to realize it was the Holy Spirit. Whether he heard the words in an audible voice or felt the impression of the words on his heart, we'll never know. But we do know for sure that the Spirit was speaking.

The Bible says God is the same yesterday, today, and forever. If He could speak to Ezekiel back then, He can and will speak to you today.

What is He speaking to your heart today?

Thank You for the reminder that You're still speaking, Lord! My ears are wide open.

EVENING
HIS GLORY FILLS THE TEMPLE

And the glory of the LORD went up from the cherub to the threshold
of the house, and the house was filled with the cloud, and the court
was filled with the brightness of the glory of the LORD.
EZEKIEL 10:4 ESV

The Bible gives us glimpses into what heaven will be like. In the book of Ezekiel, the glory of God filled the temple like a cloud, causing a curious glow to radiate across the courtyard.

Can you picture it now? Does your imagination stretch that far? Can you feel the weight of God's glory enveloping you like a cloud? Are your eyes blinded with His magnificence?

Oh, what an exquisite foretaste of what is to come!

I love to spend time in Your presence, Lord. I can't wait until I'm able to do that for
all eternity. What a day it will be, when I witness it all firsthand for the first time.

MORNING
A SHELTER FROM THE STORM

*"This is what the Sovereign Lord says: I will take a branch from the top of
a tall cedar, and I will plant it on the top of Israel's highest mountain. It will
become a majestic cedar, sending forth its branches and producing seed. Birds
of every sort will nest in it, finding shelter in the shade of its branches."*

EZEKIEL 17:22–23 NLT

What a lovely passage from the book of Ezekiel. It paints a brilliant picture, with images of birds finding shelter in the branches of a majestic cedar. Clearly, God has always cared about serving as our shelter during a storm.

Think of a time when God spread Himself out over your situation in much the same way the branches of that cedar tree were spread to welcome the birds. He's not a discriminator. The passage assures us that "birds of every sort" are welcome.

Are you ready to fly into God's arms today for some much-needed rest?

Lord, You are my shelter not just in times of storm but every day.

EVENING
HE SAID IT. THAT SETTLES IT.

*"I, the Lord, have spoken! The time has come, and I won't hold back. I will
not change my mind, and I will have no pity on you. You will be judged
on the basis of all your wicked actions, says the Sovereign Lord."*

EZEKIEL 24:14 NLT

When God says He's going to do something, He follows through. You can take it to the bank. We see this in Isaiah 55:11 (NLT) as well, where God says: "It is the same with my word. I send it out, and it always produces fruit. It will accomplish all I want it to, and it will prosper everywhere I send it."

Your God is a God of His word. And He wants you to be a woman of *your* word too. If you say you're going to do it. . .do it.

Lord, I want to be a woman of my word. If I say it, that settles it!

MORNING
TAKE ACTION

*"You are very entertaining to them, like someone who sings love
songs with a beautiful voice or plays fine music on an instrument.
They hear what you say, but they don't act on it!"*

EZEKIEL 33:32 NLT

If you've ever had friends (or, worse yet, children) who didn't take you seriously, perhaps you have an inkling of what God feels like at times. He speaks. . .but we don't always pay close attention or act on His words.

God's always speaking, and although we're decent listeners, we don't always act on what He says. We're like our own children, hearing a parental unit say, "Go clean your room!" but then refusing to budge from our spot on the sofa. How much easier life would be if we always listened and obeyed.

Today, think about the last message God laid on your heart. Did you spring into action?

Lord, thank You for speaking. May I be a doer, not just a hearer.

EVENING
RISE AGAIN

*Then he said to me, "Speak a prophetic message to these bones and say, 'Dry
bones, listen to the word of the LORD! This is what the Sovereign LORD says:
Look! I am going to put breath into you and make you live again!'"*

EZEKIEL 37:4–5 NLT

Don't give up! There are things you've been praying for that might be just around the corner. There are dreams that have died but are meant to be resurrected. There are bones lying dead in a heap that God wants to bring to life again.

No matter what dreams you've buried, it's not too late. Even now, God is longing to breathe life into your situation. Will you give it to Him?

Lord, I'm grateful for the reminder that You've come to breathe life into dry bones.

MORNING
RUSHING WATERS

Suddenly, the glory of the God of Israel appeared from the east.
The sound of his coming was like the roar of rushing waters,
and the whole landscape shone with his glory.

EZEKIEL 43:2 NLT

Can you envision being so overwhelmed by the magnitude of God's presence that it feels (and sounds) as if a mighty roaring river is about to sweep over you? That's what it's like to be caught up with Him. You're swept away—away from your troubles, your broken heart, your rocky relationships. In those moments, as those holy waters sweep over you, you're washed afresh with His power, His joy, His holiness.

God wants you to meet Him at this river, to dive in, to enjoy all that He has to offer.

Lord, may I experience Your glory right here, right now. Amen.

EVENING
A RIVER OF HEALING

He asked me, "Have you been watching, son of man?" Then he led
me back along the riverbank. When I returned, I was surprised by
the sight of many trees growing on both sides of the river.

EZEKIEL 47:6–7 NLT

Jesus is the River of Life! He's come to split the dry, parched areas of your life wide open and to pour His living water over it all so that life might return.

What dried-out areas can you turn over to God tonight? Picture Him soaking those areas with holy water. How amazing, to watch them spring to life once more!

You're a miracle worker, Lord! You take my parched life and
saturate it with Your holy presence, bringing life anew.

MORNING
THE HANDWRITING ON THE WALL

Suddenly, they saw the fingers of a human hand writing on the plaster wall of the king's palace, near the lampstand. The king himself saw the hand as it wrote, and his face turned pale with fright. His knees knocked together in fear and his legs gave way beneath him.

DANIEL 5:5–6 NLT

God will do anything necessary to get His intended's attention. When He's got a message to deliver, He does it in unforgettable ways.

Balaam got his message through a donkey (Numbers 22). The young virgin girl, Mary, received hers through the angel Gabriel (Luke 1). God spoke to Moses in a burning bush (Exodus 3). He spoke to Joseph through a dream (Genesis 37).

Think of the different ways God has gotten your attention. Perhaps He spoke through a friend. Maybe He conveyed His message through circumstances. He's got messages to convey. Messages to and for you. Make sure your eyes and ears are wide open.

I'm listening, Father. Convey Your message to my heart, I pray.

EVENING
THE LORD'S UNFAILING LOVE

"But then I will win her back once again. I will lead her into the desert and speak tenderly to her there. I will return her vineyards to her and transform the Valley of Trouble into a gateway of hope. She will give herself to me there, as she did long ago when she was young, when I freed her from her captivity in Egypt."

HOSEA 2:14–15 NLT

That same love that propelled God to chase after His beloved Israel also propels Him to chase after you. No matter how far you wander, no matter how stubborn you get, He won't give up on you. You're His daughter, His beloved.

Isn't the image of God speaking tenderly to you, the one He loves, so precious? He's not standing next to you, berating you or beating you over the head for your mistakes. Quite the opposite, in fact! His words are laced with love. And because you know you're loved, it's so easy to slip your hand into His for a happily ever after.

You love me, Lord! Thank You!

MORNING
PRESSING ON TO KNOW HIM

"Oh, that we might know the Lord! Let us press on to know him. He will respond to us as surely as the arrival of dawn or the coming of rains in early spring."
HOSEA 6:3 NLT

Press in to know God. Take the time. Linger in His presence. Listen to the messages He's whispering in your ear. This Friend of all friends will never betray you. He's incapable of bringing you harm. He will be the finest Friend you've ever known and one who will stick with you till the end—and beyond.

What an amazing Friend You are! Oh, how I long to know You even more, Lord!

EVENING
BRING YOUR CONFESSIONS

Bring your confessions, and return to the Lord. Say to him, "Forgive all our sins and graciously receive us, so that we may offer you our praises."
HOSEA 14:2 NLT

God longs to forgive all sin. In fact, Jesus died to cover the cost of all sins. But if a person refuses to acknowledge her wrong, if she blows it off or acts like she's not at fault, how can God be expected to forgive?

This is why the Bible is clear that we must bring our confessions to the Lord. And those confessions *have* to be sincere. Nothing glib. Nothing nonchalant. Come with a penitent heart, ready to confess your sin so that you can be completely forgiven.

Lord, I confess my sins. It's not easy to say, "I did wrong," but I want and need Your forgiveness.

MORNING
HE WILL POUR OUT HIS SPIRIT

"Then, after doing all those things, I will pour out my Spirit upon all people. Your sons and daughters will prophesy. Your old men will dream dreams, and your young men will see visions."

JOEL 2:28 NLT

Look around you! God is on the move. All kinds of amazing, supernatural things are taking place. Lives are being healed. Relationships are being restored. People are coming to the Lord in record numbers.

Yes, persecution will come. But the Lord is already providing a supernatural outlet for His children. Look up!

Lord, I won't be afraid. Instead, I choose to be excited to be alive during this pivotal point in church history. Thank You for pouring out Your Spirit, Lord!

EVENING
PROMISED PEACE

Israel will be abandoned until the time when she who is in labor bears a son, and the rest of his brothers return to join the Israelites. He will stand and shepherd his flock in the strength of the LORD, in the majesty of the name of the LORD his God. And they will live securely, for then his greatness will reach to the ends of the earth.

MICAH 5:3–4 NIV

Your life right now might be filled with many challenges. Though it might be different from those who had waited for and needed Jesus thousands of years ago, your need for a Messiah and the promised peace that comes with Him are just as important.

Open your hands and heart to Jesus tonight. Tell Him what is troubling you. Invite Him, your Lord and miracle worker, to be your promised peace.

Jesus, I need Your deliverance right now. Thank You for filling me with Your Holy Spirit's provision of power and peace.

MORNING
GET UP AND GO

The LORD gave this message to Jonah son of Amittai: "Get up and go to the great city of Nineveh. Announce my judgment against it because I have seen how wicked its people are." But Jonah got up and went in the opposite direction to get away from the LORD.

JONAH 1:1–3 NLT

Has God asked you, His precious daughter, to say something bold or do something that seems nearly impossible? Chances are the answer is yes. As you continue to read God's Word, consider it your mind's training manual. Soaking in scripture will prompt you to *want* to obey God and focus on the upside of this life. As you do, you will find yourself praising Him more than putting Him down.

God, wherever You lead me, I want to follow You! Give me the courage and conviction to get up and go.

EVENING
A PLACE OF PEACE

"The silver is mine, and the gold is mine, declares the LORD of hosts. The latter glory of this house shall be greater than the former, says the LORD of hosts. And in this place I will give peace, declares the LORD of hosts."

HAGGAI 2:8–9 ESV

Think back to when you accepted Jesus into your life. What was your life like then? Did you have the kind of peace you have now? Did you acknowledge God for who He is in your life and all He has given you? Take some time to find a place of peace and thank Him.

Lord, thank You for being my place and Prince of Peace. Thank You for all You've given me: this life, this breath, this time, this calm. I love You, Lord. You are and always will be my all in all.

MORNING
THE FAMILY LINE

Thus there were fourteen generations in all from Abraham to David, fourteen from David to the exile to Babylon, and fourteen from the exile to the Messiah.
MATTHEW 1:17 NIV

A lot of the details of Jesus' early life get covered in the first four chapters of the book of Matthew. So much to consider during the early life of the King. And here's something to think about as you read today's text: *you* are very much a part of this story. Why was it so important for you to read all of the Old Testament? To see how all those generations of prophets and leaders who obeyed God's call on their life were progenitors of Jesus. They paved the way for Jesus' ministry. Even though they didn't get to meet Jesus on this earth, they prepared for His presence among us.

You are a part of Jesus' family line. When you accepted Him into your life, you became an adopted daughter and an heir to all God's promises. How awesome is that?

Lord, thank You for allowing me to be a part of Your family and Your master plan.

EVENING
STRIVE FOR CONTENTMENT

"You're blessed when you're content with just who you are—no more, no less. That's the moment you find yourselves proud owners of everything that can't be bought."
MATTHEW 5:5 MSG

If you're living for God and not the world, you'll find yourself content with who you are and what you have, for none of what Jesus talks about can be bought or earned.

As a present-day Jesus follower, you are to strive for contentment in life. When you do, God's peace will overflow within and without.

Lord, help me to seek You and not the things of this world.
When I'm looking up to You, contentment reigns inside and out.

MORNING
ACCEPTING THE CALL OF MINISTRY

Come unto me, all ye that labour and are heavy laden, and I will give you rest.
Take my yoke upon you, and learn of me; for I am meek and lowly in heart: and
ye shall find rest unto your souls. For my yoke is easy, and my burden is light.
MATTHEW 11:28–30 KJV

When you accept the call of ministry and service on your life, there will be times that you will need rest from the demands and responsibilities that threaten to wear you out. Needing to rest doesn't mean it's time to quit serving the Lord. It's simply hitting the PAUSE button.

Are you feeling worn down? Or are you trudging your way through ministry? If so, hit that PAUSE button. Take time to rest. Evaluate what God has placed before you. Then ask for a new, fresh vision.

Jesus, thank You for placing a ministry in my life so I can serve You and
others, spreading Your good news and building up Your kingdom.

EVENING
UNDERDOG GRACE

"So the last will be first, and the first will be last."
MATTHEW 20:16 NIV

Tonight, consider areas in your life where you've been considered an underdog but got to experience God's grace. Think about other people in your life, underdogs to whom you can extend this same gentle love and compassion. Then, the next time you find yourself overlooking someone, look up to God. Ask Him to show you how to act and what to say as a way to serve and express God's love poured out.

Jesus, I'm not always the best at loving others
the way You did. Help me to be more like You.

MORNING
FOLLOW HIM

"Follow Me," Jesus told them, "and I will make you fish for people!"
Immediately they left their nets and followed Him.
MARK 1:17–18 HCSB

What has following Jesus been like for you over the years? Was there anything you've had to give up or let go of? Did you ever come to a point where you realized you were on the wrong path and had to completely change direction?

While the cost of following Jesus can be great, there's nothing better than believing in and trusting Him. Life is more thrilling, more abundant, more worthwhile when you surrender your life to your Creator.

Lord, I recommit to following You and Your ways. Although others around me are not living for You, I know I must. Help me stay fixed and focused on the call You have placed on my life, and give me the courage to continue in my faith walk.

EVENING
SUFFICIENT SOVEREIGNTY

And he said, Abba, Father, all things are possible unto thee; take away
this cup from me: nevertheless not what I will, but what thou wilt.
MARK 14:36 KJV

As a woman of God, chances are you have dealt with some challenging situations. More than likely, you know firsthand what it's like to witness or endure suffering. Maybe you can relate to what Jesus prayed and have found yourself praying similar words.

No matter where your faith journey is right now, trust God. Look up instead of down. Be willing to do whatever He asks of you, even if it looks or feels like it might temporarily hurt. God has good things in store for you. He'll resurrect your current suffering to reveal His sufficient sovereignty.

Lord, give me the eyes to see that whatever I'm going through right now will have a good outcome in the days, weeks, months, and years ahead.

MORNING
SENT OUT

But he replied, "I must preach the Good News of the Kingdom of God in other towns, too, because that is why I was sent."
LUKE 4:43 NLT

You have been called by God to do some amazing things for the faith. Sometimes you might receive great opposition. But keep stepping out in faith. Don't give up. Remember you were called for a divine purpose, which is to live for Christ. More specifically, God has given you a ministry to focus on. When the pressure is on and it feels like no one is supporting you, remember that *God* loves and supports you!

Lord, when I feel downcast, unsupported, or looked down upon because of my faith, please quickly open new doors of ministry for me. Give me the strength to do what You've called me to do.

EVENING
BEATITUDE ATTITUDE

"Blessed are you when people hate you, when they exclude you and insult you and reject your name as evil, because of the Son of Man."
LUKE 6:22 NIV

Sometimes you might experience seasons of being financially deprived. Sometimes you might know what it's like to not have enough to eat. Sometimes circumstances may figuratively or literally bring you to tears. Sometimes you might experience a cold shoulder because of who and what you believe in. If—or when—these things happen, look to God. Remember the beatitude attitude He desires you to have. Know He will see you through whatever your circumstances are and will bless you because of it. That's His promise!

Lord, when my attitude gets the best of me, help me to remember the blessings You have in mind for me. Help me look up to You instead of down and to rest in Your promises all around.

MORNING
STAY CALM AND CARRY ON

*When you hear of wars and insurrections (disturbances, disorder,
and confusion), do not become alarmed and panic-stricken and terrified;
for all this must take place first, but the end will not [come] immediately.*
LUKE 21:9 AMPC

No matter what kind of heart you have, Jesus tells you that when you hear all the bad news about wars and other acts of violence that humans inflict upon other humans, you are not to freak out and become terrified. These things are going to happen. Yet, once again, Jesus asks you to be patient and on your guard during these times. Don't let "your hearts be overburdened and depressed" (Luke 21:34 AMPC). Don't get fixated on the worries or on the business of life. Instead, get focused on God. Then no matter when or where the end time does come, you'll be ready.

Lord, help me stay calm and carry on no matter what's going on in this world.

EVENING
THE HEART WHISPERER

*He did not need anyone to bear witness concerning man [needed
no evidence from anyone about men], for He Himself knew what
was in human nature. [He could read men's hearts.]*
JOHN 2:25 AMPC

If Jesus knows you and what's in your heart, you can be sure He knows others and what's in their hearts. So trust Jesus, your Heart Whisperer, to lead you down the right path, the sure route to lush meadows and still waters.

*Lord, You who know all, help me navigate the maze of people
in my life by searching their hearts—as well as my own!*

MORNING
THE ENTRANCE OF GOD'S WORD

*You plan to kill Me, because My word has no entrance (makes no progress,
does not find any place) in you. . . . I assure you, most solemnly I tell you,
if anyone observes My teaching [lives in accordance with My message,
keeps My word], he will by no means ever see and experience death.*

JOHN 8:37, 51 AMPC

What kind of impression has God's Word made upon you? In what ways do you follow Jesus' teachings? How well do you keep His Word—in church and out? No matter what you need or desire, you can find the truth in God's message, a message that not only remedies but feeds and strengthens your heart, body, mind, spirit, and soul—today and every day of your life.

*I don't want to be dead to Your Word, Lord. So please, show
and tell me what You want me to see, hear, and know.*

EVENING
BECAUSE JESUS IS, YOU WILL. . .

I assure you, most solemnly I tell you, that I Myself am the Door for the sheep.

JOHN 10:7 AMPC

Because Jesus is the Bread of Life, you will never be hungry or thirsty.

Because Jesus is the Light of the World, you'll never get lost in the darkness.

Because Jesus is the Door of the sheep, you will be safe from predators.

Because Jesus is the Resurrection and the Life, you will never die.

Because Jesus is the Good Shepherd, you will never get lost.

Because Jesus is the Way, the Truth, and the Life, you will find your path through the truth and knowledge of God.

Because Jesus is the True Vine, you can attach yourself to Him, allowing His life to flow in and through you.

Thank You, Lord, for being who You are and allowing me to find all I need within You.

MORNING
LOVE

I give you a new commandment: that you should love one another. Just as I have loved you, so you too should love one another. By this shall all [men] know that you are My disciples, if you love one another [if you keep on showing love among yourselves].
JOHN 13:34–35 AMPC

Love. May that treasure lie at the very core of your being. May this precious love, springing from your Creator, God, who is Love personified (1 John 4:8), flow from Him and be continually dispersed through you to others. How else will others know and understand who God is if you, one of His adherents, do not reflect that same love to all—even those who are difficult to love?

Today, start and end your day with the greatest treasure and resource you have. Love.

I want to reflect You in this world, Lord. Help me be known as a person of love.

EVENING
JESUS' PRAYER FOR YOU

Neither for these alone do I pray [it is not for their sake only that I make this request], but also for all those who will ever come to believe in (trust in, cling to, rely on) Me through their word and teaching, that they all may be one, [just] as You, Father, are in Me and I in You.
JOHN 17:20–21 AMPC

Through the hearing of God's Word, the power of Jesus' prayer, and the teachings of believers who walked the road you're now on, you are one with other believers. So tonight, let go of all that discourages, disheartens, disturbs, and destroys. Tap into the power, prayers, promises, and presence of God the Father, Jesus the Son, and the Spirit of Comfort. And acknowledge that the same love God had for His one and only Son is the same love God has for you.

Jesus, I'm honored that You prayed for me all those years ago and that Your Father loves me just as He loves You. In the power of that prayer, I rise. In the power of that love, I live.

MORNING
LIVE IN EXPECTATION

Jesus came, though they were behind closed doors, and stood among them and said, Peace to you! . . . Jesus said to him, Because you have seen Me, Thomas, do you now believe (trust, have faith)?
JOHN 20:26, 29 AMPC

Before His ascension, Jesus showed up one final time in an unexpected time and place. It happened when the disciples went fishing. All night they'd caught nothing. Then a stranger (who was actually Jesus) from the shore told them to "Cast the net on the right side of the boat and you will find [some]. So they cast the net, and. . .hauled the net to land, full of large fish, 153 of them" (John 21:6, 11 AMPC).

Expect Jesus where and when you least expect Him.

Lord, I live in expectation of Your presence in my life! Come, Jesus! Come!

EVENING
JOY IN JESUS

I saw the Lord constantly before me, for He is at my right hand that I may not be shaken or overthrown or cast down [from my secure and happy state]. . . . You have made known to me the ways of life; You will enrapture me [diffusing my soul with joy] with and in Your presence.
ACTS 2:25, 28 AMPC

If you keep God constantly before you, keeping Him close, right by your side, you will never be shaken up. Nothing can defeat you or bring you down. All that's left for you to do is rejoice! You can say, "I'm glad from the inside out, ecstatic; I've pitched my tent in the land of hope. I know you'll never dump me in Hades; I'll never even smell the stench of death. You've got my feet on the life-path, with your face shining sun-joy all around" (Acts 2:25–28 MSG).

With You right beside me, Lord, my joy, peace, and contentment know no bounds!

MORNING
BLESSED IN OBEDIENCE

And the Lord said to him, Get up and go to the street called Straight and ask at the house of Judas for a man of Tarsus named Saul, for behold, he is praying [there]. And he has seen in a vision a man named Ananias enter and lay his hands on him so that he might regain his sight.

ACTS 9:11–12 AMPC

Although Ananias expressed his reservations, his fears of helping the bloodthirsty Saul, God told him to go anyway. So Ananias went. In the end, God blessed both men *and* the church by giving it a new apostle.

Even though God may give you a dangerous task to fulfill, when you obey Him, you can be sure He'll give you the means and courage to do it, and a blessing besides.

Lord, give me the means and courage to do what You have called me to do.

EVENING
THE POWER OF PERSISTENT PRAYER

So Peter was kept in prison, but fervent prayer for him was persistently made to God by the church (assembly). . . . When he, at a glance, became aware of this [comprehending all the elements of the case], he went to the house of Mary the mother of John, whose surname was Mark, where a large number were assembled together and were praying.

ACTS 12:5, 12 AMPC

Because of their prayers the very night before Herod was going to bring Peter out to be executed, an angel appeared, woke Peter up, and told him to get up. As Peter rose, his chains simply fell off his hands! After Peter got dressed, the angel led him straight out of the prison and down the street. Next thing Peter knew, the angel had gone.

When your future seems unfair, uncertain, and impossible, take your case and pleas before God. Prayer has the power to alert angels, change the landscape, and free imprisoned souls.

Help me, Lord, become a persistent prayer for You and those You love.

MORNING
WHAT MATTERS MOST

"What matters most to me is to finish what God started: the job the Master
Jesus gave me. . . . Now I'm turning you over to God, our marvelous God
whose gracious Word can make you into what he wants you to be and give
you everything you could possibly need in this community of holy friends."
ACTS 20:24, 32 MSG

Today, take heart, knowing that God is in control. All you need to do is finish what God started by completing the task Jesus has given you. Then turn yourself over to God, marveling at His power and thanking Him for His strength, protection, and love. Know that God's Word can and will mold you into exactly who He wants you to be and that He'll provide you with all you need to get there from here.

Oh Lord, You're what matters most in my life. For that and all things, I thank You.

EVENING
TAKE—AND SPREAD—COURAGE!

And [that same] following night the Lord stood beside Paul and said,
Take courage, Paul, for as you have borne faithful witness concerning
Me at Jerusalem, so you must also bear witness at Rome.
ACTS 23:11 AMPC

God knows all, sees all, and controls all. He made sure Paul's nephew heard about the plot to kill his uncle. The young man first let Paul know. Paul then sent the nephew to the commander, and the commander took things in hand from there to ensure Paul's safety.

Once God speaks courage into someone's ears, it has a domino effect and begins spreading to others. Tonight, allow God to speak courage into your ears. As you feel that courage strengthening you, spread it to the next person you meet!

Lord, I take the courage You so willingly offer. Help me, Lord,
to spread that same mettle to everyone I meet.

DAY 358

MORNING
AS YOU ARE

It is through Him that we have received grace (God's unmerited favor) and [our]
apostleship to promote obedience to the faith and make disciples for His name's sake. . .
and this includes you, called of Jesus Christ and invited [as you are] to belong to Him.
ROMANS 1:5–6 AMPC

When a woman gets pregnant, people might say she and her husband are "expecting." And that's true. They're expecting a child. Yet they do not know who that child will look like or how they will behave. And even when that child does appear, even when it's birthed or adopted into a (hopefully) loving family, how it will someday "turn out" is a mystery to everyone but God!

Just like that expected child, you too are no mystery to God. He has called you, invited you, to take this life journey with Him—*just "as you are."* So stop striving and begin thriving. God's got you. Your job is to simply "get" Him.

Thank You, Lord, for wanting and accepting me just as I am.

EVENING
A MIGHTY WORD KEEPER

No unbelief or distrust made him waver (doubtingly question) concerning
the promise of God, but he grew strong and was empowered by faith as
he gave praise and glory to God, fully satisfied and assured that God was
able and mighty to keep His word and to do what He had promised.
ROMANS 4:20–21 AMPC

What do you think your life would look like if you had the faith of Abraham? How would your life change if you were fully assured that God would keep the Word He's spoken to you and to you alone? What would happen if you remembered, moment by moment, that God is true to His promises to you, to each and every guarantee recorded in the Bible?

Tonight, tomorrow, and every single moment, believe like Abraham, and watch God work through His Word.

Mighty Word Keeper, it's in Your Word alone that
I believe and in Your promises only that I trust.

MORNING
THE GREATEST

And now these three remain: faith, hope and love. But the greatest of these is love.
1 CORINTHIANS 13:13 NIV

God commands us to love one another as He has loved us (John 15:12). So open your heart, and allow God's love to pour into you so you can share His love with those around you. From this day forward, make it your aim to "trust steadily in God, hope unswervingly, love extravagantly" (1 Corinthians 13:13 MSG).

Dear Lord, thank You for these encouraging words, Your unconditional love, and the faith and hope they offer me. Uplift me always with Your love, which I treasure above all.

EVENING
SHINE ON!

For God, who said, "Let light shine out of darkness," made his light shine in our hearts to give us the light of the knowledge of God's glory displayed in the face of Christ.
2 CORINTHIANS 4:6 NIV

The light of God is even *more* powerful than that of the sun. Just as He created, sustains, and brings you physical light, God has created, sustains, and can bring you spiritual light, if only you'd open your eyes to it. This "light" is the knowledge of God, which He has given us all through His Word. And with it comes the peace that this knowledge brings.

As you bask in God's awesome light, remember that it's not to be hidden under a blanket or hoarded from the crowd but to be shared with others and spread to all you encounter.

Dear Lord, let Your divine light shine upon and through me. Allow it to bring me Your peace. Help me to share Your light with those around me.

MORNING
STRENGTH TRAINING

That is why, for Christ's sake, I delight in weaknesses, in insults, in hardships, in persecutions, in difficulties. For when I am weak, then I am strong.
2 CORINTHIANS 12:10 NIV

God may not take away your hardships or afflictions, but He does give you the strength to deal with them, to endure your struggles. Through perseverance, you too will find victory. In your weakness, you too will become strong in Christ.

Dear Lord, I pray for Your strength. I know I am weak; I know I have faults and troubles. Yet I also know You will bolster me through the rough times and bless me with the grace to persevere and to triumph.

EVENING
LEAN ON ME

Carry each other's burdens, and in this way you will fulfill the law of Christ.
GALATIANS 6:2 NIV

What's the "law of Christ"? It's found in Jesus' response to a scribe's question, "Of all the commandments, which is the most important?" (Mark 12:28 NIV). Jesus said, first and foremost, "'Love the Lord your God with all your heart and with all your soul and with all your mind and with all your strength.' The second is this: 'Love your neighbor as yourself'" (Mark 12:30–31 NIV).

God knows you will have burdens in this world. But by leaning on others, you can sustain and carry each other, just as God sustains and carries all.

Dear Lord, I ask Your help to sustain me as I do my best to sustain those around me. By carrying the burdens of others, I will do my best to fulfill Your commandment.

MORNING
GRACE

For it is by grace you have been saved, through faith—and this is not from yourselves, it is the gift of God—not by works, so that no one can boast.
EPHESIANS 2:8–9 NIV

You can rejoice in the fact that God has saved you not because of anything you have done but through your faith alone. Yes, it's that simple. God's greatest gift is offered to you free of charge. Because this gift was not of your doing, you cannot boast or brag. You are just the joyful beneficiary for eternity.

So have faith, that amazing confidence in what you hope for and assurance in what you do not see (Hebrews 11:1). And leave the boasting to God, the perfect Giver of the perfect gift.

Dear Lord, thank You for Your incredible gift of salvation, given not because of anything I have said or done but solely through my faith.

EVENING
THANKSGIVING

Do not be anxious about anything, but in every situation, by prayer and petition, with thanksgiving, present your requests to God.
PHILIPPIANS 4:6 NIV

Tonight, lean into one of the most upbeat verses ever written: "This is the day the LORD has made. We will rejoice and be glad in it" (Psalm 118:24 NLT). Then rejoice as you turn your troubles over to God, thanking Him for all and trusting Him to answer your prayers and petitions. What better antianxiety approach could there be?

Dear Lord, as I come to You in prayer with my concerns, I also come with a heart full of gratitude for Your many blessings. In You I trust.

MORNING
YOU ARE INVITED!

Let us then approach God's throne of grace with confidence, so that we
may receive mercy and find grace to help us in our time of need.
HEBREWS 4:16 NIV

God's throne room is a reception hall like no other. There you receive His infinite mercy and grace not because of anything you did but because you are in need. And with this mercy and grace comes peace. "Grace and peace be yours in abundance through the knowledge of God and of Jesus our Lord" (2 Peter 1:2 NIV).

How comforting to know God's mercy, grace, and peace come hand in hand. How will you RSVP to God's invitation to approach His throne of grace?

Dear Lord, I thank You for Your grace, which works through me to regenerate
and sanctify me and inspires me to persevere during good times and bad.

EVENING
HEAVENLY HAVEN

Let us draw near to God with a sincere heart and with the full assurance
that faith brings, having our hearts sprinkled to cleanse us from a guilty
conscience and having our bodies washed with pure water.
HEBREWS 10:22 NIV

Just as ships are drawn to lighthouses, people from all over the world are drawn to the light of God. It appeals to those who have a sincere heart and a strong faith and to those who are looking for direction, for the way of life that will keep them from getting stuck, floundering, and wrecking.

As you draw near to Jesus, that "light of the world" (John 8:12 NIV), do so with a sincere heart and the confidence that when you accepted Him, God absolved you of all guilt. You have been cleansed *and* given a full pardon and a clear pathway to the Lord of Light!

Dear Lord, I am blessed beyond measure to be drawn to You.

MORNING
HAVE FAITH

Now faith is confidence in what we hope for and assurance about what we do not see.
HEBREWS 11:1 NIV

What a wonderful feeling, to have full assurance and confidence in God! This faith isn't blind but rather comes from the knowledge we have in the Word of God through His scriptures and the teachings through His Son, Jesus Christ.

So have confidence in your hopes. Have assurance and peace about what has not yet been made visible to you. Fully trust in God with all.

Dear Lord, how wonderful it is to know that I can be completely confident in You and Your promises, that I can live each day in peace, knowing I can have assurance of those things I cannot see but that You have declared to be true.

EVENING
HEAVEN

But in keeping with his promise we are looking forward to a new heaven and a new earth, where righteousness dwells.
2 PETER 3:13 NIV

Peter tells us to look forward to a *new* heaven and a *new* earth. He says righteousness will dwell there. The question is, Will this take place on our present earth? Will God cleanse the earth of evil and deliver it to the righteous? No one can know for sure the real meaning of Peter's words. But the question of "where" the new heaven and earth will be is not all that important. The knowledge of *what* is the thing that should resonate with you.

Remember that faith is the assurance of those things that we cannot see. So when God promises you that you will dwell in righteousness, be confident He will indeed deliver. When the day arrives that you see heaven for yourself, you will most certainly understand.

Dear Lord, I look forward to dwelling with righteousness in Your holy kingdom to come.

MORNING
HELP IS ON THE WAY

If anyone has material possessions and sees a brother or sister in need but has no pity on them, how can the love of God be in that person?
1 JOHN 3:17 NIV

How do you respond when you see someone in distress? John tells you that we should have pity on them. Sure, the sight of someone in distress tugs at our heartstrings. But what can we do? John answers: "Dear children, let us not love with words or speech but with actions and in truth" (1 John 3:18 NIV).

Helping is easier said than done many times. Bring attention to the situation. Make some noise. Do *something*.

Remember, *everyone* is a child of God.

Dear Lord, open my eyes to the plight of the less fortunate. Give me the courage to reach out with love and compassion and to take whatever action You'd like me to take. I offer this prayer to You who'd once had no place to lay His head.

EVENING
KNOCKING AT THE DOOR

"Here I am! I stand at the door and knock. If anyone hears my voice and opens the door, I will come in and eat with that person, and they with me."
REVELATION 3:20 NIV

In this letter Jesus dictates to John, He gives the rather apathetic and uncommitted Christians of Laodicea an open invitation to listen for His knock and His voice and allow Him entry. Jesus was extending a warm and sincere offer of love and forgiveness. In the same way. Jesus issued this invitation to the church of Laodicea. He offers it to *all* who read His words. If you let Him in, He will accept you, and all past sins will be forgiven.

Jesus is at the door of your life, regardless of past actions, spiritual journey, or even unbelief. Just open the door to Him, and He will come into your life.

Dear Lord, I accept Your gracious invitation to eat with me and to show me the way.

MORNING
HALLELUJAH!

Angels, numbering thousands upon thousands, and ten thousand times ten thousand. . . .encircled the throne and the living creatures and the elders. In a loud voice they were saying: "Worthy is the Lamb, who was slain, to receive power and wealth and wisdom and strength and honor and glory and praise!"

REVELATION 5:11–12 NIV

Jesus was sacrificed as a ransom for *all* of the sins of humankind forever. Through the killing of *this* Lamb, the ultimate price for our eternal life was paid.

Jesus is worthy of all heavenly wealth, wisdom, and strength. And He is worthy of our daily praise and honor. So today, raise your voice loudly, and joyfully sing the praise of the Lamb of God! How blessed we are that God sent His only Son to save us all. Rejoice! And sing: "Worthy is the Lamb, who was slain, to receive power and wealth and wisdom and strength and honor and glory and praise!"

Dear Lord, I praise You and I thank You for the Lamb of God.

EVENING
LIVING WATER

"For the Lamb at the center of the throne will be their shepherd; 'he will lead them to springs of living water.' 'And God will wipe away every tear from their eyes.'"

REVELATION 7:17 NIV

Are you craving for Jesus to quench your thirst? If so, remember Jesus' words, "Whoever believes in me, as Scripture has said, rivers of living water will flow from within them" (John 7:38). And allow the Lord your Shepherd to make you lie down in green meadows and to lead you beside the quiet waters (Psalm 23:1–2). Visualize the abundant water, flowing and calm, and the fact that God will truly wipe every tear from your eyes, bringing you the peace and comfort you're longing for.

Dear Lord, I pray there is a place for me at Your springs of living water.
Guide me and console me, that I may live in Your kingdom forever.

1-Jan	Gen. 1–2	Matt. 1	Ps. 1
2-Jan	Gen. 3–4	Matt. 2	Ps. 2
3-Jan	Gen. 5–7	Matt. 3	Ps. 3
4-Jan	Gen. 8–10	Matt. 4	Ps. 4
5-Jan	Gen. 11–13	Matt. 5:1–20	Ps. 5
6-Jan	Gen. 14–16	Matt. 5:21–48	Ps. 6
7-Jan	Gen. 17–18	Matt. 6:1–18	Ps. 7
8-Jan	Gen. 19–20	Matt. 6:19–34	Ps. 8
9-Jan	Gen. 21–23	Matt. 7:1–11	Ps. 9:1–8
10-Jan	Gen. 24	Matt. 7:12–29	Ps. 9:9–20
11-Jan	Gen. 25–26	Matt. 8:1–17	Ps. 10:1–11
12-Jan	Gen. 27:1–28:9	Matt. 8:18–34	Ps. 10:12–18
13-Jan	Gen. 28:10–29:35	Matt. 9	Ps. 11
14-Jan	Gen. 30:1–31:21	Matt. 10:1–15	Ps. 12
15-Jan	Gen. 31:22–32:21	Matt. 10:16–36	Ps. 13
16-Jan	Gen. 32:22–34:31	Matt. 10:37–11:6	Ps. 14
17-Jan	Gen. 35–36	Matt. 11:7–24	Ps. 15
18-Jan	Gen. 37–38	Matt. 11:25–30	Ps. 16
19-Jan	Gen. 39–40	Matt. 12:1–29	Ps. 17
20-Jan	Gen. 41	Matt. 12:30–50	Ps. 18:1–15
21-Jan	Gen. 42–43	Matt. 13:1–9	Ps. 18:16–29
22-Jan	Gen. 44–45	Matt. 13:10–23	Ps. 18:30–50
23-Jan	Gen. 46:1–47:26	Matt. 13:24–43	Ps. 19
24-Jan	Gen. 47:27–49:28	Matt. 13:44–58	Ps. 20
25-Jan	Gen. 49:29–Exod. 1:22	Matt. 14	Ps. 21
26-Jan	Exod. 2–3	Matt. 15:1–28	Ps. 22:1–21
27-Jan	Exod. 4:1–5:21	Matt. 15:29–16:12	Ps. 22:22–31
28-Jan	Exod. 5:22–7:24	Matt. 16:13–28	Ps. 23
29-Jan	Exod. 7:25–9:35	Matt. 17:1–9	Ps. 24
30-Jan	Exod. 10–11	Matt. 17:10–27	Ps. 25
31-Jan	Exod. 12	Matt. 18:1–20	Ps. 26
1-Feb	Exod. 13–14	Matt. 18:21–35	Ps. 27
2-Feb	Exod. 15–16	Matt. 19:1–15	Ps. 28
3-Feb	Exod. 17–19	Matt. 19:16–30	Ps. 29
4-Feb	Exod. 20–21	Matt. 20:1–19	Ps. 30
5-Feb	Exod. 22–23	Matt. 20:20–34	Ps. 31:1–8

6-Feb	Exod. 24–25	Matt. 21:1–27	Ps. 31:9–18
7-Feb	Exod. 26–27	Matt. 21:28–46	Ps. 31:19–24
8-Feb	Exod. 28	Matt. 22	Ps. 32
9-Feb	Exod. 29	Matt. 23:1–36	Ps. 33:1–12
10-Feb	Exod. 30–31	Matt. 23:37–24:28	Ps. 33:13–22
11-Feb	Exod. 32–33	Matt. 24:29–51	Ps. 34:1–7
12-Feb	Exod. 34:1–35:29	Matt. 25:1–13	Ps. 34:8–22
13-Feb	Exod. 35:30–37:29	Matt. 25:14–30	Ps. 35:1–8
14-Feb	Exod. 38–39	Matt. 25:31–46	Ps. 35:9–17
15-Feb	Exod. 40	Matt. 26:1–35	Ps. 35:18–28
16-Feb	Lev. 1–3	Matt. 26:36–68	Ps. 36:1–6
17-Feb	Lev. 4:1–5:13	Matt. 26:69–27:26	Ps. 36:7–12
18-Feb	Lev. 5:14–7:21	Matt. 27:27–50	Ps. 37:1–6
19-Feb	Lev. 7:22–8:36	Matt. 27:51–66	Ps. 37:7–26
20-Feb	Lev. 9–10	Matt. 28	Ps. 37:27–40
21-Feb	Lev. 11–12	Mark 1:1–28	Ps. 38
22-Feb	Lev. 13	Mark 1:29–39	Ps. 39
23-Feb	Lev. 14	Mark 1:40–2:12	Ps. 40:1–8
24-Feb	Lev. 15	Mark 2:13–3:35	Ps. 40:9–17
25-Feb	Lev. 16–17	Mark 4:1–20	Ps. 41:1–4
26-Feb	Lev. 18–19	Mark 4:21–41	Ps. 41:5–13
27-Feb	Lev. 20	Mark 5	Ps. 42–43
28-Feb	Lev. 21–22	Mark 6:1–13	Ps. 44
1-Mar	Lev. 23–24	Mark 6:14–29	Ps. 45:1–5
2-Mar	Lev. 25	Mark 6:30–56	Ps. 45:6–12
3-Mar	Lev. 26	Mark 7	Ps. 45:13–17
4-Mar	Lev. 27	Mark 8	Ps. 46
5-Mar	Num. 1–2	Mark 9:1–13	Ps. 47
6-Mar	Num. 3	Mark 9:14–50	Ps. 48:1–8
7-Mar	Num. 4	Mark 10:1–34	Ps. 48:9–14
8-Mar	Num. 5:1–6:21	Mark 10:35–52	Ps. 49:1–9
9-Mar	Num. 6:22–7:47	Mark 11	Ps. 49:10–20
10-Mar	Num. 7:48–8:4	Mark 12:1–27	Ps. 50:1–15
11-Mar	Num. 8:5–9:23	Mark 12:28–44	Ps. 50:16–23
12-Mar	Num. 10–11	Mark 13:1–8	Ps. 51:1–9
13-Mar	Num. 12–13	Mark 13:9–37	Ps. 51:10–19
14-Mar	Num. 14	Mark 14:1–31	Ps. 52
15-Mar	Num. 15	Mark 14:32–72	Ps. 53
16-Mar	Num. 16	Mark 15:1–32	Ps. 54

17-Mar	Num. 17–18	Mark 15:33–47	Ps. 55
18-Mar	Num. 19–20	Mark 16	Ps. 56:1–7
19-Mar	Num. 21:1–22:20	Luke 1:1–25	Ps. 56:8–13
20-Mar	Num. 22:21–23:30	Luke 1:26–56	Ps. 57
21-Mar	Num. 24–25	Luke 1:57–2:20	Ps. 58
22-Mar	Num. 26:1–27:11	Luke 2:21–38	Ps. 59:1–8
23-Mar	Num. 27:12–29:11	Luke 2:39–52	Ps. 59:9–17
24-Mar	Num. 29:12–30:16	Luke 3	Ps. 60:1–5
25-Mar	Num. 31	Luke 4	Ps. 60:6–12
26-Mar	Num. 32–33	Luke 5:1–16	Ps. 61
27-Mar	Num. 34–36	Luke 5:17–32	Ps. 62:1–6
28-Mar	Deut. 1:1–2:25	Luke 5:33–6:11	Ps. 62:7–12
29-Mar	Deut. 2:26–4:14	Luke 6:12–35	Ps. 63:1–5
30-Mar	Deut. 4:15–5:22	Luke 6:36–49	Ps. 63:6–11
31-Mar	Deut. 5:23–7:26	Luke 7:1–17	Ps. 64:1–5
1-Apr	Deut. 8–9	Luke 7:18–35	Ps. 64:6–10
2-Apr	Deut. 10–11	Luke 7:36–8:3	Ps. 65:1–8
3-Apr	Deut. 12–13	Luke 8:4–21	Ps. 65:9–13
4-Apr	Deut. 14:1–16:8	Luke 8:22–39	Ps. 66:1–7
5-Apr	Deut. 16:9–18:22	Luke 8:40–56	Ps. 66:8–15
6-Apr	Deut. 19:1–21:9	Luke 9:1–22	Ps. 66:16–20
7-Apr	Deut. 21:10–23:8	Luke 9:23–42	Ps. 67
8-Apr	Deut. 23:9–25:19	Luke 9:43–62	Ps. 68:1–6
9-Apr	Deut. 26:1–28:14	Luke 10:1–20	Ps. 68:7–14
10-Apr	Deut. 28:15–68	Luke 10:21–37	Ps. 68:15–19
11-Apr	Deut. 29–30	Luke 10:38–11:23	Ps. 68:20–27
12-Apr	Deut. 31:1–32:22	Luke 11:24–36	Ps. 68:28–35
13-Apr	Deut. 32:23–33:29	Luke 11:37–54	Ps. 69:1–9
14-Apr	Deut. 34–Josh. 2	Luke 12:1–15	Ps. 69:10–17
15-Apr	Josh. 3:1–5:12	Luke 12:16–40	Ps. 69:18–28
16-Apr	Josh. 5:13–7:26	Luke 12:41–48	Ps. 69:29–36
17-Apr	Josh. 8–9	Luke 12:49–59	Ps. 70
18-Apr	Josh. 10:1–11:15	Luke 13:1–21	Ps. 71:1–6
19-Apr	Josh. 11:16–13:33	Luke 13:22–35	Ps. 71:7–16
20-Apr	Josh. 14–16	Luke 14:1–15	Ps. 71:17–21
21-Apr	Josh. 17:1–19:16	Luke 14:16–35	Ps. 71:22–24
22-Apr	Josh. 19:17–21:42	Luke 15:1–10	Ps. 72:1–11
23-Apr	Josh. 21:43–22:34	Luke 15:11–32	Ps. 72:12–20
24-Apr	Josh. 23–24	Luke 16:1–18	Ps. 73:1–9

25-Apr	Judg. 1–2	Luke 16:19–17:10	Ps. 73:10–20
26-Apr	Judg. 3–4	Luke 17:11–37	Ps. 73:21–28
27-Apr	Judg. 5:1–6:24	Luke 18:1–17	Ps. 74:1–3
28-Apr	Judg. 6:25–7:25	Luke 18:18–43	Ps. 74:4–11
29-Apr	Judg. 8:1–9:23	Luke 19:1–28	Ps. 74:12–17
30-Apr	Judg. 9:24–10:18	Luke 19:29–48	Ps. 74:18–23
1-May	Judg. 11:1–12:7	Luke 20:1–26	Ps. 75:1–7
2-May	Judg. 12:8–14:20	Luke 20:27–47	Ps. 75:8–10
3-May	Judg. 15–16	Luke 21:1–19	Ps. 76:1–7
4-May	Judg. 17–18	Luke 21:20–22:6	Ps. 76:8–12
5-May	Judg. 19:1–20:23	Luke 22:7–30	Ps. 77:1–11
6-May	Judg. 20:24–21:25	Luke 22:31–54	Ps. 77:12–20
7-May	Ruth 1–2	Luke 22:55–23:25	Ps. 78:1–4
8-May	Ruth 3–4	Luke 23:26–24:12	Ps. 78:5–8
9-May	1 Sam. 1:1–2:21	Luke 24:13–53	Ps. 78:9–16
10-May	1 Sam. 2:22–4:22	John 1:1–28	Ps. 78:17–24
11-May	1 Sam. 5–7	John 1:29–51	Ps. 78:25–33
12-May	1 Sam. 8:1–9:26	John 2	Ps. 78:34–41
13-May	1 Sam. 9:27–11:15	John 3:1–22	Ps. 78:42–55
14-May	1 Sam. 12–13	John 3:23–4:10	Ps. 78:56–66
15-May	1 Sam. 14	John 4:11–38	Ps. 78:67–72
16-May	1 Sam. 15–16	John 4:39–54	Ps. 79:1–7
17-May	1 Sam. 17	John 5:1–24	Ps. 79:8–13
18-May	1 Sam. 18–19	John 5:25–47	Ps. 80:1–7
19-May	1 Sam. 20–21	John 6:1–21	Ps. 80:8–19
20-May	1 Sam. 22–23	John 6:22–42	Ps. 81:1–10
21-May	1 Sam. 24:1–25:31	John 6:43–71	Ps. 81:11–16
22-May	1 Sam. 25:32–27:12	John 7:1–24	Ps. 82
23-May	1 Sam. 28–29	John 7:25–8:11	Ps. 83
24-May	1 Sam. 30–31	John 8:12–47	Ps. 84:1–4
25-May	2 Sam. 1–2	John 8:48–9:12	Ps. 84:5–12
26-May	2 Sam. 3–4	John 9:13–34	Ps. 85:1–7
27-May	2 Sam. 5:1–7:17	John 9:35–10:10	Ps. 85:8–13
28-May	2 Sam. 7:18–10:19	John 10:11–30	Ps. 86:1–10
29-May	2 Sam. 11:1–12:25	John 10:31–11:16	Ps. 86:11–17
30-May	2 Sam. 12:26–13:39	John 11:17–54	Ps. 87
31-May	2 Sam. 14:1–15:12	John 11:55–12:19	Ps. 88:1–9
1-Jun	2 Sam. 15:13–16:23	John 12:20–43	Ps. 88:10–18
2-Jun	2 Sam. 17:1–18:18	John 12:44–13:20	Ps. 89:1–6

3-Jun	2 Sam. 18:19–19:39	John 13:21–38	Ps. 89:7–13
4-Jun	2 Sam. 19:40–21:22	John 14:1–17	Ps. 89:14–18
5-Jun	2 Sam. 22:1–23:7	John 14:18–15:27	Ps. 89:19–29
6-Jun	2 Sam. 23:8–24:25	John 16:1–22	Ps. 89:30–37
7-Jun	1 Kings 1	John 16:23–17:5	Ps. 89:38–52
8-Jun	1 Kings 2	John 17:6–26	Ps. 90:1–12
9-Jun	1 Kings 3–4	John 18:1–27	Ps. 90:13–17
10-Jun	1 Kings 5–6	John 18:28–19:5	Ps. 91:1–10
11-Jun	1 Kings 7	John 19:6–24	Ps. 91:11–16
12-Jun	1 Kings 8:1–53	John 19:25–42	Ps. 92:1–9
13-Jun	1 Kings 8:54–10:13	John 20:1–18	Ps. 92:10–15
14-Jun	1 Kings 10:14–11:43	John 20:19–31	Ps. 93
15-Jun	1 Kings 12:1–13:10	John 21	Ps. 94:1–11
16-Jun	1 Kings 13:11–14:31	Acts 1:1–11	Ps. 94:12–23
17-Jun	1 Kings 15:1–16:20	Acts 1:12–26	Ps. 95
18-Jun	1 Kings 16:21–18:19	Acts 2:1–21	Ps. 96:1–8
19-Jun	1 Kings 18:20–19:21	Acts 2:22–41	Ps. 96:9–13
20-Jun	1 Kings 20	Acts 2:42–3:26	Ps. 97:1–6
21-Jun	1 Kings 21:1–22:28	Acts 4:1–22	Ps. 97:7–12
22-Jun	1 Kings 22:29– 2 Kings 1:18	Acts 4:23–5:11	Ps. 98
23-Jun	2 Kings 2–3	Acts 5:12–28	Ps. 99
24-Jun	2 Kings 4	Acts 5:29–6:15	Ps. 100
25-Jun	2 Kings 5:1–6:23	Acts 7:1–16	Ps. 101
26-Jun	2 Kings 6:24–8:15	Acts 7:17–36	Ps. 102:1–7
27-Jun	2 Kings 8:16–9:37	Acts 7:37–53	Ps. 102:8–17
28-Jun	2 Kings 10–11	Acts 7:54–8:8	Ps. 102:18–28
29-Jun	2 Kings 12–13	Acts 8:9–40	Ps. 103:1–9
30-Jun	2 Kings 14–15	Acts 9:1–16	Ps. 103:10–14
1-Jul	2 Kings 16–17	Acts 9:17–31	Ps. 103:15–22
2-Jul	2 Kings 18:1–19:7	Acts 9:32–10:16	Ps. 104:1–9
3-Jul	2 Kings 19:8–20:21	Acts 10:17–33	Ps. 104:10–23
4-Jul	2 Kings 21:1–22:20	Acts 10:34–11:18	Ps. 104:24–30
5-Jul	2 Kings 23	Acts 11:19–12:17	Ps. 104:31–35
6-Jul	2 Kings 24–25	Acts 12:18–13:13	Ps. 105:1–7
7-Jul	1 Chron. 1–2	Acts 13:14–43	Ps. 105:8–15
8-Jul	1 Chron. 3:1–5:10	Acts 13:44–14:10	Ps. 105:16–28
9-Jul	1 Chron. 5:11–6:81	Acts 14:11–28	Ps. 105:29–36
10-Jul	1 Chron. 7:1–9:9	Acts 15:1–18	Ps. 105:37–45

11-Jul	1 Chron. 9:10–11:9	Acts 15:19–41	Ps. 106:1–12
12-Jul	1 Chron. 11:10–12:40	Acts 16:1–15	Ps. 106:13–27
13-Jul	1 Chron. 13–15	Acts 16:16–40	Ps. 106:28–33
14-Jul	1 Chron. 16–17	Acts 17:1–14	Ps. 106:34–43
15-Jul	1 Chron. 18–20	Acts 17:15–34	Ps. 106:44–48
16-Jul	1 Chron. 21–22	Acts 18:1–23	Ps. 107:1–9
17-Jul	1 Chron. 23–25	Acts 18:24–19:10	Ps. 107:10–16
18-Jul	1 Chron. 26–27	Acts 19:11–22	Ps. 107:17–32
19-Jul	1 Chron. 28–29	Acts 19:23–41	Ps. 107:33–38
20-Jul	2 Chron. 1–3	Acts 20:1–16	Ps. 107:39–43
21-Jul	2 Chron. 4:1–6:11	Acts 20:17–38	Ps. 108
22-Jul	2 Chron. 6:12–7:10	Acts 21:1–14	Ps. 109:1–20
23-Jul	2 Chron. 7:11–9:28	Acts 21:15–32	Ps. 109:21–31
24-Jul	2 Chron. 9:29–12:16	Acts 21:33–22:16	Ps. 110:1–3
25-Jul	2 Chron. 13–15	Acts 22:17–23:11	Ps. 110:4–7
26-Jul	2 Chron. 16–17	Acts 23:12–24:21	Ps. 111
27-Jul	2 Chron. 18–19	Acts 24:22–25:12	Ps. 112
28-Jul	2 Chron. 20–21	Acts 25:13–27	Ps. 113
29-Jul	2 Chron. 22–23	Acts 26	Ps. 114
30-Jul	2 Chron. 24:1–25:16	Acts 27:1–20	Ps. 115:1–10
31-Jul	2 Chron. 25:17–27:9	Acts 27:21–28:6	Ps. 115:11–18
1-Aug	2 Chron. 28:1–29:19	Acts 28:7–31	Ps. 116:1–5
2-Aug	2 Chron. 29:20–30:27	Rom. 1:1–17	Ps. 116:6–19
3-Aug	2 Chron. 31–32	Rom. 1:18–32	Ps. 117
4-Aug	2 Chron. 33:1–34:7	Rom. 2	Ps. 118:1–18
5-Aug	2 Chron. 34:8–35:19	Rom. 3:1–26	Ps. 118:19–23
6-Aug	2 Chron. 35:20–36:23	Rom. 3:27–4:25	Ps. 118:24–29
7-Aug	Ezra 1–3	Rom. 5	Ps. 119:1–8
8-Aug	Ezra 4–5	Rom. 6:1–7:6	Ps. 119:9–16
9-Aug	Ezra 6:1–7:26	Rom. 7:7–25	Ps. 119:17–32
10-Aug	Ezra 7:27–9:4	Rom. 8:1–27	Ps. 119:33–40
11-Aug	Ezra 9:5–10:44	Rom. 8:28–39	Ps. 119:41–64
12-Aug	Neh. 1:1–3:16	Rom. 9:1–18	Ps. 119:65–72
13-Aug	Neh. 3:17–5:13	Rom. 9:19–33	Ps. 119:73–80
14-Aug	Neh. 5:14–7:73	Rom. 10:1–13	Ps. 119:81–88
15-Aug	Neh. 8:1–9:5	Rom. 10:14–11:24	Ps. 119:89–104
16-Aug	Neh. 9:6–10:27	Rom. 11:25–12:8	Ps. 119:105–120
17-Aug	Neh. 10:28–12:26	Rom. 12:9–13:7	Ps. 119:121–128
18-Aug	Neh. 12:27–13:31	Rom. 13:8–14:12	Ps. 119:129–136

19-Aug	Esther 1:1–2:18	Rom. 14:13–15:13	Ps. 119:137–152
20-Aug	Esther 2:19–5:14	Rom. 15:14–21	Ps. 119:153–168
21-Aug	Esther 6–8	Rom. 15:22–33	Ps. 119:169–176
22-Aug	Esther 9–10	Rom. 16	Ps. 120–122
23-Aug	Job 1–3	1 Cor. 1:1–25	Ps. 123
24-Aug	Job 4–6	1 Cor. 1:26–2:16	Ps. 124–125
25-Aug	Job 7–9	1 Cor. 3	Ps. 126–127
26-Aug	Job 10–13	1 Cor. 4:1–13	Ps. 128–129
27-Aug	Job 14–16	1 Cor. 4:14–5:13	Ps. 130
28-Aug	Job 17–20	1 Cor. 6	Ps. 131
29-Aug	Job 21–23	1 Cor. 7:1–16	Ps. 132
30-Aug	Job 24–27	1 Cor. 7:17–40	Ps. 133–134
31-Aug	Job 28–30	1 Cor. 8	Ps. 135
1-Sep	Job 31–33	1 Cor. 9:1–18	Ps. 136:1–9
2-Sep	Job 34–36	1 Cor. 9:19–10:13	Ps. 136:10–26
3-Sep	Job 37–39	1 Cor. 10:14–11:1	Ps. 137
4-Sep	Job 40–42	1 Cor. 11:2–34	Ps. 138
5-Sep	Eccles. 1:1–3:15	1 Cor. 12:1–26	Ps. 139:1–6
6-Sep	Eccles. 3:16–6:12	1 Cor. 12:27–13:13	Ps. 139:7–18
7-Sep	Eccles. 7:1–9:12	1 Cor. 14:1–22	Ps. 139:19–24
8-Sep	Eccles. 9:13–12:14	1 Cor. 14:23–15:11	Ps. 140:1–8
9-Sep	SS 1–4	1 Cor. 15:12–34	Ps. 140:9–13
10-Sep	SS 5–8	1 Cor. 15:35–58	Ps. 141
11-Sep	Isa. 1–2	1 Cor. 16	Ps. 142
12-Sep	Isa. 3–5	2 Cor. 1:1–11	Ps. 143:1–6
13-Sep	Isa. 6–8	2 Cor. 1:12–2:4	Ps. 143:7–12
14-Sep	Isa. 9–10	2 Cor. 2:5–17	Ps. 144
15-Sep	Isa. 11–13	2 Cor. 3	Ps. 145
16-Sep	Isa. 14–16	2 Cor. 4	Ps. 146
17-Sep	Isa. 17–19	2 Cor. 5	Ps. 147:1–11
18-Sep	Isa. 20–23	2 Cor. 6	Ps. 147:12–20
19-Sep	Isa. 24:1–26:19	2 Cor. 7	Ps. 148
20-Sep	Isa. 26:20–28:29	2 Cor. 8	Ps. 149–150
21-Sep	Isa. 29–30	2 Cor. 9	Prov. 1:1–9
22-Sep	Isa. 31–33	2 Cor. 10	Prov. 1:10–22
23-Sep	Isa. 34–36	2 Cor. 11	Prov. 1:23–26
24-Sep	Isa. 37–38	2 Cor. 12:1–10	Prov. 1:27–33
25-Sep	Isa. 39–40	2 Cor. 12:11–13:14	Prov. 2:1–15
26-Sep	Isa. 41–42	Gal. 1	Prov. 2:16–22

27-Sep	Isa. 43:1–44:20	Gal. 2	Prov. 3:1–12
28-Sep	Isa. 44:21–46:13	Gal. 3:1–18	Prov. 3:13–26
29-Sep	Isa. 47:1–49:13	Gal. 3:19–29	Prov. 3:27–35
30-Sep	Isa. 49:14–51:23	Gal. 4:1–11	Prov. 4:1–19
1-Oct	Isa. 52–54	Gal. 4:12–31	Prov. 4:20–27
2-Oct	Isa. 55–57	Gal. 5	Prov. 5:1–14
3-Oct	Isa. 58–59	Gal. 6	Prov. 5:15–23
4-Oct	Isa. 60–62	Eph. 1	Prov. 6:1–5
5-Oct	Isa. 63:1–65:16	Eph. 2	Prov. 6:6–19
6-Oct	Isa. 65:17–66:24	Eph. 3:1–4:16	Prov. 6:20–26
7-Oct	Jer. 1–2	Eph. 4:17–32	Prov. 6:27–35
8-Oct	Jer. 3:1–4:22	Eph. 5	Prov. 7:1–5
9-Oct	Jer. 4:23–5:31	Eph. 6	Prov. 7:6–27
10-Oct	Jer. 6:1–7:26	Phil. 1:1–26	Prov. 8:1–11
11-Oct	Jer. 7:27–9:16	Phil. 1:27–2:18	Prov. 8:12–21
12-Oct	Jer. 9:17–11:17	Phil. 2:19–30	Prov. 8:22–36
13-Oct	Jer. 11:18–13:27	Phil. 3	Prov. 9:1–6
14-Oct	Jer. 14–15	Phil. 4	Prov. 9:7–18
15-Oct	Jer. 16–17	Col. 1:1–23	Prov. 10:1–5
16-Oct	Jer. 18:1–20:6	Col. 1:24–2:15	Prov. 10:6–14
17-Oct	Jer. 20:7–22:19	Col. 2:16–3:4	Prov. 10:15–26
18-Oct	Jer. 22:20–23:40	Col. 3:5–4:1	Prov. 10:27–32
19-Oct	Jer. 24–25	Col. 4:2–18	Prov. 11:1–11
20-Oct	Jer. 26–27	1 Thess. 1:1–2:8	Prov. 11:12–21
21-Oct	Jer. 28–29	1 Thess. 2:9–3:13	Prov. 11:22–26
22-Oct	Jer. 30:1–31:22	1 Thess. 4:1–5:11	Prov. 11:27–31
23-Oct	Jer. 31:23–32:35	1 Thess. 5:12–28	Prov. 12:1–14
24-Oct	Jer. 32:36–34:7	2 Thess. 1–2	Prov. 12:15–20
25-Oct	Jer. 34:8–36:10	2 Thess. 3	Prov. 12:21–28
26-Oct	Jer. 36:11–38:13	1 Tim. 1:1–17	Prov. 13:1–4
27-Oct	Jer. 38:14–40:6	1 Tim. 1:18–3:13	Prov. 13:5–13
28-Oct	Jer. 40:7–42:22	1 Tim. 3:14–4:10	Prov. 13:14–21
29-Oct	Jer. 43–44	1 Tim. 4:11–5:16	Prov. 13:22–25
30-Oct	Jer. 45–47	1 Tim. 5:17–6:21	Prov. 14:1–6
31-Oct	Jer. 48:1–49:6	2 Tim. 1	Prov. 14:7–22
1-Nov	Jer. 49:7–50:16	2 Tim. 2	Prov. 14:23–27
2-Nov	Jer. 50:17–51:14	2 Tim. 3	Prov. 14:28–35
3-Nov	Jer. 51:15–64	2 Tim. 4	Prov. 15:1–9
4-Nov	Jer. 52–Lam. 1	Titus 1:1–9	Prov. 15:10–17

5-Nov	Lam. 2:1–3:38	Titus 1:10–2:15	Prov. 15:18–26
6-Nov	Lam. 3:39–5:22	Titus 3	Prov. 15:27–33
7-Nov	Ezek. 1:1–3:21	Philemon	Prov. 16:1–9
8-Nov	Ezek. 3:22–5:17	Heb. 1:1–2:4	Prov. 16:10–21
9-Nov	Ezek. 6–7	Heb. 2:5–18	Prov. 16:22–33
10-Nov	Ezek. 8–10	Heb. 3:1–4:3	Prov. 17:1–5
11-Nov	Ezek. 11–12	Heb. 4:4–5:10	Prov. 17:6–12
12-Nov	Ezek. 13–14	Heb. 5:11–6:20	Prov. 17:13–22
13-Nov	Ezek. 15:1–16:43	Heb. 7	Prov. 17:23–28
14-Nov	Ezek. 16:44–17:24	Heb. 8:1–9:10	Prov. 18:1–7
15-Nov	Ezek. 18–19	Heb. 9:11–28	Prov. 18:8–17
16-Nov	Ezek. 20	Heb. 10:1–25	Prov. 18:18–24
17-Nov	Ezek. 21–22	Heb. 10:26–39	Prov. 19:1–8
18-Nov	Ezek. 23	Heb. 11:1–31	Prov. 19:9–14
19-Nov	Ezek. 24–26	Heb. 11:32–40	Prov. 19:15–21
20-Nov	Ezek. 27–28	Heb. 12:1–13	Prov. 19:22–29
21-Nov	Ezek. 29–30	Heb. 12:14–29	Prov. 20:1–18
22-Nov	Ezek. 31–32	Heb. 13	Prov. 20:19–24
23-Nov	Ezek. 33:1–34:10	James 1	Prov. 20:25–30
24-Nov	Ezek. 34:11–36:15	James 2	Prov. 21:1–8
25-Nov	Ezek. 36:16–37:28	James 3	Prov. 21:9–18
26-Nov	Ezek. 38–39	James 4:1–5:6	Prov. 21:19–24
27-Nov	Ezek. 40	James 5:7–20	Prov. 21:25–31
28-Nov	Ezek. 41:1–43:12	1 Pet. 1:1–12	Prov. 22:1–9
29-Nov	Ezek. 43:13–44:31	1 Pet. 1:13–2:3	Prov. 22:10–23
30-Nov	Ezek. 45–46	1 Pet. 2:4–17	Prov. 22:24–29
1-Dec	Ezek. 47–48	1 Pet. 2:18–3:7	Prov. 23:1–9
2-Dec	Dan. 1:1–2:23	1 Pet. 3:8–4:19	Prov. 23:10–16
3-Dec	Dan. 2:24–3:30	1 Pet. 5	Prov. 23:17–25
4-Dec	Dan. 4	2 Pet. 1	Prov. 23:26–35
5-Dec	Dan. 5	2 Pet. 2	Prov. 24:1–18
6-Dec	Dan. 6:1–7:14	2 Pet. 3	Prov. 24:19–27
7-Dec	Dan. 7:15–8:27	1 John 1:1–2:17	Prov. 24:28–34
8-Dec	Dan. 9–10	1 John 2:18–29	Prov. 25:1–12
9-Dec	Dan. 11–12	1 John 3:1–12	Prov. 25:13–17
10-Dec	Hos. 1–3	1 John 3:13–4:16	Prov. 25:18–28
11-Dec	Hos. 4–6	1 John 4:17–5:21	Prov. 26:1–16
12-Dec	Hos. 7–10	2 John	Prov. 26:17–21
13-Dec	Hos. 11–14	3 John	Prov. 26:22–27:9

14-Dec	Joel 1:1–2:17	Jude	Prov. 27:10–17
15-Dec	Joel 2:18–3:21	Rev. 1:1–2:11	Prov. 27:18–27
16-Dec	Amos 1:1–4:5	Rev. 2:12–29	Prov. 28:1–8
17-Dec	Amos 4:6–6:14	Rev. 3	Prov. 28:9–16
18-Dec	Amos 7–9	Rev. 4:1–5:5	Prov. 28:17–24
19-Dec	Obad.–Jonah	Rev. 5:6–14	Prov. 28:25–28
20-Dec	Mic. 1:1–4:5	Rev. 6:1–7:8	Prov. 29:1–8
21-Dec	Mic. 4:6–7:20	Rev. 7:9–8:13	Prov. 29:9–14
22-Dec	Nah. 1–3	Rev. 9–10	Prov. 29:15–23
23-Dec	Hab. 1–3	Rev. 11	Prov. 29:24–27
24-Dec	Zeph. 1–3	Rev. 12	Prov. 30:1–6
25-Dec	Hag. 1–2	Rev. 13:1–14:13	Prov. 30:7–16
26-Dec	Zech. 1–4	Rev. 14:14–16:3	Prov. 30:17–20
27-Dec	Zech. 5–8	Rev. 16:4–21	Prov. 30:21–28
28-Dec	Zech. 9–11	Rev. 17:1–18:8	Prov. 30:29–33
29-Dec	Zech. 12–14	Rev. 18:9–24	Prov. 31:1–9
30-Dec	Mal. 1–2	Rev. 19–20	Prov. 31:10–17
31-Dec	Mal. 3–4	Rev. 21–22	Prov. 31:18–31